D1275293

THE
ARMOURER
AND HIS CRAFT

VENUS AT THE FORGE OF VULCAN. JAN BRUEGHEL AND HENDRICK VAN BALEN. CIRCA 1600

KAISER FRIEDRICH MUSEUM, BERLIN

THE ARMOURER AND HIS CRAFT

FROM THE XIth TO THE XVIth CENTURY

BY CHARLES FFOULKES

DOVER PUBLICATIONS, INC., New York

Published in Canada by General Publishing Company, Ltd., 30 Lesmill
Road, Don Mills, Toronto, Ontario.
Published in the United Kingdom by Constable and Company, Ltd.

This Dover edition, first published in 1988, is an unabridged republica-
tion of the work originally published by Methuen & Co. Ltd., London, in
1912. For reasons of space, the plates have been slightly rearranged in the
present edition.

Manufactured in the United States of America
Dover Publications, Inc., 31 East 2nd Street, Mineola, N.Y. 11501

Library of Congress Cataloging-in-Publication Data

Ffoulkes, Charles John, 1868–1947.
    The armourer and his craft from the XIth to the XVIth century / by
Charles Ffoulkes.
        p.   cm.
    Reprint. Originally published: London : Methuen, 1912.
    Bibliography: p.
    Includes index.
    ISBN 0-486-25851-3 (pbk.)
    1. Arms and armor—History. 2. Armorers. I. Title.
U810.F46   1988
739.7′5—dc19   88-22874
                                                                    CIP

TO THE RIGHT HONOURABLE

THE VISCOUNT DILLON, Hon. M.A. Oxon.

V.P.S.A., Etc. Etc.

CURATOR OF THE TOWER ARMOURIES

PREFACE

I DO not propose, in this work, to consider the history or development of defensive armour, for this has been more or less fully discussed in works which deal with the subject from the historical side of the question. I have rather endeavoured to compile a work which will, in some measure, fill up a gap in the subject, by collecting all the records and references, especially in English documents, which relate to the actual making of armour and the regulations which controlled the Armourer and his Craft. At the same time it is impossible to discuss this branch of the subject without overlapping in some details the existing works on Arms and Armour, but such repetition has only been included because it bears directly on the making, selling, or wearing of armour.

I have intentionally omitted all reference to the sword and other weapons of offence, for this would have unduly increased the size of the present work, and the subject is of such importance that it deserves a full consideration in a separate volume.

The original limits of this work have been considerably enlarged since it was offered as a thesis for the Degree of Bachelor of Letters in the University of Oxford in the Michaelmas Term, 1911. A polyglot glossary has been included, as this is a detail which has been practically overlooked by all English writers. The subject of Arms and Armour has not, up to the present time, received the attention in England that it deserves, but I would be the first to admit the value of the works of Meyrick and Hewitt, which are the foundations upon which German and French as well as all English authors have based their investigations. At the same time it should be remembered that these two authors were pioneers, and statements which they made have been contradicted or modified by more recent research. Two examples of this will suffice. Meyrick named the upstanding neck-guards on the pauldron the " passguards " and the neck-armour of the horse the " mainfaire." From the researches of Viscount Dillon we learn that the passguard was a reinforcing piece for the joust and the mainfaire was a gauntlet (*main de fer.*) Both these mistakes are still perpetuated in foreign works on the subject, which shows the influence of Meyrick's work even at the present day.

The subject of the Armourer and his Craft has never received much attention in England, even at the hands of Meyrick and Hewitt. On the Continent, however, writers like the late Dr. Wendelin Boeheim, Gurlitt, Buff, and Angellucci have all added greatly to our store of information on the subject. Boeheim's work on the Armourers of Europe (*Meister der Waffenschmiedekunst*) is the only work in any language which has given us some account of the armour craftsmen of the fifteenth and sixteenth centuries, and I should be indeed remiss if I did not take this opportunity of acknowledging the assistance which this collection of biographies has been in the preparation of the present work. Signori Gelli and Moretti have collected interesting documents relating to the Missaglia family, but apart from this no other writers have made a study of the Armourer.

Gay's *Encyclopædia*, which unfortunately was cut short after the letter G by the death of the author, is also invaluable as far as it goes, in that it gives in every case contemporary references relating to the use of each word. The late J. B. Giraud published certain records dealing with the Armourer in various French archæological journals, and M. Charles Buttin has placed all those interested in the subject under a deep obligation for his minute researches on the subject of the proving of armour.

Of living English writers I would express the indebtedness not only of myself, but also of all those who are true *amateurs d'armes*, to Baron de Cosson, who, with the late J. Burges, A.R.A., compiled the Catalogue of Helmets and Mail which is to this day the standard work on the subject. Last of all I would offer my sincere thanks to

PREFACE

Viscount Dillon, Curator of the Tower Armouries, not only for his minute researches printed in the *Archæologia* and *Archæological Journal*, which have brought to light much valuable information respecting the Armourer and his Craft in English records, but also for very great personal interest and assistance in the compilation of this work.

CHARLES FFOULKES

S. John's College,
Oxford, 1912

CONTENTS

LIST OF ILLUSTRATIONS IN THE TEXT

LIST OF PLATES

ACKNOWLEDGMENT

THE author desires to express his thanks for permission to reproduce illustrations contained in this work to the following :—

Viscount Dillon, Curator of the Tower Armouries ; Mr. Guy Laking, M.V.O., King's Armourer ; M. Charles Buttin, Paris ; Mr. Albert Calvert, London ; The Society of Antiquaries ; The Archæological Institute ; The Burlington Fine Arts Club ; The Curators of the Musée d'Artillerie, Paris ; and of the Johanneum, Dresden ; Messrs. Mansell and Co., Hanfstaengl, Griggs and Co., London ; Sgi. Fratelli Alinari, Florence ; Sig. Anderson, Rome ; Herren Teufel, Munich ; Löwy, Vienna (publishers of Boeheim's *Waffensammlungen*) ; Moeser, Berlin (publishers of Boeheim's *Meister der Waffenschmiedkunst*) ; Christof Müller, Nuremberg ; Seeman, Leipzig (publishers of Boeheim's *Waffenkunde*) ; and Sen. Hauser and Menet, Madrid.

WORKS OF REFERENCE

Allgemeine Zeitung. Various vols.

Angellucci. Doccumenti inediti.

Antiquarian Repertory.

Archæologia. Various vols.

Archæological Journal. Various vols.

Archives Civiques de Lille.

Archives Camerales di Torino.

Armourers' Company, London, Records of.

Beckman. History of Inventions. 1846.

Belleval, Marquis de. Costume Militaire Français de 1445

Boeheim. Waffenkunde. 1890.

„ Meister der Waffenschmiedekunst. 1897.

„ Articles in Jahrbuch des Kunsthist. Sammlungen.

Boileau, Étienne. Livres des Métiers. Edit. 1837.

Buff, A. Augsburger Platner Allge. Zeit. 1892.

Buttin. Notes sur l'Épreuve. (Rev. Savoisienne, 1906, fasc. 4.)

„ Le Guet de Genève. 1910.

Calendar of State Papers. Various entries.

Carteggio ined. artisti.

Cellini, Benvenuto. Arte Fabrile, Plon. 1883.

„ „ Life ,Cust. 1910.

Chambres des Comptes, Paris. Various entries, 1765.

Chronique de Bertrand du Guesclin. Edit. 1837.

City of London Letter Books.

Cosson, Baron de :—

    Arch. Journ., XXXVII. Catalogue of Helmets and Mail.

    „ „ XLI. Gauntlets.

    „ „ XLVIII. Arsenals and Armouries of Southern Germany.

    Catalogue of the Duc de Dino's Collection.

Daniele, Père Gabriel. Hist. de la Milice Français. 1721.

Demmin. Guide des Amateurs d'Armes.

Dillon, Viscount :—

    Archæologia, LI.   Arms and Armour at Westminster, the Tower, and Greenwich. 1547.

        ,,   LI.   Trial of Armour. 1590.

        ,,   LVII.   Ordinances of Chivalry, XV cent.

    Arch. Journ., XLIV. The Besague or Moton.

        ,,   ,,   XLVI.   The Pasguard and the Volant Piece.

        ,,   ,,   LI.   An Elizabethan Armourer's Album, 1590.

        ,,   ,,   LV.   Tilting in Tudor Times.

        ,,   ,,   LX.   Armour Notes.

        ,,   ,,   LXV.   Armour and Arms in Shakespeare.

        ,,   ,,   LXIX. Horse Armour.

    An Almain Armourer's Album, Introduction and Notes. 1905.

Dudley, Dud. Metallum Martis. 1665.

Essenwein. Die Helm. 1892.

Fauchet, Claude. Origines des Chevaliers, etc. 1610.

ffoulkes, Charles :—

    Armour and Weapons. 1909.

    Gaya's Traité des Armes. 1911.

    Arms and Armour at Oxford. 1912.

    Archæologia, LXII, LXIII.

    Arch. Journ., LXVIII.

    Burlington Mag. April, 1911.

    Connoisseur. June, Sept., Nov., 1909.

    Zeitschrift für Historische Waffenkunde, V. 10.

Forestie. Livres des Comptes des Frères Bonis.

Garnier. L'Artillerie des Ducs de Bourgogne.

Gay. Glossaire Archéologique.

Gaya. Traité des Armes, 1687. (Edit. by C. ffoulkes.) 1911.

Gazette de Beaux Arts. Various articles.

Gelli, J. Guida del Amatore di Armi Antiche. 1900.

Gelli and Moretti. I Missaglia. 1903.

Giraud. Les Armuriers Français et Étrangers, 1898.

Gurlitt. Deutschen Turniere, Rüstungen und Plattner. 1889.

Gwynne, John. Memoirs of the Great Civil War. 1822 edit.

Hastings MS. Ordinances of Chivalry. (Archæologia, LVII.)

Hefner-Altneck. Tracten des Christlichen Mittelalters. 1840.

Herbert, William. Hist. of 12 Livery Companies of London. 1834–7.

Hewitt. Ancient Armour. 1855.

Holinshed, R. Chronicles

Jahrbuch des Kunsthistorische Sammlungen des Allerhöchster Kaiserhause. Various vols.

Langey.   Discipline Militaire.

La Noue.   Discours Politiques et Militaires, trans. by E. A.   1587.

Letters and Papers Foreign and Domestic, Record Office.   Various entries.

Markham, G.   Decades of Epistles of War.   1662.   Souldiers' Accidence.   1643.

Memorials of the Verney Family.

Mémoires de la Soc. Arch. de Touraine.

Meyrick.   Antient Armour.

Montgomery.   Milice Français.

Morigia.   Hist. dell' Antichita di Milano.

Oliver de la Marche.   Memoirs, etc.   1616 edit.

Ordonnances des Métiers de Paris.

Ordonnances des Rois.

Patent Office, London, Records of.

Pennant.   History of London.

Pelegrini.   Di un Armajuolo Bellunese.   Arch. Venez., X.

René.   Traicté d'un Tournoi.

Revue Savoisienne.   Various vols.

Rogers, J. Thorold.   History of Agriculture and Prices.   1866.

Rymer.   Fœdera.   Various entries.

Saulx-Tavannes.   Mém. rel. à l'hist. de France, Vol. VIII.   1866.

Saxe, Marshal.   Rêveries.   Edit. 1756.

Scott, Sir S.   History of the British Army.

Speculum Regale.   Edit. 1768.

Smith, Sir John.   Instructions and Orders Militarie.   1593.   Discourses.   1590.

Sussex Archæological Journal.   Various articles.

Walsingham.   Historia Anglicana, Rolls Series.

Wardroom Accounts of Edward I.   Soc. of Ant.

Zeitschrift für Historische Waffenkunde.   Various articles.

Catalogues of Windsor Castle; the Tower; Wallace Collection; Rotunda, Woolwich; Musée d'Artillerie, Paris; Armeria Reale, Turin; Real Armeria, Madrid; Waffensammlung, Vienna; Zeughaus, Berlin; Porte de Hal, Brussels; Historische Museum, Dresden; Ashmolean and Pitt-Rivers Museums, Oxford; British Museum; etc. etc.

Articles in various Journals and Periodicals by Viscount Dillon, Baron de Cosson, Burgess, Waller, Way, Meyrick, Hewitt, ffoulkes, Boeheim, Angellucci, Beaumont, Buttin, Yriarte, Giraud.

Various MSS. from the British Museum; Bib. Nat., Paris; Königl. Bibliothek, Berlin; Bodleian Library; etc. etc.

THE
ARMOURER
AND HIS CRAFT

So yff hit stoode than no wer ware
Lost were the craffte of Armoreres

LYDGATE, *The hors, the shepe & the gosse*, line 127

THE ARMOURER
AND HIS CRAFT

THE ARMOURER

THE importance of the craft of the armourer in the Middle Ages can hardly be overestimated, for it is, to a large extent, to the excellence of defensive armour and weapons that we owe much of the development of art and craftsmanship all over Europe. The reason for this somewhat sweeping statement is to be found in the fact that up to the sixteenth century the individual and the personal factor were of supreme importance in war, and it was the individual whose needs the armourer studied. In the days when military organization was in its infancy, and the leader was endowed by his followers with almost supernatural qualities, the battle was often won by the prowess of the commander, or lost by his death or disablement. It would be tedious to quote more than a few instances of this importance of the individual in war, but the following are typical of the spirit which pervaded the medieval army.

At the battle of Hastings, when William was supposed to have been killed he rallied his followers by lifting his helmet and riding through the host crying, "I am here and by God's grace I shall conquer!" The success of Joan of Arc need hardly be mentioned, as it is an obvious example of the change which could be effected in the spirit of an army by a popular leader. This importance of the individual was realized by the leaders themselves, and, as a safeguard, it was often the custom to dress one or more knights like the sovereign or commander to draw off the attack. At Bosworth field Richmond had more than one knight who personated him; Shakespeare gives the number as five, for Richard says, "There be six Richmonds in the field; five have I slain instead of him."

When the importance of the leader is realized it will be obvious that the craft of the man who protected him in battle was of the utmost importance to the State; and when once this is admitted, we may fairly consider that, in an age of ceaseless wars and private raids, the importance of all the other applied arts which followed in the train of a victorious leader depended to a very great extent on the protection afforded him by his armourer.[1]

It would be indeed superfluous to dwell upon the artistic influences which may be traced directly to the military operations of the Assyrians, Greeks, Romans, and at a later date the Northern tribes of Europe, for every writer on the subject bases his opinions upon this foundation. In more modern periods the conquest of Spain by the Moors introduced a type of design which has never been wholly eradicated from Spanish Art, and in our own country the Norman Conquest gave us a dignified strength of architecture which would never have been established as a national phase of art if the victory had been to Harold and the English. The improvements in the equipment and military organization of the foot-soldier in the thirteenth and fourteenth centuries necessitated a more complete style of defensive armour for the mounted man, and the elaborate leg armour of plate may be directly traced to the improvement in the weapons of the former. As is the case at the present day in the navy, the race between weapon and defence was ceaseless, each improvement of the one being met by a corresponding improvement in the other, till the perfection of the firearm ruled any form of defence out of the competition. More peaceful influences were at work, however, due to the interchange of visits between European princes; and German and Italian fashions of armour, as well as of the other applied arts, competed with each other all over Europe, though their adoption may generally be traced to a ruler of note like Maximilian or Charles V.

So without undue exaggeration we may fairly claim for the craft of the armourer a foremost place as one of the chief influences in the

---

[1] See Regulations of the "Heaumers," Appendix B, p. 171.

evolution of modern art and, as such, an important factor in the development of all the arts which follow in the train of conquest.

There are certain essential rules which must be observed in the practice of every craft; but in most cases only one or two are necessary for the production of good work, because of the limitations either of the craft or of the needs of those for whom it is practised. It would be out of place to go through the various applied arts and to consider the rules which guide them ; but, on examination of these rules as they apply to the craft of the armourer, it will be seen how each and all are essential for the production of satisfactory work.

The rules are these :—

    1. Suitability for purpose.
    2. Convenience in use.
    3. Recognition of material.
    4. Soundness of constructional methods.
    5. Subservience of decoration to the preceding rules.

It may be advantageous to examine these rules one by one and see how they are observed to the full in the best specimens of armour and how their neglect produced inferior work.

1. **Suitability for purpose.**—The object of defensive armour was to protect the wearer from attack of the most powerful weapon in use at the period when it was made. This was obtained not only by thickness of metal, but also by so fashioning the planes of the metal that they presented a " glancing surface " to the blow. An early example of this consideration of the needs of the wearer is to be found in the first additions of plate to the suit of mail which were made in the leg armour of the thirteenth century (Fig. 38). The reason for this was the increased efficacy of the weapons of the foot-soldier, who naturally attacked the legs of the mounted man. The use of mail was far from practical, except in the form of gussets or capes, which could not be made so conveniently in plate. The mail armour of the thirteenth century was only a partial protection, for although it defended the wearer from arrows and from sword-cut or lance-thrust, it was but little protection against the bruise of the blow, even when, as was always

the case, a padded garment was worn underneath. Up to the sixteenth century the shield was used for this reason and provided a smooth movable surface which the knight could oppose to the weapon and thus present a glancing surface to the blow.

An examination of a suit of armour of the fifteenth century will show how this glancing surface was studied in every part. The lames of the arm-pieces are overlapped downwards so that the blow might slip off, and the elbow-cop presents a smooth rounded surface which will direct the blow off the arm of the wearer. The breastplate, which was at first simply smooth and rounded, became in the sixteenth century fluted ; and a practical experiment will show that when the thrust of a lance—the favourite weapon at that time—met one of these flutings it was directed to the strong ridge at neck or arm hole and thence off the body (Plate 30, 2). The upstanding neck-guards, wrongly called " passe-guards," were also intended to protect the weak part where helmet and gorget met. The fan-plate of the knee-piece protected the bend of the knee, especially when bent in riding, the normal position of the mounted man, and the sollerets were so fashioned that the foot was best protected when in the stirrup.

The helm and helmet are especially good examples of the craft of the armourer in this respect. The early flat-topped helm of the thirteenth century was soon discarded because it was found that the full force of the downward blow was felt, which was not the case when the skull of the head-piece was pointed or rounded (Fig. 1). A treatise on the subject of Military Equipment in the fifteenth century (Appendix D) distinctly enjoins that the

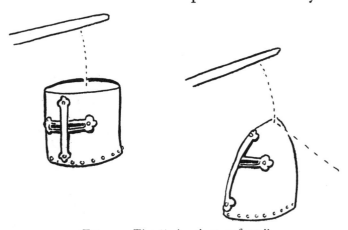

FIG. 1. The " glancing surface."

rivets on the helm should be filed flat : " Et les autres ont la teste du clou limée affin que le rochet ny prengne." This is not often found in existing helms, but the fact that it is mentioned shows that the smooth surface of the helm was an important consideration. In

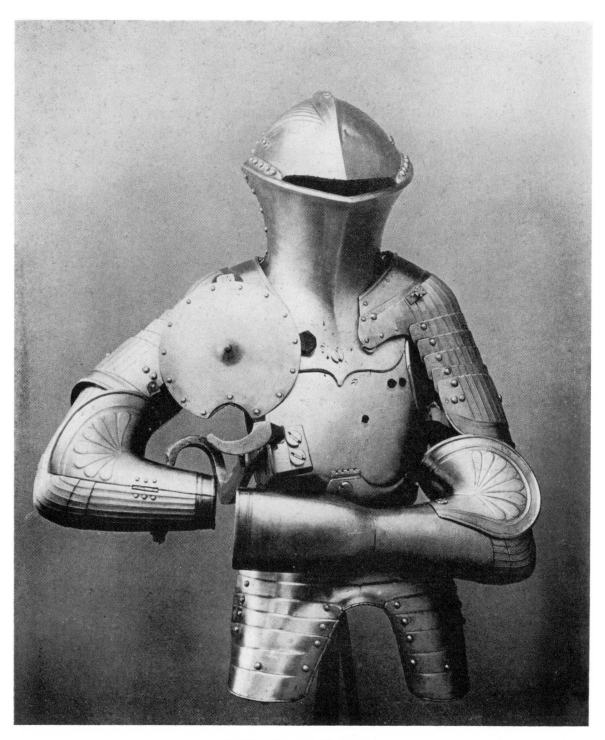

ARMOUR FOR THE STECHZEUG
XV--XVI CENT.

PLATE I

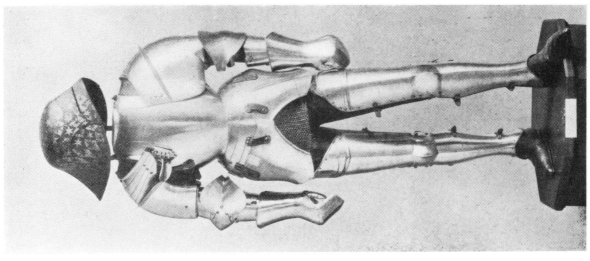

ARMOUR BY ANTONIO DA MISSAGLIA, 1480

S. GEORGE, BY MANTEGNA, 1431-1506
ACCADEMIA, VENICE

PLATE II

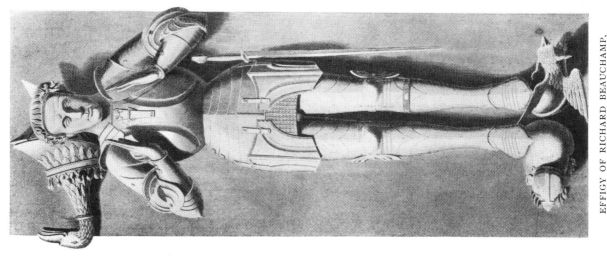

EFFIGY OF RICHARD BEAUCHAMP,
EARL OF WARWICK
S. MARY'S CHURCH, WARWICK, 1454

helms made for jousting these considerations were minutely studied by the armourer, for the object of jousters in the sixteenth century was simply to score points and not to injure each other. The occularium of the jousting-helm is narrow and is so placed that it is only of use when the wearer bends forward with his lance in rest. The lance was always pointed across the horse's neck and was directed to the left side of his opponent, therefore the left side of the helm is always smooth with no projection or opening (Fig. 2). These are found,

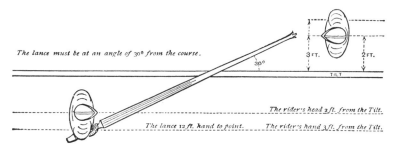

FIG. 2. Position of lance in jousting (*Arch. Journ.*, LV).

in cases where they occur, on the right side, where there would be no chance of their catching the lance-point. Again, the skull and front plate of the helm are generally thicker than those at the back, where there is no chance of a blow being delivered.

2. **Convenience in use.**—Besides protecting the fighting man the armourer had to remember that his patron had to ride, sometimes to walk, and always to use his arms with convenience, and at the same time had to be protected while so doing. At first the cuirass was made simply in two pieces, the back and the front fastened under the arms with straps. In the middle of the fifteenth century each of these was made in two or more pieces joined with a rivet, working loose in a slot cut in the uppermost of the plates, so that a certain amount of movement of the torse was possible. The pauldrons, which often appear unnecessarily large, almost meeting in front and, as is the case in the statue of Colleoni in Venice, crossing at the back, are so made that they would protect the armpit when the arm was raised in striking a blow (Fig. 3). The upper part of the arm-piece or rerebrace is made of overlapping lames held together by sliding rivets, which allow a certain amount of play outwards and forwards, but the defence becomes rigid if the arm

is moved backwards, for this movement is not necessary in delivering a blow (see page 52). The arm and leg pieces are hinged with metal hinges on the outside of the limb and fastened with straps or hooks and

FIG. 3.   Back of Pauldrons of A. Statue of Colleoni, Venice.
B. Missaglia Suit, Waffensammlung, Vienna.

staples on the inside. In most cases modern theatrical armour errs in this respect, for it is obvious that if the straps were on the outside the first object of the enemy would be to cut them and render the armour useless. The vambrace or cannon and the lower portion of the rerebrace are in single cylindrical plates, for here no movement is possible independently from the shoulder and elbow. The rerebrace, however, is generally formed with a collar which turns in a groove bossed out in the upper portion, so that the arm can turn outwards or inwards without moving the shoulder (see page 54). The cuisse and the front and back of the jamb are for the same reasons each made in one piece, joined to

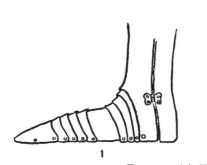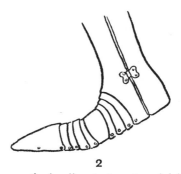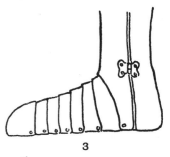

FIG. 4.   (1) The practical solleret at rest and (2) in action.
(3) Unpractical solleret, late sixteenth century.

the knee-cop and solleret by narrow lames working loose on rivets. The cuisse only covers the top part of the thigh for convenience on horseback, and wherever a cuisse is found that protects the back of the thigh we may be sure that the owner fought on foot (Plate IX). The solleret is made so that the foot can move naturally in walking. The upper part is formed of small lames working on loose rivets and overlapping downwards towards a centre-plate which covers the tread of the foot; beyond this the toe-plates overlap upwards and thus perfect freedom of movement is obtained.

The various forms of head-piece all more or less exemplify this need of convenience in use, for they protected the head and at the same time gave as much opportunity for seeing, hearing, and breathing as was compatible with their defensive qualities. The armet or close helmet is perhaps the most ingenious, with its single or double visor, which could be lifted up so as to leave the face completely exposed till the moment of attack, when it was closed and fastened with a locking hook (Plate XIII). Examples of the armourer adapting his work to the requirements of his patrons are to be found in the globose helm for fighting at barriers made by one of the Missaglia family (Tower, II, 29). Here the vision-slits were evidently found to be too large and too dangerous to the wearer. An inner plate was added with smaller holes through which no weapon used at barriers could penetrate (Plate X). A second example shown in Fig. 14 has a plate added at the lower edge to increase the height of the helm, which suggests that the last wearer had a longer neck than the original owner. This convenience in use is also to be noticed in the gauntlet, which, as the science of sword-play developed, was gradually discarded in favour of a defence formed of the portes or rings on the sword-hilt (Plate XXII). In jousting-armour there was only one position to be considered, namely, the position with hand on bridle and lance in rest. The armourer therefore strove to protect his patron when he assumed that position alone. The arm defences of jousting-armour with elbow-guard and poldermitton would be useless if the wearer had to raise his arm with a sword, but, when the lance was held in rest, the plates of the defences were so arranged that every blow slipped harmlessly off. As the right hand was protected with the large shield or vamplate fixed to the lance a gauntlet for this hand was frequently dispensed with, and, as the left hand was only employed to hold the reins, a semi-cylindrical plate protected the hand instead of the articulated gauntlet in use on the field of war (Plate I).

Horse armour or "barding" was of necessity more cumbrous and but little was attempted beyond the covering of the vital parts of the body with plates or padded trappings (Fig. 5). Mail was used for the

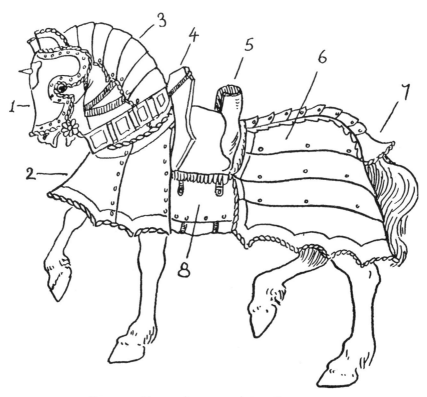

FIG. 5. Horse Armour, sixteenth century.

	ENGLISH	FRENCH	GERMAN	ITALIAN	SPANISH
1.	chanfron	chanfrein	ross-stirn	testiera	testera
2.	peytral	poitrail	brust panzer	pettiera	pechera
3.	crinet	crinière	{ mähnen panzer kanze	} collo	cuello
4.	pommel	{ pommeau arcade de devant	} sattel-knopf	primo arcione	pomo del arzon
5.	cantel	{ troussequin arcade de derrière	rückenstück pausch	} secondo arcione	zaguero
6.	crupper	croupière	{ krup panzer lenden panzer	} groppa	grupera
7.	tail-guard	garde-queue	schwanzriem panzer	guardacorda	guardamalso
8.	flanchard	{ flançois flanchière	} flanken panzer	fiancali	flanqueras

whole "bard" in the thirteenth century, as we know from the decorations in the "Painted Chamber" at Westminster.[1] It was still in use for the neck-defence or "crinet" in the middle of the fifteenth century. Examples of the latter are to be found in Paris (Plate XXIII) and in the

---

[1] *Vetusta Monumenta*, **VI**, and *Armour and Weapons*, p. 88, C. ffoulkes.

Wallace Collection, No. 620. Some attempt to make an articulated suit was evidently made; for we have a portrait of Harnischmeister Albrecht

FIG. 6. Harnischmeister Albrecht, 1480.
From a painting in the Arsenal, Vienna.

(1480) mounted on a horse whose legs are completely covered by articulated plates similar to those on human armour (Fig. 6). A portion of the leg-piece of this or of a similar suit is in the Musée Porte de Hal,

Brussels (Fig. 7).   Besides the obvious advantage of plate armour over mail for defensive purposes, it should be noted that in the former the weight is distributed over the body and limbs, while with the latter the whole equipment hangs from the shoulders, with possibly some support at the waist. Hence the movements of the mail-clad man were much hampered both by the weight of the fabric, and also by the fact that in bending the arm or leg the mail would crease in folds, and would thus both interfere with complete freedom and would probably produce a sore from chafing.

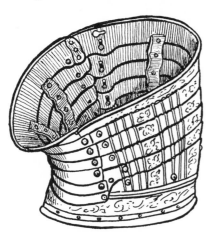

FIG. 7.   Cuissard for the off hock of a horse.   Musée Porte de Hal, Brussels, IV, 9.

3. **Recognition of material.**—It would seem at first sight superfluous to give examples of this when considering armour ; but in the sixteenth century, when the craftsman desired to show off his technical skill, we find many suits made to imitate the puffed and slashed velvets and silks of civilian dress.   A notable example of this is to be found on the famous " Engraved Suit " made by Conrad Seusenhofer for Henry VIII in the Tower, in which the cloth " bases " or skirts of civilian dress are imitated in metal (Plates XII, XXI).   The human form, head and torse, were also counterfeited in metal in the sixteenth century, with no great success from the technical point of view.

4. **Soundness of constructional methods.**—This rule is really contained in those that have preceded it, but some notice should be paid to the various methods of fastening different plates and portions of the suit together.   There are many ingenious forms of turning hook and pin by which these plates can be joined or taken apart at will (page 55). The sliding rivet is one of the most important of these constructional details.   The lower end of the rivet is burred over the back of the lower plate, and the upper plate has a slot cut of less width than the rivet-head, but sufficiently long to allow the plate to move backwards and forwards, generally from three-quarters to one inch (page 52).

5. **Subservience of decoration to the preceding rules.**—The best suits are practically undecorated, but at the same time there are many

which are ornamented with incised or engraved lines and gilding which do not detract from the utility of the armour. This last rule is best understood by examples of the breach rather than the observance; so we may take the rules in order and see how each was broken during that period known as the Renaissance.

(1) The "glancing surface" was destroyed by elaborate embossing, generally of meaningless designs, in which the point or edge of a weapon would catch.

(2) The convenience was also impaired by the same methods, for the lames and different portions of the suit could not play easily one over the other if each had designs in high relief. Plates were set at unpractical angles, sometimes overlapping upwards, in which the weapon would catch and would not glance off. We find that foot-armour was made in the sixteenth and seventeenth centuries with the lames all overlapping upwards or downwards, and with no centre-plate for the tread. In the suit given to Henry, Prince of Wales, by the Prince de Joinville in 1608 (Tower, II, 17) the lames of the solleret all overlap downwards (see also Fig. 4). It will be obvious that with such a foot-covering it would be impossible to walk with ease.

(3) The observance of this rule may be taken as a matter of course and its neglect has been noticed above.

(4) The careless arrangement of the foot-armour, as mentioned in No. 2, is an example of the disregard of this rule. Another instance is the embossing the metal of various parts of the suit so as to simulate lames or separate plates. They do not ornament the suit and of course do not add to its convenience; they merely create a false impression and save the craftsman some labour. The same may be said of the "clous perdus" or false rivets, which are found in late suits, doing no work in the construction of the suit, but giving an appearance of constructional work which is lacking.

(5) One has only to keep the above rules in mind and then to examine an embossed suit by Piccinino or Peffenhauser to see how this rule was broken to the detriment of the work as a good piece of craftsmanship, though perhaps the result may have increased the artistic reputation of the craftsman (Plate XIV).

It should be noticed that the craftsman of the Renaissance, in spite of his disregard of the craft rules, did not deteriorate as a worker; for some of the suits of the Negrolis or of the two above-mentioned armourers could hardly be equalled at the present day as specimens of metal-work. But his energies were directed into different channels and his reputation as an honest craftsman suffered.   By the sixteenth century everything concerned with the defensive qualities and the constructional details of armour had been discovered and carried to a high pitch of perfection. The craftsman therefore had to find some way of exhibiting his dexterity.   Add to this the love of ostentation and display of his patron, one of the most noticeable traits of the so-called Renaissance, and we find that by degrees the old craft-excellence became neglected in the advertisement of the craftsman and the ostentation of his patron.

In dealing with the first rule no mention was made of the defensive qualities of armour against firearms, and this from the middle of the sixteenth century was an important detail in the craft of the armourer.   The glancing surface was of some use; but the armed man could not afford to take chances.   So his equipment was made to resist a point-blank shot of pistol or arquebus.   This will be noticed with details as to the proof of armour on page 65.   It was the fact that armour *was* proof against firearms which led to its disuse, and not that it was of no avail against them, as is the generally accepted idea.   The armourer proved his work by the most powerful weapons in use, and by so doing found that he had to increase the weight of metal till it became insupportable (see page 117).

In the days when travelling was difficult and the difficulties of transportation great, both on account of the condition of the roads and also because of the insecurity of life and property, due to national and personal wars, it was but natural that each country and district should be in a large measure self-supporting, especially with respect to armour and weapons.   At the same time, by degrees, some localities produced superior work, either because they possessed natural resources or because some master founded a school with superior methods to those of his neighbours.   Thus we find Milan famous for hauberks, Bordeaux[1] for swords, Colin cleeves (Cologne halberds), Toulouse swords, misericordes of Versy, chapeaux de Montauban (steel hats), Barcelona bucklers,

---

[1] Haute Savoye, near Aix-les-Bains.

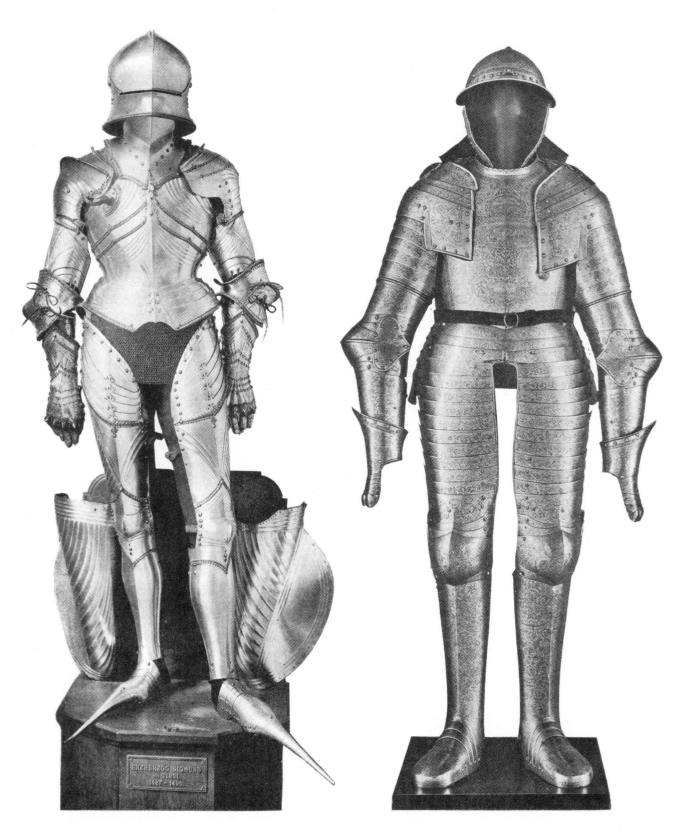

ARMOUR OF SIGISMOND OF TIROL, 1427-96   ARMOUR OF LOUIS XIV, BY GARBAGNAUS, 1668

PLATE III

ARMOURERS AT WORK. XV CENT.

BRIT. MUS. ROY. MS. 16, G. V, FOL. II

WOODCARVING OF DUKE WILLIAM OF AQUITAINE
AND HIS ARMOURER. XV CENT.

VENUS AND VULCAN. XIII CENT.

BERLIN, KÖNIGL. BIB. CODEX MS. GERM. 282, 79

PLATE IV

arbalests of Catheloigne, and of course swords of Solingen, Toledo, and Passau.

The principal centres for the making of armour were Italy and Germany, and it is quite impossible to say which of the two was the superior from the craftsman's point of view. If anything, perhaps the German school favoured a rather heavier type of equipment, due, no doubt, to the natural characteristics of the race as compared with the Italian, and also, when the decadence of armour began, perhaps the German armourer of the Renaissance erred more in respect of useless and florid ornamentation than did his Italian rival. But even here the types are so similar that it is almost impossible to discriminate. France produced no great armourers, at least we have no records of craft-princes such as the Colmans, the Seusenhofers, the Missaglias, or the Negrolis, and the same may be said of England. We have isolated examples here and there of English and French work, but we have no records of great schools in either country like those of Milan, Brescia, Nuremberg, Augsburg, and Innsbruck. A few scattered entries from state or civic documents will be found under the various headings of this work and portions of regulations respecting the trade ; but of the lives of the craftsmen we know but little. At a time when personal safety in the field was of the utmost importance, it can be easily under-stood that the patron would take no risks, but would employ for choice those craftsmen who held the highest repute for their work, just as till recently the prospective motorist or airman would not risk a home-made machine, but patronized French makers. It may seem strange that the local craftsmen did not attempt to improve their work when examples of foreign skill were imported in great quantities ; but against this we must set the fact that the detail of the first importance in the craft of the armourer was the tempering of the metal and this the craftsman kept a close secret. We have various accounts of secret processes, miraculous springs of water, poisoned ores, and such-like which were employed, fabulously no doubt, to attain fine temper for the metal, but no details are given. It may be that the metal itself was superior in some districts, as witness the Trial of Armour given on page 66. Seusenhofer when provided with inferior metal from the mines by Kugler suggested that it should be classed as "Milanese," a clear proof that the German craftsmen, at any rate, considered the Italian material to be inferior to their own.   Little is known as to the production of the

Florentine armourers.   Mr. Staley in his *Guilds of Florence* has unfortunately found little of importance under this heading in the civic records of the city.

The "Corazzi e spadai" of Florence will, however, be always known by their patron S. George, whose statue by Donatello stood outside the gild church of Or San Michele.   At the base of the niche in which it stood are carved the arms given in Fig. 8.

Armourers were imported by sovereigns and princes to produce armour

FIG. 8. Arms of the Armourers' Gild, from the church of Or San Michele, Florence.

for their personal use and thus to avoid the difficulties of transit, but they seem to have kept their craft to themselves and to have founded no school.   Henry VIII brought over the "Almain Armourers" to Greenwich at the beginning of his reign, but most of them went back in time to their own country, and few took out denization papers.   In 1624 we find that only one of the descendants of these foreigners was left and he resolutely refused to teach any one the "mysterie of plating" (page 188).   A colony of armourers migrated from Milan to Arbois towards the end of the fifteenth century, but no celebrated craftsmen seem to have joined them except the Merate brothers, who worked for Maximilian and Mary of Burgundy.   It is difficult, in fact impossible, to say which country led in the beginnings of the armourer's craft.   We have the suit of Roberto di Sanseverino (Vienna, Waffensamm-lung, No. 3) signed with the mark of Antonio Missaglia, *circ.* 1470, and we also have a statuette by Hans Multscher at Augsburg, *circ.* 1458,

FIG. 9. S. George, by Hans Multscher, 1458, Augsburg.

which represents S. George in a suit of armour of precisely the same design (Fig. 9). It should be noted, however, that the treatment of this figure shows a strong Italian influence. In European history of the fifteenth century we have few records of German armourers being employed, during the first half, at any rate, by the rulers of other states. We know that Richard Beauchamp, Earl of Warwick, travelled in Italy and wore armour of a distinctly Italian style, for it is depicted in the *Beauchamp Pageants* (Fig. 10) and is also shown on his magnificent monument in S. Mary's Church, Warwick. The likeness of the armour on this monument to that shown in the picture of S. George, by Mantegna, in the Accademia, Venice, is so striking that we are bound to admit that the two suits must have been produced by the same master, and on comparison with the suit in Vienna above alluded to, that master must have been one of the Missaglia family. The Earl of Warwick died in 1439 and Mantegna was born about 1431, so that it is quite possible that the former purchased a suit of the very latest fashion when in Italy, and that the latter, realizing the beauty of work produced when he was but a boy, used a similar suit as a model for his picture (Plate II). As early as 1398 the Earl of Derby had armour brought over to England by Milanese armourers, and by the year 1427 Milan had become such an important factory town that it supplied in a few days armour for 4000 cavalry and 2000 infantry.

FIG. 10. Richard Beauchamp, Earl of Warwick (Cot. Jul. E, IV, F, 12 b).

The impetus given to the craft in Germany was due to the interest of the young Emperor Maximilian, who encouraged not only the armourer, but every other craftsman and artist in his dominions. In the *Weisz Künig* we find him teaching the masters of all crafts how best to do their own work, though this is probably an exaggeration of the sycophantic author and illustrator. Still we are forced to admit that the crafts in Germany attained to a very high level during his reign. In the description of his visit to Conrad Seusenhofer, the armourer, it is recorded that the latter wished to employ certain devices of his own in the making of armour, to which the young Emperor replied, "Arm me according to my own wish, for it is I and not you who will take part in the tournament." From Germany came armour presented by the Emperor to Henry VIII, and it is clear that such a master as Seusenhofer, working so near the Italian frontier as Innsbruck, must have influenced the Milanese work, just as the Milanese in the first instance influenced the German craftsmen. With the succession of Charles V to the thrones of Spain and Germany we find a new impetus given to German armourers. In Spain there seems to have been a strong feeling in favour of Milanese work, and the contest between the two schools of craftsmen was bitter in the extreme. So personal did this feud become that we find Desiderius Colman in 1552 making a shield for Charles V on which the maker is represented as a bull charging a Roman soldier on whose shield is the word "Negrol," a reference to the rivalry between the Colmans and the Negrolis of Milan (Plate XXIV). With the demand for decorated armour the rivalry between the two centres of trade increased, and there is little to choose between the works of the German and Italian craftsmen, either in the riotous incoherence of design or in the extraordinary skill with which it was produced and finished.

From entries in the State Papers preserved in the Record Office, it would seem that Milanese armourers were employed by Henry VIII during the first years of his reign. By the year 1515 the Almain or German armourers from Brussels had evidently taken their place, for they are entered as king's servants with liveries. Only one Milanese name is found in the list of armourers, Baltesar Bullato, 1532, so that it is clear that Henry, owing, no doubt, to the influence of Maximilian, had definitely committed himself to German armour as opposed to Italian. England seems to have remained faithful to this German influence, but her rulers and nobles never indulged in the exaggerated and over-elaborate productions which held favour in Spain and Germany, a fact which is noticeable even at the present day, when the so-called "Art Nouveau" disfigures many German and Italian cities but has never obtained a serious foothold in England. Simplicity and practicality were always the chief features in English armour. The few known

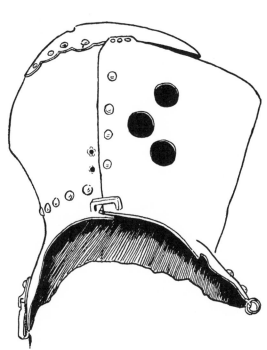

FIG. 11. The Westminster Helm, *circ.* 1500.
Westminster Abbey. 17 lb. 12 oz.

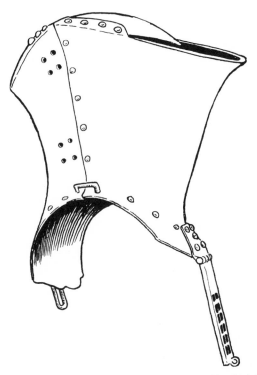

FIG. 12. The Brocas Helm, Rotunda, Woolwich.
22 lb. 8 oz.

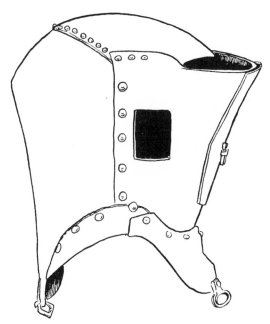

FIG. 13. The Fogge Helm, Ashford, Sussex.
24 lb.

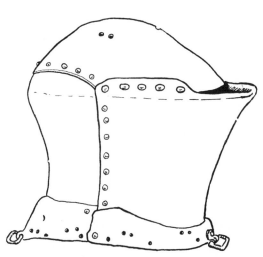

FIG. 14. The Barendyne Helm, Great Haseley,
Oxon. 13 lb. 8 oz.

specimens of English work of the late fifteenth and early sixteenth centuries, the jousting-helms at Westminster, Woolwich, Ashford, Petworth, and the Wallace Collection, are examples of this, and the armour of later years has the same qualification (Figs. 11–14). Even the suits of Topf, who worked in England at the end of the sixteenth century and produced the magnificent work that is shown at the Tower, Windsor, and elsewhere, the designs for which are contained in an album in the Art Library at South Kensington, are marked by a restraint which is not found in the works of Piccinino and Peffenhauser. The decoration never impairs the utility of the armour, and the designs are always those suitable for work in tempered steel, and are not in any way suggestive of the goldsmith's work of his foreign contemporaries. In the English national collections we have but little eccentric armour, which is so common in Continental museums; all is severe and yet graceful, practical even if decorated, a tribute to the characteristics of the English race of fighting men.

The ornamentation of armour with gilding had obtained such a firm hold that in the seventeenth century James II was obliged to make an exception in its favour in his proclamation against the use of "gold and silver foliate," an extract of which is given in Appendix I, page 187. In discussing the craft of the armourer it should be remembered that we can only base our conclusions on the scattered entries of payments, inventories, and other documents in State or private collections, and by examination of suits which have been preserved in the armouries and collections of Europe and England. These suits represent but a very small percentage of the large stores of armour of all kinds which must have been in existence at the beginning of the seventeenth century, and it is only the fine and exceptional examples which have survived. The material was so costly in the making that it was made and remade over and over again; which will account for the absence of complete suits of the fourteenth century and the scarcity of those of the fifteenth and sixteenth centuries now in existence. Occasionally we have local collections which give us a suggestion of what the standing armoury must have been, such as the armour stores at Gratz, Zurich, the collection of helmets and armour found in the castle of Chalcis,[1] and village

---

[1] Charles ffoulkes "Italian Armour at Chalcis," *Archæologia*, LXII.

armouries like that at Mendlesham, Suffolk. Two examples of the treatment of armour must suffice. In the Inventory of the Tower, taken in 33 Hen. VI, 1455, is the entry: "Item viij habergeons some of Meleyn and some of Westewale of the which v of Melyn were delyv'ed to the College of Eyton and iij broken to make slewys and voyders and ye's." Here clearly the hauberk is cut up and used to make sleeves and gussets, which were more useful when the complete plate body-defences had come into fashion than the shirt of mail. This is also another example of the competition between Milan and Germany (Westphalia) in the matter of armour-making. As an example of the other reason for the absence of armour in national and private collections in any great quantities, we may cite Hearne's account of his visit to Ditchley, given in his *Remains* under the date 1718. He says: "In one of the outhouses I saw strange armour which belonged to the ancestors[1] of the Earl of Litchfield, some of the armour very old." In the steward's accounts of but a few weeks later Viscount Dillon has discovered an entry, "received of Mr. Mott, the brazier for the old armour wayed 14 cwt. 1 qr. 21 lb. at 10s. the cwt. £7. 4. 6." The saddles had been previously cut up to nail up the fruit trees.[2] From the weight of armour sold there were probably about twenty suits, some of which must certainly have been of value, possibly one or more of the missing suits designed by Topf for Sir Henry Lee and illustrated in the *Almain Armourer's Album* now in the South Kensington Art Library. It can be readily understood that when the historic or artistic value of armour was not appreciated it was a cumbrous and useless possession, which soon deteriorated if not kept clean and bright, and therefore it was melted down just as are the broken stoves and domestic ironmongery which litter the rubbish-heaps to-day. We find interesting examples of the application of munitions of war to peaceful purposes in the use of sword-pommels as weights for steelyards, helmets for buckets and scale-bowls, and portions of body armour cut up and fashioned into lock-covers in the Stibbert Museum, Florence, in the collection of the Marchese Peruzzi, and elsewhere.[3] Even as late as the year 1887 the value of armour was not realized, for in that year two half-suits, stamped

[1] Sir Henry Lee.   [2] *Arch. Journ.*, June, 1895.
[3] Sir Thomas Gresham's steelyard in the London Museum is decorated with portions of sword hilts.

with the college mark, were sold from New College, Oxford, as old iron (*Arms and Armour in Oxford*, C. ffoulkes).

State and civic records have frequent entries of regulations and disputes connected with the various craft-gilds, and the armourers were no exception. The right of search was a privilege jealously guarded, for it prevented the competition of those outside the gild and was also a check against foreign competition, which was always a thorn in the side of the armourer. Every country enacted laws against importation of arms, and yet for really fine work every country had to look to Italy or Germany. But this was probably the case only among the richest, and it is the elaborate workmanship on the armour which has ensured the survival of many suits of this type. The ordinary hosting or war-harness was made quite as well in England as elsewhere; just as the Englishwoman of to-day can be dressed as well in London as in Paris; but, if she can afford it, elects to pay large sums for the *cachet* of the Parisian name. With regard to the documents bearing on the life of individual armourers, we have such records as wills, registers of baptisms and marriages, and also trade accounts and bills. In the latter the armourer seems to have been no better off than the painter or sculptor of the Middle Ages and Renaissance. He was always in financial difficulties and was ceaselessly pressing his patron for payment. An example of this is given on page 59, where we find that W. Pickering was paid £200 in 1614, the balance of his bill for £340, for a suit made for Henry, Prince of Wales, who died in 1612; so that he had to wait at least two years before he received the whole amount. Conrad Seusenhofer suffered in the same way and his life was one long struggle with Maximilian and the Diet for payments for his work. The armourer, however, had the advantage over his fellow-craftsmen; for when a war or a tournament was imminent he made his own terms and refused delivery till he had received payment.

The craft of the armourer merits far more study than has hitherto been bestowed upon it, for in its finest examples it fulfils all the essential laws of good craftsmanship to the uttermost. Added to this the works of the armourer have what may be called a double personal interest. In the first place, they are the actual wearing apparel of kings, princes, and other persons of note, made to their measure and often exhibition

ARMOURER'S ANVIL AND PINCERS. XVI CENT.
BRITISH MUSEUM, BURGES BEQUEST

ANVIL. XIV CENT.
IN THE POSSESSION OF MME. BELLON, AVIGNON

PLATE V

MAXIMILIAN AND HIS ARMOURER, CONRAD SEUSENHOFER
FROM THE WEISZ KÜNIG

PLATE VI

some peculiarity of their owner. Owing to the perishable nature of fabrics but little of wearing apparel has survived to us of the periods anterior to the seventeenth century, and therefore the suit of armour is most valuable as an historical record, especially when taken in conjunction with portraits, historical paintings, and sculpture. In addition to this we have the personality of the maker. The boldly grooved breastplate, the pauldrons, and the wide elbow-cops of the Missaglia, the distinctive hook for the armet which appears only on Topf suits can be recognized at once, and besides this we have the *poinçon* or signature of the craftsman, which it is almost impossible to imitate, and which at once proclaims the authorship of the armour.

The whole subject of the armourer and his craft, his limitations, his success at his best period, and his decadence in later years can be best summed up in the illustration given on Plate III. Here we have the graceful and light yet serviceable suit of Sigismond of Tirol, made by an unknown armourer about the year 1470, placed side by side with the cumbrous defence made for Louis XIV by Garbagnus of Brescia in 1668. Though this craftsman must have had fine work by his forefathers at hand to study, and though the other arts and crafts were tending towards a light and flowing, if meaningless, style of design, the craft of the armourer had by this time reached a depth of sheer utilitarian ugliness which was never equalled even in the most primitive years of its history.

TOOLS, APPLIANCES, ETC.

THE tools used by the armourers of all nations differ but little from the implements of the blacksmith and, as will be seen in considering the various inventories that survive, these have scarcely varied in form during the centuries. When once invented the hammer, the anvil, the vice, the chisel, and the pincers are open to but few improvements, and even with the advent of steam and mechanical power, the functions of the tool remain and are simply guided by a machine instead of by the hand.

The chief work of the armourer was the beating out of plates from the solid ingot of metal and therefore we find that all illustrations dealing with this craft show the workmen engaged in this operation. When once the rough shape of the piece was obtained a great deal of the work was done when the metal was cold, as will be seen from examination of the illustrations.

When the craft of the armourer became important and when a large trade was done in these munitions of war, it was found more convenient to have the plates beaten out in special mills before they were handed over to the armourer to make up into armour. These battering-mills are noticed on pages 35, 188.

In many instances they were probably owned by the armourers and were often under the same roof; but the fact that we find hammermen, millmen, platers, and armourers mentioned together in records and bills of payment to armouries seems to suggest that they had different duties assigned to them.

That the work of the plater was quite distinct from that of the armourer in the sixteenth century we gather from entries in the State Papers Domestic, and in the reign of James I, which will be discussed more fully farther on in this chapter.

The earliest European illustration of an armourer at work at present known is to be found in the thirteenth-century *Aeneid* of Heinrich von Waldec (codex MS. Germ. fol. 282, p. 79) in the Königl. Bib. Berlin

22

(Plate IV). From the fact that the armourer (Vulcan) is holding the helm with pincers we may infer that he is working it hot. The anvil as shown in this miniature (Plate IV) is square and of primitive form and would seem to be quite useless for the work, but this may be due to the inexperience of the artist. The hammer, however, is carefully drawn and is evidently from some real example in which the face is rounded in a slightly convex form and the toe ends in a small blunted point which may be for riveting small objects or for making small bosses.

In the fifteenth century we find more care as to details and more operations shown in the illustration on the same plate, taken from a miniature by Boccace in *Les Clercs et Nobles Femmes* (Bib. Reg. 16, G, v. fol. 11) in the British Museum. Here we have several men at work under the superintendence of a lady who is generally supposed to be the Countess Matilda, while their labours are enlivened by a flute-player. The man at the bench appears to be putting together a defence composed of circular plates laced to a leather or linen foundation which strongly resembles the culet of so-called "penny plate" armour in the Tower (III, 358). The helm-smith is working on a bascinet which he holds with pincers, but he is using the toe of the hammer and not the face, which hardly seems a likely operation. He holds the helmet on a helmet-stake which probably has a rounded surface for finishing off the curves. The seated man is perhaps the most interesting figure, for he is a rare example of a mail-maker at work, closing up the rings with a pair of pincers. Up to the present we have no definite idea as to how the intricate operation of mail-making was accomplished so as to turn out rapidly coats of mail. It is probable that

FIG. 15. The Mail-maker (from Jost Amman's *Stände und Handwerker*), *circ.* 1590.

some form of pincer was used which pierced the flattened ends of the ring and closed up the rivet when inserted. Possibly investigations in the East, where mail is still made, may throw some light upon the subject.[1]

---

[1] The present writer is commissioning research to this end in Syria, where the craft still survives.

The illustration by Jost Amman (Fig. 15) certainly shows the craftsman using a punch and hammer for his work and the only other tool shown is a pair of shears. Mail was in use up to the first years of the seventeenth century, so we may be sure the artist drew his figure from life.

FIG. 16. The Armourer (from the same source as Fig. 15).

Few of the actual tools of the armourer survive to us at the present day. In the Burges Bequest in the British Museum is a fine anvil decorated with figures of saints in relief of the sixteenth century, which appears to have been used by a craftsman dealing with metal in plates or sheets, for the face of the anvil is burred over in a manner that would not be the case if the smith had worked with bars or rods, the usual materials of the blacksmith. In the same case is a pair of armourer's pincers which resemble the *multum in parvo* tools of to-day, for they include hammer, wire-cutter, nail-drawer, and turnscrew (Plate V). A similar pair of pincers exists in the Rotunda Museum, Woolwich (XVI, 200). In the Wallace Collection (No. 88) is an armourer's hammer of the sixteenth century with a faceted copper head, the reason for which was probably the need for avoiding scratching the surface when finishing a piece. In the same collection is a finely decorated farrier's hammer (1002), which also includes a nail-drawer and turn-nut. The handle is inlaid with brass and mother-of-pearl and is decorated with engravings of S. George and a musketeer of about 1640. A decorated anvil and vice which were catalogued as those of an armourer, the property of Mr. Ambrose Morell, were exhibited in the Metropolitan Museum, New York, in 1911, but from the form and size of the tools they would appear to have been rather those of the silver-smith than of the armourer. Jost Amman's "Armourer" (Fig. 16) calls for no special notice, as no tools are shown in the workshop, and is merely of interest as being included in this *Book of Trades*, published in 1590.

The earliest inventory containing armourers' tools is found in the archives of the city of Lille. It is dated 1302 and refers to the effects of the Constable de Nesle in the Hôtel de Soissons, Paris. The inventory is a long one and includes many interesting details of furniture, fabrics, and armour. That portion relating to the tools runs as follows :—

Arch. Dept. du Nord. Fonds de la Chambre des Comptes de Lille, No. 4401.

Une englume et fos a souffler   lx s.
Unes tenailes bicournes, i martel et menus instruments de forge   xiii s. vi d.
Item unes venterieres   v s.
„   xxxviii fers faites   xii s. viii d.
„   sas a cleus, tenons environs v sommes   xxi l. v s.
„   xiii douzaines de fer de Bourgoyne   xxii s. vi d.

Another early inventory is that of Framlingham Castle, Norfolk, of the year 1308 :—

ix capellae ferratae   at iv s.
iii vices ad eandem tendentes   at ii s.

The earliest complete English inventory of tools connected with the craft of the armourer occurs in the *Accounts of the Constable of Dover Castle.* Two separate lists are given at different dates, which may be studied with more convenience if placed side by side :—[1]

Dec. 20. 17 Edw. III, 1344.	*Jan. 26. 35 Edw. III, 1361.*
Item in Fabrica.	En la Forge.
ij maides[2]	ij andefeltes de fer[2]
ij bicorn[3]	j andefelte debruse
iij martellos magnos	j bikore[3]
iij martellos parvos	iij slegges[4]
ij tenaces magnas[5]	iiij hammeres
v tenaces parvas[5]	vj paires tanges dount deux grosses
ij instrumenta ad ferram cinendum[6]	iiij pensons febles[5]
iiij instrumenta ferrea ad claves inficiendos[7]	iij nailetoules per clause en icels fair[6]
ij paria flaborum[8]	iij paire bulghes dount une nouvell[8]
j folour de ferro[9]	j peer moler[10]
j mola de petra versatilis pro ferreo acuendo[10]	ij fusels de feer aicele[11]
ij ligamina de ferreo pro	j paire de wynches[13] as meme la peer
j buketto[12]	j trow de peer pur ewe[14]
	j hurthestaf de feer[15]
	j cottyngyre[16]
	j markingyre[17] une cable vels et pourz

---

[1] *Arch. Journ.,* XI, 380.

[2] Anvils.	[6] Tools for closing rivets.	[10] Grindstone.
[3] Bickiron.	[7] Shears.	[11] Spindles (?).
[4] Sledge-hammer.	[8] Bellows.	[12] Bucket-hoops.
[5] Pincers and tongs.	[9] Rammer (bellows ?).	[13] Winches.

[14] Stone water-trough.
[15] Hearth-stick, poker.
[16] Cutting-iron, shears or cold-chisel.
[17] Marking-iron.

All the above tools are in use at the present day, except perhaps the "nailetoules" for closing the rivets, and, as has been stated above, if we could but discover what this implement was we might find that it is also used at the present day for some other purpose. The nearest approach to such a tool is the eyelet-hole maker and riveter used by bootmakers. The "bicornes" are still known to-day as bickirons. They are small anvils with long horns which are used when riveting tubes or turning over long pieces of metal. It is a little uncertain as to whether the "folour" derives its name from the same root as the modern French "fouloir," a "rammer," or from the Latin "follis," "bellows." The former would seem more probable, as it was made of iron. The "fusels de feer aicele" present some difficulty, but they may be taken to be spindles of some kind, possibly for the grindstones. The "wynches" explain themselves, but the addition of "as meme la peer" is not so clear, for from the next item "peer" evidently means "stone," for it is a trough of stone for water ; at the same time the word "pair" is often written "peer" at this period, so it may refer to a pair of winches. The bellows, shears, and grindstone call for no special comment, but the "hurthestaff" presents some difficulty. It would seem to be derived from the word "hearth" or "herth," in which case it would probably be a long iron rod, rake, or poker, used for tending the forge-fire. This seems to be borne out in the inventory of 1514, where it is spelt "harth stake." The "cottyngyr" and "markingyre" may be found in every blacksmith's shop to-day as cold-chisels and marking-iron.

The next entry bearing upon the subject of tools and workshop requirements is found in an *Inventory under Privy Seal of Henry VI*, dated 1485, at which time John Stanley, of Wyrall, Cheshire, was Sergeant of the Armoury of the Tower.[1] Here we find the following items recorded :—

> it'm ij yerds iij q'ters of corse rede sylke
> It'm d'yerds d'q'reters of rede vele wet
> It'm iiij grosses of poyntes[2]
> It'm vj armyng nales[3]

⎫
⎬ All splendid and moch
⎭ more to coom of the
king's harneys

> It'm hamer, j bequerne, j payr of pynsonys, iij pounde of wyre
>   which was sold by Mastr. Wylliam Fox armerer

[1] *Archæologia*, XIV, 123 ; also Meyrick, *Antient Armour*, II, 119.   [2] See page 109.   [3] Rivets.

The " bequerne " is the same as the " bicorn " mentioned in the Dover Castle inventory.

In the earlier periods we have no records as to the material used or the quantities required. It is only when we come to the sixteenth century that we find detailed accounts kept to assist our investigations respecting the making of armour.

The next inventory worthy of note contains a list of payments made to John Blewbery, who was in charge of the workshops in 3 Henry VIII, 1514.

Public Record Office.

xviii September   Also payde by Owre Commandement to John Blewbery for the new fforge at Greenwiche made for the Armarers of Brussells these peces ensuynge.

	s.	d.
a vyce	xiii	iv
a greate bekehorne	lx	
a smalle bekehorne	xvi	
a peyre of bellowes	xxx	
a pype stake[1]	iii	iv
a Creste stake[2]	iv	
a vysure stake[3]	iv	
a hanging pype stake[4]	iv	iv
a stake for the hedde pecys[5]	v	
ii curace stakes[6]	x	
iv peyre of Sherys[7]	xl	
iii platynge hamers[8]	viii	
iii hamers for the hedde pecys	v	
a creste hamer for the hedde peces		xx
ii hamers	ii	viii
ii greve hamers[9]	iii	iv
a meeke hamer[10]		xvi
ii pleyne hamers	ii	
ii platynge hamers	ii	
ii chesels wt. an halve		viii
a creste hamer for the curace		xii
ii Rewetinge hamers[11]		xvi
a boos hamer[12]		xii
xi ffylys[13]		xi

[1] Round-horned anvil for making tubes.
[2] For beating up a helmet-crest.
[3] For visors.
[4] Uncertain.
[5] Helmet-stake.
[6] For the cuirass.
[7] Shears.
[8] Heavy hammers.
[9] Hammers for greaves.
[10] (?)
[11] Riveting-hammer.
[12] Embossing-hammer.
[13] Files.

	s.	d.
a payre of pynsors		xviii
ii payre of tongs		xvi
a harth stake[1]		vi
ii chesels & vi ponchons	ii	
a watr. trowgh		xviii
a temperinge barrelle		xii
one Andevyle	xx	
vi stokks to set the Tolys	x	
xvi dobles at xvi d every doble	xxi	iv
xviii quarters of Colys	vi	ix
in alle	xiii li. xvi s.	xi d.

Here we find the outfit more elaborate than that scheduled at Dover.   The various " stakes " in use show that there were special appliances for making every part of the armour, both as regards the anvils and the hammers.   The " halve " with the two chisels is, of course, the haft or handle, which could be fitted to either.   The " vi stokks to set the Tolys " are presumably handles in which the tools were fixed.   The "ponchons " are punches used in the repoussé work.   The " xvi dobles " were probably heavy iron models on which the various pieces were shaped.   Two specimens in the Tower (a morion, IV, 227, and a breastplate, III, 209), are considered by the present Curator to be dobles, for they are cast and not wrought, are far too heavy for actual use, and have no holes for rivets or for attaching the lining.

In the illustration given on Plate VI, taken from Hans Burgmair's *Weisz Künig*, many of these tools are shown in use.   The engraving was produced by an artist who was also a designer of armour, so they would certainly be correctly drawn.   The various small stakes are all in use and all the work is being done with the metal cold, for the men are holding it with their hands.   This working of the cold metal tends to compress the crystals and to make the metal hard, and is more than once alluded to in works upon armour.   Gaya, in his *Traité des armes*,[2] mentions this detail, and again Jean de Saulx-Tavannes[3] mentions " cuirasses battues à froid" when speaking of armour of " proof," which is also noticed in the present work under that heading.

---

[1] Poker.
[2] Reprint (Clar. Press, Oxon, 1911), edited by Charles ffoulkes.
[3] *Mém. rel. à l'hist. de France* (Paris, 1866), p. 191, col. 1.

ARMOUR OF KURFÜRST MORITZ. BY MATTHAÜS FRAUENPREIS, 1548

PLATE VII

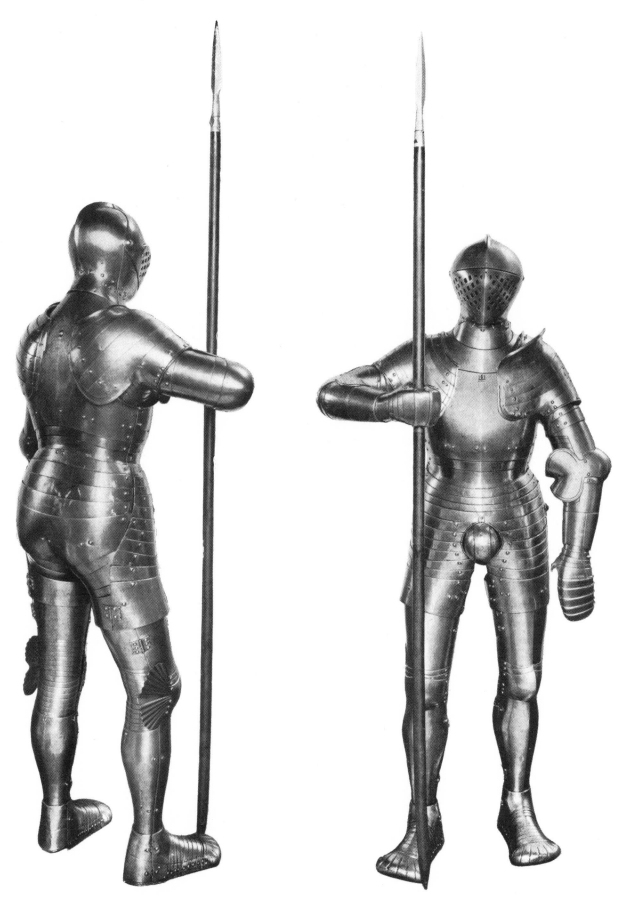

ARMOUR OF HENRY VIII FOR FIGHTING ON FOOT IN THE LISTS

PLATE VIII

The following extracts from various books and documents relate to the tools and appliances of the armourer :—

1278. *Roll of Expenses for a Tournament in Windsor Park.*

It qualibet cresta   j per chaston

These chastones or clavones were rivets for fastening the crests of the knights and also of the horses. Most of the items in this roll were supplied by curriers or tailors, for the weapons and armour were of wood or leather, and metal does not seem to have been used.

1300. *Wardrobe Expenses of Edward I.*[1]

Una Cresta cum clavis argenti pro eodem capello.

1301. *An indenture on the delivery of the Castle of Montgomery by William de Leyburn to Hugo de Knoville.*[2]

Unum incudem et i martellum et ii suffletis ovi valoris.

These are evidently the contents of the castle armourer's workshop : an anvil, a hammer, and a small pair of bellows of no value. Perhaps such items are hardly worth chronicling, but in a work of this nature it seems to be advisable to collect every entry bearing upon the subject, so as to make it a complete study of the craft of the armourer both technically and historically, as far as is possible with the very limited material obtainable.

1369. *Dethe Blaunche, l.* 9964. Chaucer.

As hys brothres hamers ronge
upon hys anuelet up and doon.

1386. *Knight's Tale, l.* 1649. Chaucer.

Faste the armurers also
with fyle and hamer prikynge to and fro.

This refers to the travelling armourer who accompanied his lord to the tournament or to war.

1465. *Acts. of Sir John Howard.*

20,000 Bregander nayle   11s. 8d.

These are the small rivets used in making the brigandine. A brigandine with sleeves at Madrid (c. 11) is composed of 3827 separate plates and over 7000 rivets were used in putting it together.

---

[1] *Archæologia*, XVIII, 305.   [2] Cott. MS., Vit. c. 10, fol. 154.

1460 (?). *Ordinances of Chivalry, fol. 123b.*[1]

> Also a dosen tresses of armynge poyntis.
> Also a hamyr and pynsones and a bicorne.
> Also smale nayles a dosen.

The "tresses" were plaited laces for fastening the various portions of armour to the wearer. These may be seen in the portrait of the Duc de Nevers (?) at Hampton Court, the picture of S. Demetrius by L'Ortolano in the National Gallery, and more clearly in the portrait of an unknown navigator in the Fortnum Room of the Ashmolean Museum, Oxford. The arming-points will be found described and illustrated on page 109.

1513. *Equipage of Henry, Earl of Northumberland.*[2]

> Emmery & oile for dressing my Lord's harnes.
> Leather, bokills & naylles for mendyng my Lords harnes.
> Towles conserning the mending of my Lord's harnes. Item a payre of nyppers, a payre of pynsores, a pomyshe,[3] & ij fylles. Item a small sti'the, a hammer, and all ouy^r stuffe and tooles belonginge an armorer. Item viij yards of white blaunkett for trussing of my Lord's harnes in.

The emery and oil were used in cleaning the armour and will be noticed in due course on page 78. The nippers, pincers, etc., have been alluded to before. The "sti'the" is an anvil, a term used up to Shakespeare's time, as may be found in *Hamlet*, iii. 2, 89. All these "Towles" or tools would be part of the travelling equipment of the armourer who accompanied his lord on active service.

1514. *Record Office, 9 July, to John Blewbery.*

For a millwheel with stondard, 2 beams & brasys [braces] belonging thereto and two small wheels to drive the glasys	40s.	
For two elm planks for lanterns for the same mill	5s.	
13 lbs. of tin at 5d. a lb.	5s.	5d.
28 lbs. of white soap for tempering the said mill at 2d. lb.	4s.	10d.
500 gauntlet nailes		8d.
100 & a half of iron 4/8, 3 rivetting hamers 2/-	6s.	8d.
a payre of pynsers 2/8, 4 crest fylys 4/-	6s.	8d.
2 greate fylys	5s.	
100 & a half of steele for vambraces & gaunteletes	60s.	

[1] *Archæologia*, LVII, also *Arch. Journ.*, IV, 226.
[2] *Antiquarian Repertory*, IV, 367.   [3] Pumice-stone.

The mill-wheel was for the water-power used for turning the grind-stones and other appliances which will be noticed later on in this chapter. The "glasys" are probably the glazing-wheels for putting the final polish upon the finished armour. The white soap was for lubricating the axle of the mill-wheel or for the final polish of the metal on the wheel or buff. The "gauntlet nailes" are small rivets for gauntlets which, being of thinner metal, would require a smaller-sized rivet than the rest of the body armour. The steel for vambraces and gauntlets was probably thinner than that used for other portions of the suit.

> 1514. *Record Office, 22 July, to John Blewbery.*
>
> for the glasyers of the said mill and one spindle to
> the same glasyers   £4   0   0
> for a grind stone & the beam for the same mill   1   0   0
>
> *King's Book of Payments, Record Office.*
>
> 1516. *Feb., to Edith, widow of Fountain, millman.*
>
> for milling & carriage of harness   15   0   0
>
> 1516. *Record Office, loc. cit., May, John Hardy, fishmonger.*
>
> 4 bundles of Isebrooke stuff for making parts of
> harness   £8   6   8

It is difficult to see why this payment should have been made unless the fishmonger had imported the Innsbruck metal in one of his boats. The term "Isebroke" will be found mentioned under the chapter dealing with the Proving of Armour.

> 1517. *Record Office, loc. cit., April, to John de Mery.*
>
> 2541 lbs. of steel plates of Isebroke and Lymbrickes
> stuff   £26   12   0

The "Lymbricke" metal came from Limburg, in North Brabant.

> 1517. *Record Office, loc. cit., May, to Sir Edw. Guylford.*
>
> making two forges & the repairs in the Armory at
> Southwark   £19   2   0
>
> 1520. *Record Office,*[1] *April, Richd. Pellande, Rauffe Brand, Richd. Cutler, and
> Hans,* four of the King's armourers, brought to the Field of the Cloth
> of Gold all sorts of necessaries for armour, such as buckles, files,
> chisels, punches, hinges, hides, and rivets.
>
> The glazing-mill was taken down at Greenwich and was set up at
> Guisnes with four forges.

---

[1] Expenses of Sir Edw. Guilford, Master of the Armoury.

1544. *Cott. App. XXVIII, f.* 69, *Brit. Mus.*

Working in the privy Armoury upon the filing of the king's Majestie's harnes & other necessaries from May 11–July 16. (This is part of the account of Erasmus, the King's armourer, who is noticed elsewhere.)

1544. *Loc. cit., f.* 76. *Charges of the King's Armoury.*

Item 8 bundles of steel to the said Armoury for
the whole year 38/- the bundle   li. xv   iiii

(Lockers and Millmen are mentioned in this entry.)

On page 31 it was noted that in 1516 four bundles of steel cost £8 6s. 8d., in 1517 2541 lb. cost £26 12s., that is about 2½d. per lb. From these three entries taken together we gather that the "bundle" was about 20 lb.

1544. *Cott. App.*[1] XXVIII, f. 76.

Item for 16 bundles of steel to serve both shops a whole year at 38/- per bundle	li. xxx	viii	
Item i hide of buff leather every month for both shops at 10/- the hide		vi	x
Item to every of the said shops 4 loads of charcoal a month 9/- the load		xl	xix
Item for both shops i cowhide every month at 6/8 the hide		iv	vi	viii
Item 100 of iron every month for both shops at 6/8 the 100		iv	vi	viii
Item in wispe steel for both shops every month 15 lbs. at 4d. lb.			lxv
Item in wire monthly to both shops 12 lb. monthly at 4d. the lb.			lii
Item in nayles & buckles for both shops monthly			lxv

This record contains other details in connection with the two workshops of Greenwich and Westminster, in which 12 armourers, 2 locksmiths, and 2 millmen and 2 prentices are employed who " will make yearly, with the said 16 bundles of steel and the other stuff aforesaid, 32 harnesses complete, every harness to be rated to the king's Highness at £12, which amounteth in the year towards his Grace's charge iii^c iiii^{xx} iiii^{li} " (£384).

From these details we can find approximately that the 32 suits required 13 hundred of iron and 195 lb. of whisp steel. Therefore each suit took 40¾ lb. of iron and about 6 lb. of whisp steel.

[1] See also Appendix F.

The leather was either for straps and linings for the armour, or may have been used for facing the polishing-wheels or "buffs." The year was divided into thirteen lunar months.

1559. *Henry V, iv, chorus.* Shakespeare.
> The Armourers accomplishing the knights
> With busy hamers closing riuets up.

This is more or less a poetic licence, for the riveting was only done on each separate piece, and these were joined on the wearer with straps, arming-points, or turning-pins. Of course this entry should be taken as made at the year when Shakespeare wrote, and not as representing an actual occurrence at Agincourt.

1562. *State Papers Domestic, Elizabeth, Vol. XXI,* 14.
> Due also to the armorers of the Tower for their wages
> & for leather, buckels, nailes & other paiments in indent
> to the said armory at the feast of Christmas last past   vj^{li} xv^{s}

In this entry are mentioned arming nails, butret nails, hammers, punshions, sheres, fyles, sand for scouring, cords, points, oyletholes, tow and butten nails.

1574. *State Papers Domestic, Elizabeth, Vol. XCIX,* 50.
> The monthly charge ordinary, vez coles, stele
> Iron nayles, buckills & lether &c.   vij^{li}

1593. *Auditor's Privy Seal Book,* 353.
> Elizabeth to the Treasurer & Chamberlain of the Exchequer.
> Whereas we . . . are informed that the mills serving for our Armoury at Greenwich are decayed, you are to pay to Sir H. Lee such sums as are necessary for the repairs . . . for the mills not to exceed £80.

1622. *Record Office, Sir Henry Lee's Accounts of the Armoury.*

The following details are mentioned :—
> Redskins for bordering of armour, calfskins for the same, leather for gauntlets, Round headed nails, Tynned nails, flat headed nails, white nails, yellow nails, double buckels, buckels, nails and taches for gantlets, copper nails, brockases, tacejoyntz.

The "nails" here mentioned are rivets of iron or brass or copper. Some were tinned to prevent rusting, a custom which was practised as early as 1361, for we find in one of the inventories of Dover Castle[1]

[1] *Arch. Journ.,* XI.

under that date "xiii basynetz tinez." The "taches" for gauntlets were fastenings of some kind, possibly turning-pins. The " brockases" were also probably brooches or fastenings of some sort, and the "tacejoyntz" hinges for attaching the tassets to the taces.

1624. *State Papers Domestic, Jac. I, Vol. CLXXX, 71, 72. Erection of Plating-mills by Capt. Martin at Erith.* (This document is quoted at length in Appendix J, p. 188.)

The rates for Plaetes and armors exectly examined for the prices the strength and lightness considered are thus reduced.

The chardge of a tun of Armer plaetes	£18	0	0
Two chaldron of coles wt. carriadge will be	11	2	0
Reparation for the mill		12	0
The workmen for battering this tun of plaetes	4	0	0
The armourers may make them wt due shape black nayle and lether them for	7	10	0

etc. etc.

The entries in this document will be examined fully on page 41.

1631. *Fœdera, xix, p. 312.* Rymer.

Unstriking new fyling russetting new nayling lethering and lyning of a cuirassiers armor	i	iii	0

This entry occurs in a document under the Privy Seal of Charles I, dated Westminster, June 29, which refers to the using of a hall-mark for armour. The principal portion of this is given in Appendix K, page 191.

1643. *State Papers Domestic, Car. I, Nov. 20.*

Letter from Privy Seal to treasurer & under Treasurer of Exchequer to pay Wm. Legg Master of the Armoury £100 by way of imprest upon account to be employed in building a mill at Woolvercote near Oxford for grinding swords & for building forges providing tools & other necessaries for sword blade makers to be employed to make swords for our service.

1644. *State Papers Domestic, Car. I, D, Feb. 26.*

Warrant of the Privy seal to Exchequer.

By our special command Legg has caused to be erected a mill for grinding swords at Woolvercote co Gloucester & forges at Gloucester Hall, you are therefore to pay upon account to Wm. Legg Master of the Armory a sum not exceeding £2000 for grinding swords and belts in the office of the armory the same to be made at the usual price and according to pattern as by us appointed also to provide tools and other necessaries for sword blade making employed by the said Master of the Armory.

In the second of these extracts "co Gloucester" is a slip of the pen due to the close proximity of "Gloucester Hall." It should of course read "Oxford." The mill was originally owned by the nuns of Godstow, who received it from Henry I. It is now used by the Clarendon Press for paper-making. Gloucester Hall is now Worcester College. There are no records either in the city or university to throw more light on these entries.

> 1649. *Parliamentary Survey, Feb., No.* 30.
>
> > The Armory Mill consisted of two little rooms and one large one in which stood two mills, then lately altered. The mill with stables stood in an acre of ground abutting on Lewisham Common and was used till about twelve years before the above date for grinding armour and implements for the King's tilt-yard.

The mill is described in the rental of the manor, 44 Edw. III, 1371, as one for grinding steel and valued at 3s. 4d. per ann.

> 1660. *Harl. MSS.* 7457.
>
> > A view and Survey of all the Armour and other Munitions or Habiliaments of Warr remayneing at the Tower of London.[1]
> >
> > Armorers Tooles.
> >
> > Small bickernes, Tramping stakes,[2] Round stake,[3] Welting stake,[4] straite sheres,[5] fileing tonges, Hamers, Old tew iron,[6] Great square anvill, Bellows, Smiths vices, Threstles.

The entry which refers to the loss of the " Great Bear," a large anvil formerly at Greenwich, is given in full in Appendix M.

Before leaving the subject of tools and appliances, some notice should be taken of the picture by Jan Breughel (1575–1632) entitled "Venus at the Forge of Vulcan" (Kais. Friedrich Mus., Berlin, No. 678), which measures 54 cm. by 93 cm. Here all the various operations of the armourer and gun-founder are shown, with a large quantity of armour, weapons, bells, coins, and goldsmith's work. The details of especial interest are the grindstones and "glazing-wheels," and the "tilt-hammers" worked by water-power, which were probably the machines used in the "battering-mills" more than once alluded to above. These water-turned hammers continued in use in England up

---

[1] Given in full, Meyrick, *Antient Armour*, III, 106.
[2] A pick? (*Eng. Dialect Dict.*)
[3] Bottom stake.
[4] For turning over edges of iron.
[5] This shows that curved shears were also used.
[6] Possibly a nozzle for bellows (*N.E. Dict.*).

to the first quarter of the nineteenth century,[1] and are still found in Italy at the present day. They are raised by wooden cams or teeth set round the axle of the water-wheel, to which a handle is fixed on the near side for use when water-power was not available. The chisel-edge of the hammer is for stretching the metal by means of a series of longitudinal hammerings. Of the grindstones actuated by the same water-power, the larger would be for rough work, the second for finer finish, and the smallest, which is probably a wooden " buff," would be used for the high polish at the end.

It is impossible here to give a detailed description of this very interesting picture, which has been considered elsewhere by the present author.[2] At the same time the tools shown in this workshop are worthy of notice as being part of the stock-in-trade of the armourer of the seventeenth century.

To the left of the tilt-hammers, in the foreground, are a pair of large bench-shears, and above them, on a cooling-trough, just below

the magpie, is a long-handled swage for stamping grooves and edgings on metal plates. Tongs, pincers, and hammers are found in many parts of the picture, and dies for stamping coins or medals are seen immediately below the bench-shears. Directly under the right foot of Vulcan is a tracing-wheel, similar to that shown on Jost Amman's engraving of the " Compass Maker " in his *Book of Trades*. A small bench-vice lies near the lower margin of the picture under the figure of Cupid, and a hand-vice and repoussé hammer on the three-legged stool to the left. In the distance, over the figure of Venus, is the primitive contrivance for boring a

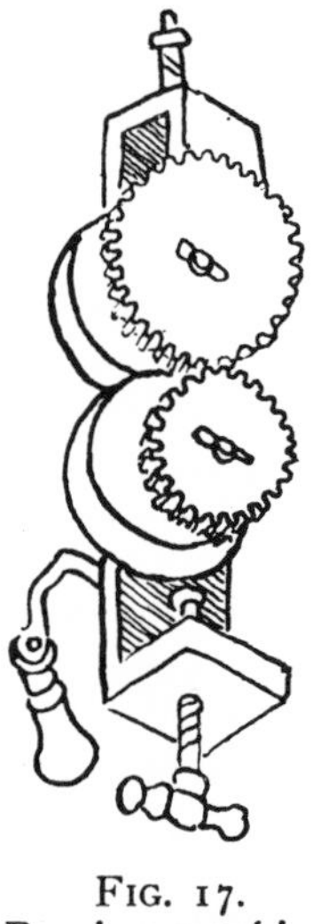

FIG. 17. Burring-machine or " Jenny " (see frontispiece).

cannon, the mould for casting which is seen close by in the floor. The most interesting detail is to be found in the machine which lies at the foot of the small anvil at Cupid's right hand. This bears a strong resemblance to the modern burring-machine or " jenny," used for turning up the edge of thin metal plates (Fig. 17).

The armour shown, with its strongly marked volutes and decoration,

---

[1] *Cabinet Cyclopædia*, " Manufacture of Metals," Lardner, 1831.
[2] *Burlington Magazine*, April, 1911. *Zeitschrift für Historische Waffenkunde*, V, 10.

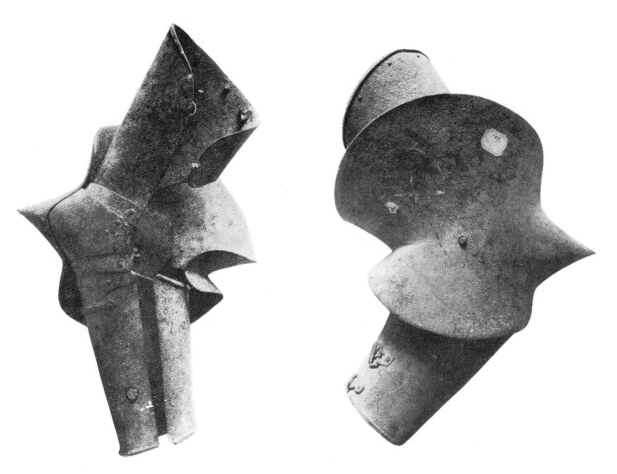

FRONT AND BACK OF BRASSARD, 1470

INSIDE OF LEG ARMOUR OF SUIT ON PLATE VIII

CUISSE, 1470

PLATE IX

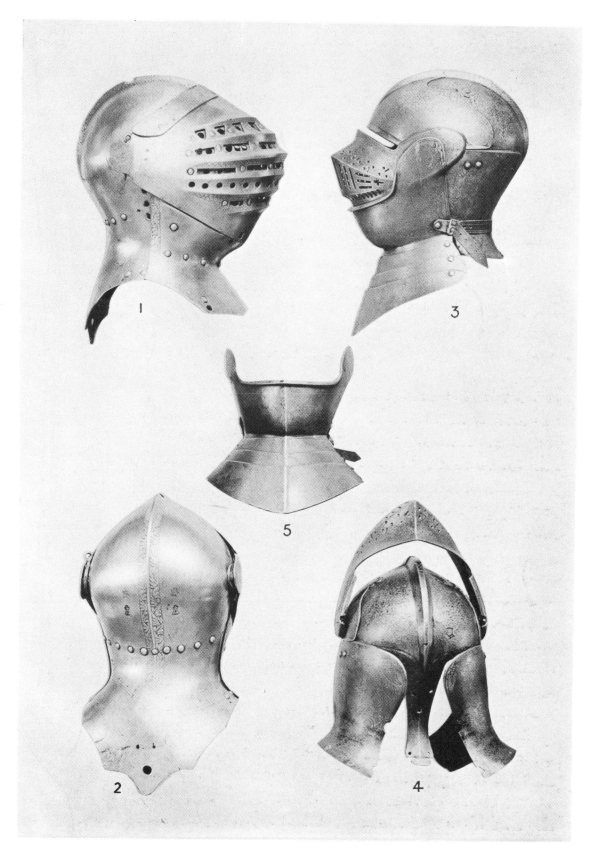

HELMETS OF HENRY VIII

1, 2. FRONT AND BACK OF HELMET BY THE MISSAGLIAS
3, 4.   „   „   „   PART OF THE SUIT SHOWN ON PLATE XII, BY CONRAD SEUSENHOFER
5. BEVOR FOR THE LATTER

THE ARMOURER'S MARKS APPEAR ON 2 AND 4

PLATE X

is of a type very common in the Madrid and Turin armouries, some of which has been ascribed to Pompeo della Chiesa. We have no clue as to whose workshop this picture represents, but if taken from life, it must certainly have been that of some master like Bartolomeo Campi, who, besides being an armourer, was a bronze-founder and goldsmith as well (see Frontispiece).

IRON AND STEEL

THERE is but little information to be obtained regarding the actual materials used by the armourer. The chief source from which he drew his supplies seems to have been Innsbruck. Why this was so is not clear from the contemporary records, but we may be sure that the German metal was harder and better tempered than that of other countries, or there would not have been the demand for it that there evidently was. In the various entries in the State Papers Domestic we find specific mention of " Isebruk " iron, and the merits of this metal must have been appreciated even in Shakespeare's time, for we have in *Othello*, v. 2, 253, " a sword of icebrook's temper." In the earliest editions of the play the word is " Isebrooke," which is obviously the anglicized version of Innsbruck.[1]

Sheffield steel must have been appreciated as early as Chaucer's time, for the Miller carries a " Sheffield thwyrtel " (knife), and in 1402 the arrows used at the battle of Homildon were pointed with Sheffield steel, so sharp that no armour could repel them.

It is possible that the German iron-smelters had discovered the properties of manganese, which hardens steel, and thus obtained a superior metal to that produced in other countries.

The discovery of steel was probably a fortuitous accident, due to the fact that the first smelting-works were fuelled with charcoal, which deoxidizes iron and turns some portion of the metal into natural steel. The Germans themselves realized the superiority of their material, for in 1511 Seusenhofer complained that his merchant was not giving him good metal, and advised that it should be classed as " Milanese," so as not to lessen the fame of Innsbruck iron.

Till the seventeenth century English iron seems to have been largely used for domestic purposes, for we find on examining Professor Rogers's *Agriculture and Prices* that German iron is never mentioned, but there

---

[1] The quotation continues : " a sword of Spain." We find many Solingen and Passau blades bearing the marks of Spanish sword-smiths.

are frequent references to English and Spanish metal. The following prices from the above work show the fluctuations in prices of iron in England.

1436. Spanish iron, 24 lb., 1s. 6d., or about £14 the ton.
1462. Iron, 42 lb. at 5d., or £17 10s. the ton.
1562. Raw English iron, £12 10s. the ton.
     Bilbow (Bilboa), £11 8s. the ton.
     Spanish, £12 the ton.
1570. Iron gun-stocks, made up, £28 the ton.
1571. Steel bar, £10 the ton.
     Bar steel, £37 4s. the ton.
1584. Spanish iron, £14 the ton. 50 bars to the ton, or about
     45 lb. to the bar.
1622. Steel, £32 the ton.
1623. Spanish iron, £14 10s. to £15 10s.
1624. Iron bars of 24 lb. at £37 4s. the ton.

These prices vary so greatly that we must be sure that there was a great difference in the quality, and also in the state in which the metal is delivered. In some cases there must have been a great deal of preparation and finishing of the raw material to account for the high price paid.

In 1517 an entry in the State Papers Domestic, given on page 31, states that 2541 lb. of Isebroke steel cost £26 12s., which gives about £23 for the ton.

In the *Sussex Archæological Journal*, II, 200, Walter Burrel gives an account of Sussex ironworks in the seventeenth century. He states that when once the furnace was lit it was kept going sometimes for forty weeks, the period being reckoned in " foundays." During each founday eight tons were made with twenty-four loads of charcoal. The metal was cast into " sows " weighing from 600 to 2000 lb. He states that " they melt off a piece of the sow about three quarters of a hundredweight and beat it with sledges near a fire so that it may not fall to pieces, treating it with water they thus bring it to a ' bloom,' a four square piece 2 ft. long."[1] Modern bar-iron 1 in. by 1 in. by 12 in. weighs 3·4 lb. Therefore this bloom would approximately make a plate 33 sq. ft. by $\frac{1}{16}$ in. thick.[2] Even with these data it is impossible to tell

---

[1] This would be a piece about 2 ft. by $3\frac{1}{2}$ in. by $3\frac{1}{2}$ in.
[2] Large plates of horse-armour are about $\frac{1}{16}$ in. thick.

the size of the plates delivered to the armourer ; for the appliances in the Middle Ages were but crude, and it is doubtful if rolling-mills were used in the sixteenth century. From the picture by Breughel, given as the frontispiece, we know that tilt-hammers were in use, but these would hardly have been used to flatten plates of any great size.

It would appear that iron in some localities was tainted with some poison ; for in a *Géographie d'Edrisi* quoted in Gay's *Encylopædia*, 699, reference is made to a mountain in Armenia where the iron ore is poisoned and which, when made into knives and swords, produced mortal wounds. It may have been that this was actually the case, but it is more probable that it was an invention of the owner of the mine designed to give his productions a fictitious value.

A few details of interest in connection with the manufacture of iron in England may be gathered from the *Metallum Martis* of Dud Dudley, a natural son of Edward, Lord Dudley. The treatise was printed in 1665 and refers to the author's endeavours to interest the Crown in his project for smelting iron with sea-coal instead of wood or charcoal. In his address to the King (Charles II) and Council he prefaces his technical remarks as follows :—

" Our predecessors in former Ages had both serious Consultations and Considerations before they made these many Wholesome and Good Lawes for the preservation of Wood and Timber of this Kingdome. 1 Eliz. 15, 23 Eliz. 5, 27 Eliz. 19, 28 Eliz. 3, 5. . . . Therefore it concerns His Sacred Majesty, his high Court of Parliament . . . to lay it to heart and helping hands upon fit occasions in these laudable Inventions of making Iron & melting of mines and refyning them with Pitcoal, Seacoal, Peat, and Turf ; . . . for maintenance of Navigation, men of War, the Fishing and Merchants trade, which is the greatest strength of Great Britain . . . whose defence and offence next under God consists by his sacred Majestie's assisting care and view of his men of War . . . Ordinance of Copper, Brass and Iron, Armories, Steels, and Irons of all sorts."

In his letter to the King he mentions Shippings, Stores, Armories, Ordnance, Magazines, and Trade. He mentions several counties as mining centres, but does not include Sussex or Shropshire. The first of these two was probably ruled out, as the industry there depended on the use of wood, against which Dudley's introduction of coal was levelled. We find Shropshire mentioned in the Trial of Armour given in the chapter on " Proof" (page 66).

Dudley seems to have formed a company in May, 1638, into which he took one Roger Foulke, "a Counsellor of the Temple and an ingenious man," as partner.

Before this his father, Lord Dudley, had employed a certain Richard Parkes or Parkhouse to carry iron merchandise to the Tower, which James I ordered to be tested by his " Artists," that is, of course, his armourers. Parkes made a sample fowling-piece of the new " Dudley Ore," smelted from pit-coal, and signed his name in gold upon the barrel. The gun was taken from him by Colonel Levison and was never returned.

Dudley gives three qualities of iron : grey iron, the finest, and best suited for making bar-iron; motley iron, a medium quality; and white iron, the least refined.

It is curious that in all his calculations and specifications he never actually mentions the making of armour and but seldom the casting of ordnance.

In considering the weights of suits as given in Appendix J we find the following details. By the prices given 20 cwt. make one ton. The cwt. at the time of James I was 112 lb.

Now we are told that " Six hundred of iron will make five hundred of plates," so we gather that in turning the pig-iron into plates one hundredweight was lost. The above entries give the following weights per suit or portion of a suit scheduled :—

Five hundred (weight) of plates will make 20 cuirasses
  of pistol proofe with pauldrons.
Therefore one set will weigh . . . . 28 lb.

Four hundred (weight) of plates will make 20 pair (or 40
  sets) of cuirasses without pauldrons.
Therefore one set will weigh . . . . 11 lb. 3 oz.

Sixteen hundred (weight) of plates will make 20 lance-
  armours.
Therefore one lance-armour[1] will weigh . . . 89 lb. 10 oz.

---

[1] For particulars of " lance-armour " see Appendix I.

Five hundred (weight) of plates will make 20 proof
  targets.

Therefore one target will weigh .   .   .   .   28 lb.

Twelve hundred (weight) of plates will make 20 pairs
  (40 sets) of strong cuirasses with caps.

Therefore one set of cuirass and cap will weigh   .   .   33 lb. 10 oz.

Four "platers" will make up 3700 weight or 37 cwt. of plates in one week, therefore one plater will make up 9 cwt. 28 lb. in a week or 1 cwt. 57 lb. or thereabouts in one day.

For comparison with existing suits of which the weights are known we may use the following details :—

		lb.	oz.
Paris (G, 80), *circ.* 1588. Cuirass, arm-pieces, and tassets .	.	73	0
Head-piece . . .	.	22	0
		95	0
Stanton Harcourt, Oxon, *circ.* 1685. Cuirass .	.	25	0
Head-piece . .	.	22	10
Arm-pieces (2) .	.	6	0
		53	10
Tower (II, 22), *circ.* 1686. Cuirass .	.	27	4
Head-piece . .	.	7	8
Long gauntlet .	.	3	0
		37	12
Tower (II, 92), of XVII cent. Cuirass .	.	24	0
Head-piece . .	.	6	8
The whole of this suit weighs .	.	48	8

It should be noted that two of the items in the Appendix are described as of "proof" and one is described as "strong." The lance-armours are not qualified in any way, but from their weight they must have been proof against musket or arquebus.

It is impossible to discover what size the "plates" were made before they were handed over to the armourers. The largest single plate in the Tower is a portion of the horse-armour of II, 5, known as the "Engraved Suit." This piece measures $27\frac{1}{2}$ in. at top and $28\frac{1}{4}$ in. at bottom by 17 in. and $18\frac{1}{2}$ in. high, or roughly speaking $28\frac{1}{4}$ in. by $18\frac{1}{2}$ in., about $\frac{1}{16}$ in. thick, weighing about 6 lb. 4 oz. If the numbers given on page 41 represent plates and not hundredweights, each plate

$\frac{1}{16}$ in. thick would be 6 in. by 11 in., and this is obviously absurd. It is more likely that, with the crude appliances in use, an ingot of metal was beaten out into such a plate as the weight of the ingot might give, larger or smaller as the case might be, and not standardized in any way. Dud Dudley writing in 1665 describes the methods of ironworkers before his introduction of sea-coal.

"They could make but one little lump or bloom of Iron in a day, not 100 weight and that not fusible, nor fined, or malliable, until it were long burned and wrought under hammers."[1]

[1] *Metallum Martis*, p. 37.

THE CRAFT OF THE ARMOURER

THE actual craft-work of the armourer differed but little from that of the smith, but there are some details which the armourer had to consider which were not part of ordinary blacksmith's work. There are no contemporary works of a technical nature, and our investigations can only be based on actual examination of suits, assisted by scattered extracts from authorities who mention the subject in military works. In 1649 J. Cramer printed a work, *De Armorum Fabricatione*, but it throws no light upon the subject and quotes from Roman authorities.

In the first place, the making of mail was a distinct craft which had no counterpart in other branches of smithing. At first the wire had to be beaten out from the solid, and thus the few fragments which remain to us of early mail show a rough, uneven ring of wire, clumsily fashioned and thicker than that of later dates. The invention of wire-drawing is generally ascribed to Rudolph of Nuremberg, about the middle of the fourteenth century,[1] but there were two corporations of wire-drawers in Paris in the thirteenth century mentioned in Étienne Boileau's *Livre des Métiers*, written about 1260.

When the wire was obtained, either hammered out or drawn, it was probably twisted spirally round a rod of the diameter of the required ring. It was then cut off into rings, with the ends overlapping. The two ends were flattened and punched or bored with holes through the flat portion. A small rivet, and in some cases two, was then inserted, and this was burred over with a hammer or with punches (Fig. 15, 18 ; also Plate IV). It is possible that some kind of riveting-pincers were used, but no specimens of this kind of tool are known.[2] Sometimes the ends of the rings are welded, which would be done by heating them and hammering them together. Before the rings were joined up they were interlaced one with another, each ring passing through

---

[1] *The History of Inventions.* Beckman.
[2] See *Dover Castle Inventory*, p. 25. The "nailtoules" may have been used for this purpose.

BRIGANDINE, OUTSIDE AND INSIDE. XV CENT.

BREASTPLATE FOR BRIGANDINE, 1470,
SHOWING ARMOURER'S MARK

RIGHT CUISSE OF ARMOUR FOR BARRIERS
SHOWING ARMOURER'S MARK

PLATE XI

ARMOUR PRESENTED TO HENRY VIII BY THE EMPEROR MAXIMILIAN,
MADE BY CONRAD SEUSENHOFER, 1514

PLATE XII

four others. Occasionally, to obtain increased strength, two rings were used for every one of the ordinary mail, but representations of this double mail are rare. The terms " haubert doublier," "haubert à maille double," and " haubert clavey de double maille " are found in French inventories, and in the inventory of Louis X which has been quoted before we find " 33 gorgieres doubles de Chambli, un pans et uns bras de roondes mailles, une couverture de mailles rondes demy cloies." These different items suggest that there were various ways of making mail and of putting it together. The double mail has been noticed, and the mail "demy cloues" was probably mail in which the ends of the links were closed with only one rivet. The " maile roond " being specially scheduled points to the fact that sometimes mail was made of flat rings, but whether cut from the

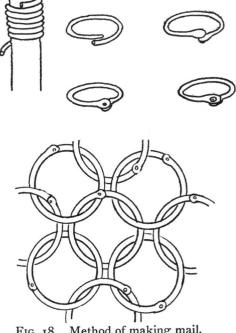

FIG. 18. Method of making mail.

sheet of metal or merely of flattened wire it is impossible to say.

Where the covering of mail was not made in one piece—that is, when the shirt, leggings, sleeves, or coif were made to open—they were fastened by laces. The chausses, or leggings of mail, were often laced at the back of the leg, as is shown in the sketchbook of Wilars de Honecourt, thirteenth century, figured in *Armour and Weapons* (Plate I) by the present author. The coif of mail was generally kept close to the head by a thong round the temples (Fig. 23, 8), and was in some instances fastened in front with an overlapping flap and a lace (Fig. 20).

FIG. 19. Sculptured representation of (1) double and (2) single mail on the effigy of R. de Mauley, 1242, formerly in York Minster (*Archæologia*, XXXI).

The Camail, or tippet of mail, which is the distinctive detail of the armour of the late fourteenth and early fifteenth century, was either hung from a flat plate of metal which was fitted over the vervelles or staples on the bascinet and kept in place by a lace or a thick wire, or the mail itself was hung over the vervelles and the plate fitted over it and secured in the same way.   This latter method appears to have been more commonly in use, to judge from sculptured effigies and brasses.   A bascinet in the Ethnological Museum, Athens,[1] shows the vervelles, plate, and wire that secured it still in place, but the mail has all corroded and disappeared.   A good restoration of the camail on a bascinet with a leather band instead of a flat plate is to be found in the Wallace Collection (No. 74).

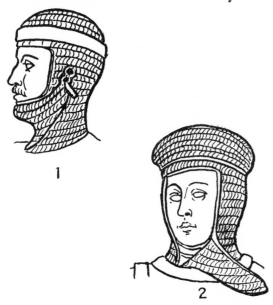

FIG. 20.   Coif of Mail.   (1) Effigy of William Mareschal, Earl of Pembroke, Temple Church. (2) Effigy in Pershore Church, Worcs (from Fairholt).

In the thirteenth century we find one of the most unpractical of all the armourer's contrivances in the nasal flap—hinged or laced to the camail, hanging down over the chin when not in use, and fastened, when required, to the bascinet by a pin or hook.   The nasal of the eleventh century, figured on the Bayeux Tapestry and elsewhere, was practical because it provided a defence for the nose and face which was as rigid as the helmet itself; but this later nasal could only protect the wearer from the actual cutting of the skin, for the full force of the blows would be felt almost as much as if there were no defence at all.   These nasals are figured so frequently in Hewitt, Hefner, and elsewhere that no special illustration is necessary in the present work.

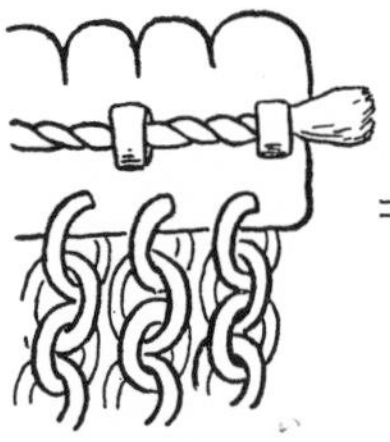

FIG. 21.
Attachment of Camail, effigy of Sir R. Pembridge, Clehonger Church, Hereford.

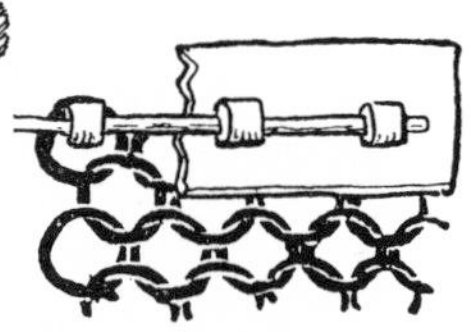

FIG. 22.
Attachment of Camail.

A variety of mail which, from the sculptured effigies and from miniatures of the thirteenth century, appears to have been in high favour, has come to be known as "Banded Mail."

In both painted and sculptured records the methods of representa-

[1] *Archæologia*, LXII.

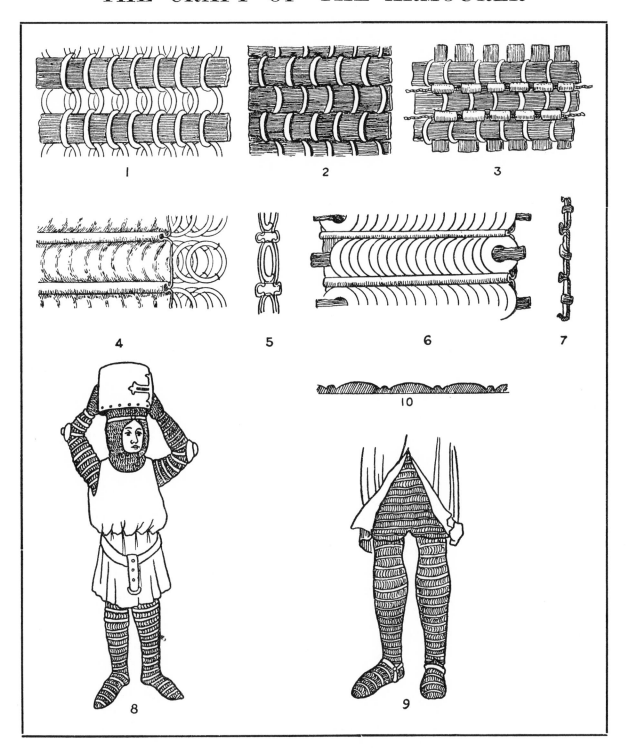

FIG. 23.   Banded Mail.

1, 2, 3. Suggested reinforcements of chain mail by leather thongs.
4. Rings covered with leather ; 5, section of same.
6. Meyrick's suggestion ; 7, section of same.
8. From *Romance of Alexander*, Bib. Nat., Paris, *circ.* 1240.
9. Effigy at Newton Solney, Derbs ; 10, section of same.

tion differ considerably from those employed to suggest the ordinary mail of interlaced rings.

In the middle of the last century, when the subject of armour began to be seriously studied, this banded mail was the subject of many theories and suggestions. Meyrick considered that it was composed of rings sewn on to a fabric, overlapping each other sideways; but a practical experiment will prove that such an arrangement would be impossible, as the weight would be excessive and the curve of the body would cause the rings to "gape." Other writers have considered that the same arrangement of rings, covered with leather which would prevent the "gaping," is the correct solution; but here again the heat would be a grave drawback.[1]

An important point on all representations of banded mail is that, when part of the garment is shown turned back, the back is the same as the front. The most practical suggestion was put forward by the late J. G. Waller,[2] who considered that it was simply chain mail with leather thongs threaded through every row or every alternate row of links. This would give a solidity to an otherwise too-pliant fabric, and would keep the mail in its place, especially on the arms and legs. It would also show the same arrangement of rings back and front.

The drawing from the *Romance of Alexander* goes far to prove that Waller's theory is the right one, for here the thongs are not shown on hands and head, where greater pliability of the mail was required, and yet these defences appear to be part of the same garment which shows the "banded" lines.

It is almost superfluous to add that no specimen of this kind of defence survives to-day, but Oriental mail is sometimes found stiffened in this manner with leather thongs.

The wearing of mail survived longer than is generally supposed. Holinshed, writing in 1586 (page 90 of the present work), mentions shirts of mail as part of the ordinary equipment of the foot-soldier. On Plate 8 of Derricke's *Image of Ireland* the mounted officer wears mail sleeves, and in an inventory of Hengrave Hall, Suffolk, taken in 1603, we find gorgets and shirts of mail, and barrels for cleaning the same. Edward Davies, writing in 1619 (*The Art of Warre*), distinctly states that the arquebussiers wore a shirt of mail (see page 115).

[1] *Arch. Journ.*, XXXVII.   [2] *Archæologia*, LIX.

The Brigandine and splinted armour were made by riveting small plates or horizontal lames on to a fabric foundation. In the former the fabric was outside, and rich ornamentation was obtained by the gilt rivet-heads which held the plates to the outer covering (see page 150). In the latter case the metal was on the outside and was riveted on to a foundation of linen. In some cases the rows of small plates are divided by strips of fine mail. There was no particular craft needed in making the brigandine, but the metal used was often of proof and was marked with the maker's name to attest it.

As may be seen on Plate XI and Fig. 36, the small plates of the brigandine are wider at the top than at the bottom, and overlap upwards. The reason for this is that the human torse is narrower at the waist than at the chest, and the plates could not overlap each other and yet conform to the lines of the figure if they overlapped downwards.

Although lighter and more pliable defences than the cuirass, the brigandine and jack were very effectual for protection against arrows, for we find, according to Walsingham,[1] that the rioters under Wat Tyler shot at a jack belonging to the Duke of Lancaster, but were unable to damage it, and eventually cut it to pieces with swords and axes.

FIG. 24. Figure wearing Jack (from *Chasse of S. Ursula*, by Memling, 1475–85, Bruges).

The jack or canvas coat of Sir John Willoughby, *temp*. Elizabeth, now at Woolaton Hall, is formed of stout canvas inside and out stuffed with two layers of tow with horn discs in between. The whole is kept together by a series of lacings which appear on the outside as lines and triangles of the same kind as those shown on Fig. 25. It is composed of six panels, two for the breast, two for the back, and two small ones for the shoulders. A portrait of Willoughby in the Painted Gallery at Greenwich shows such a jack with red cords. The jack was generally lined with metal plates and examples of this may be seen in the Tower (III, 335, 336). These are also made up of six panels and weigh about 17 lb. each. They are composed of about

---

[1] *Historia Anglicana*, Rolls Series, p. 457.

1164 metal plates[1] (Fig. 25).   In the Shuttleworth accounts published by the Chetham Society are to be found entries of $9\frac{1}{4}$ yards of linen to make a "steel coat," a pound of slape or pitch, two dozen points or laces for two coats, and 1650 steel plates.   The cost of the coat, inclusive of making, would come to about £1.   A cap, constructed in the same manner of small plates, is shown in the Burges Collection at the British Museum and is figured in the *Guide to the Mediæval Room* on page 62.

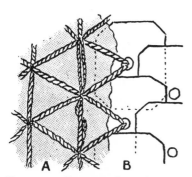

FIG. 25.   Construction of Jack.
A. Outside.
B. Plates with cover and cords removed.

The brigandine was sometimes reinforced with large placcates of steel, one on each breast, riveted to the fabric which composed the whole defence.   An example of this nature exists in the Waffensammlung at Vienna, and there are also several of these reinforcing plates, the brigandines of which have perished, in the Ethnological Museum at Athens (Fig. 26).   These latter were found in the castle of Chalcis, which was taken by the Turks from the Venetians in 1470, so they can be dated with accuracy.[2]   On one of the plates is a mark which strongly resembles the mark of Antonio Missaglia (see Plates XI, XVI). These brigandines with solid breast-pieces are described in Appendix D, page 177.   Both these plates and the example at Vienna are fitted with lance-rests which seem to be eminently unpractical, as the garment is more or less pliant and would not be of much use in sustaining the weight of a lance.   The most curious of these reinforcing plates is to be found in the picture of S. Victor by Van der Goes, *circ.* 1450, which is now in the Municipal Gallery at Glasgow.   Here the uppermost part of the torse is protected by strong plates of steel, but the abdomen is only covered by the brigandine (Fig. 27).   As an example of this fashion of armour and as

FIG. 26.   Brigandine at Vienna, No. 130.

---

[1] *Arch. Journ.*, LX.   [2] "Italian Armour at Chalcis," C. ffoulkes, *Archæologia*, LXII.

a most careful representation of detail this picture is as valuable as it is unique. Splinted armour is practically the brigandine without a covering, but made usually of stronger plates or lames. The fact that the body was covered by a series of small plates ensured greater freedom and ease in movement than was possible with

FIG. 27. S. Victor, by Van der Goes, Glasgow.

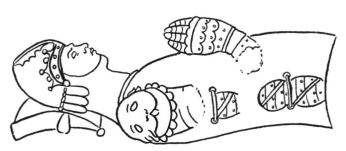

FIG. 28. Effigy at Ash Church, Kent, fourteenth century.

solid breast and back plates. The monument in Ash Church and the statue of S. George at Prague are good examples of the splinted armour of the fourteenth century (Figs. 28, 29).

That the skill of the sixteenth-century ar-

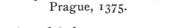

FIG. 29. Statue of S. George, Prague, 1375.

mourer surpassed that of the present-day crafts-man is evident after careful examination of some of the triple-combed Burgonets and Morions of the middle of the century. They are often found forged in one piece with no sign of join or welding, and what is more remarkable still, there is but little difference in the thickness of the metal all over the piece. Now, when a smith hollows out a plate of metal into a bowl-like form, the edges are generally thicker than the inside of the bowl; but in many of these head-pieces the metal is almost of equal thickness all over, a *tour de force* which few metal-workers to-day could imitate.[1] This thinning of the metal was utilized to a great extent in the different portions of the suit which were not exposed to attack. As will be found in the chapter

[1] Cf. Baron de Cosson, *Arch. Journ.*, XXXVII, p. 79.

on "Proof," the back-plates were generally thinner than the breasts. In jousting-helms the top of the skull, which, from the position of the rider when jousting, was most exposed to the lance, was generally much thicker than the back of the helm, where there was no chance of attack.

Again, the left side of both jousting and war harness is frequently thicker than the right, for it was here that the attack of both lance and sword was directed. Up to the middle of the fifteenth century the shield, hung on the left arm, was used as an extra protection for this the more vulnerable side of the man-at-arms, but it seriously interfered with the management of the horse. By the sixteenth century it was discarded and the armour itself made stronger on the left side both by increased thickness and also by reinforcing pieces such as the Grandgarde, the Passgarde, and the Manteau d'armes.

Perhaps the most ingenious contrivance used in making the suit of armour is the sliding rivet (Fig. 30). This contrivance has come to be called the "Almain rivet" in modern catalogues in a sense never found in contemporary documents. In these documents the "Almain rivet" is a light half-suit of German origin, made up of breast, back, and tassets, with sometimes arm - pieces. The word "rivet" was employed in the sixteenth century for a suit of armour, for Hall uses the word

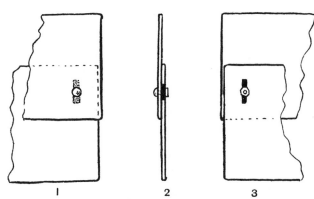

FIG. 30.   Sliding rivet showing (1) front, (2) side, (3) back.

frequently in his Chronicles. This word is therefore more probably derived from the same root as the French *revêtir*, rather than from the rivets which were used in the making of the suit. Up to the sixteenth century the rivet as we know it to-day is always called an "arming-nail," and it is only in the middle of the sixteenth century that we find the word rivet used as part of the armourer's stock-in-trade. These light suits were put together with sliding rivets, which have at the present day received the name originally given to the whole suit. The head of the rivet is burred over and fixed in the upper plate, but the lower plate is slotted for about three-quarters of an inch, so that it will play up and down on the shank

ARMET OF SIR HENRY LEE, BY JACOB TOPF, 1530-1597

PLATE XIII

PARADE ARMOUR
1. FOR KING SEBASTIAN OF PORTUGAL, BY ANTON PEFFENHAUSER, 1525-1603
2. FOR CHARLES V, BY BARTOLOMEO CAMPI, 1546

PLATE XIV

of the rivet and give more freedom of action than the fixed rivet; at the same time it will not allow the two plates to slide so far apart as will uncover the limb or body of the wearer. These sliding rivets were used to join the upper and lower portions of the breastplate which was in fashion in the last years of the fifteenth century, so as to allow a certain amount of movement for the torse backwards and forwards. They were also employed to join the taces, which needed a certain amount of play when mounting a horse or when sitting. When the "lobster-tail" cuisse superseded the taces and tassets in the late sixteenth and seventeenth centuries they were used instead of the fixed rivets for joining the lames of the cuisse.

The most ingenious arrangement of sliding rivets, however, is to be found on the brassards of the late fifteenth to the seventeenth century. As has been noticed on page 6, the armourer had to consider in this case both the defensive needs of his patron and also the necessity for using his arm as conveniently as was consistent with safety.

Now the only actions needed for the right arm are those of holding the lance in rest and of striking with the sword. The arm-defence therefore had to be so constructed that the arm could be bent for the former and raised for the latter. To do this the lames of the rerebrace are joined with sliding rivets at the hinder corners, but at the front corners they are joined with a strap fastened vertically to the top plate of the brassart and riveted, when extended straight, to each lame.

This allows play for the lames in the two above-mentioned positions, but when the arm is dropped, after the blow has been delivered, the lames automatically close one over the other and completely protect the arm and allow no backward movement.

The same arrangement is found on the laminated cuisses and tassets, in which the inner edges of the lames are joined by a strap and the outer by sliding rivets. This combination of sliding rivet and strap is shown on Fig. 7 and on Plate IX.

Another ingenious arrangement on the brassard is the turned-over edge or the embossed rim fitting in a collar, both of which allow the lower part of the rerebrace to turn horizontally to adapt it to the outward action of the hand and arm. In most suits the bossings of the rims are outside, but on the "Engraved Suit" (II, 5) in the Tower they are inside. The former gives a smooth surface to the wearer's arm and the latter presents a smooth surface to the opposing weapon (Fig. 31).

A similar rim and collar are found on close helmets and gorgets of the sixteenth century (Plate XIII).   Meyrick,[1] misreading Fauchet's[2] reference to the burgonet, considered this helmet with a lower edge fitting into the gorget to be the burgonet, but he brought no real evidence to support his assertion. Although the helmet and gorget fitted one over the other and therefore surmounted one of the chief dangers in war or joust, when the lance might penetrate the space between these two portions of the suit, it will be seen on examination of any suit of this kind that from the oblique position of the gorget the embossed rim of the helmet could not possibly turn in the hollowed rim of the gorget, so that it can only be considered as a defensive improvement which in no way added to the convenience in use, if anything it rather hampered the wearer, as he could only turn his head inside the helmet and that to no great extent. In some late suits a pin fixed at the back of the gorget comes through a hole in the lower edge of the helmet and *prevents* any possible movement.

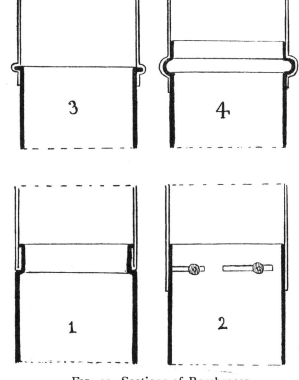

FIG. 31. Sections of Rerebraces.

1. " Engraved Suit," Tower, II, 5, 1514.
2. Tower, II, 6, 1540.
3. Tower, II, 7, 1570.
4. Wallace Collection, 340.

It is almost superfluous to mention the straps which join the various portions of the suit.   These are always placed, where possible, in positions where they are protected from injury ; as, for example, on the jambs they are on the inside of the leg, next to the horse when the wearer is mounted, and the hinge of the jamb being of metal is on

---

[1] *Antient Armour*, II, 164.   [2] *Origines des Chevalivers, etc.*, 1606, p. 142.

the outside. In some cases the end of the strap after being buckled fits into a " shoe " bossed out of the armour plate (Fig. 33).

It is practically impossible to notice the various forms of turning or locking pins used for joining parts of a suit. The general principle is that of a turning rivet with a flat, fan, or hook shaped head which, fitting into an oblong slot in the upper plate, can be turned at right angles to hold the two plates together. There are many varieties of this fastening, based upon the same principle, but those existing at the present day are often modern restorations. In suits for the joust or tourney these adjustable fastenings could not always be depended upon, and the great helm, the manteau d'armes, and the passgarde were often screwed on to the suit with square or polygonal headed bolts tightened with a spanner.

The gauntlet was sometimes capable of being locked, for the unfingered flap which covered the fingers was prolonged

Fig. 32. Locking Gauntlet of Sir Henry Lee, Armourers' Hall, London.

so as to reach the wrist, where it fastened over a pin. This was used in foot jousts to prevent the weapon from being struck out of the hand and is sometimes called the " forbidden gauntlet," an absurd term when we consider that many fine suits are provided with this appliance, which would not be the case if its use were not allowed (Fig. 32, also Plate XXII).

A few of the fastenings used to hold the different parts of the suit together are shown on Fig. 33. The

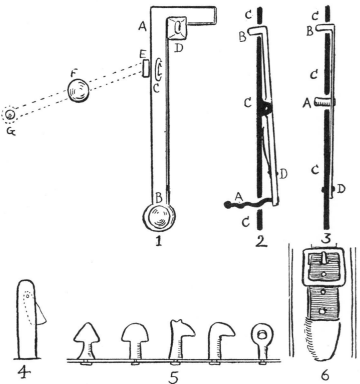

Fig. 33. Locking hooks, turning pins, and strap-cover.

hook (No. 1) is found on the armets made by Topf (page 21 and Plate XIII). Here the hook A is shown in position fastening the visor over a button D. When it is necessary to open the visor a leather thong which was attached at C is pulled and at the same time the button F is pressed. This depresses a spring riveted to the visor at G and projecting with a small tongue at E. The depression of E allows the hook to be moved back and the visor to be raised. When the hook is moved forward to close the visor the tongue E springs up and locks the whole firmly. No. 2 of the same figure is another contrivance for locking plates together, and is found on 695, Wallace Collection, and elsewhere. C C C is the section of the armour plate. The hook is pivoted at C and is fitted with a spring at D. When the leather lace at A is pulled the tongue of the hook B is brought back flush with the plate C and allows the visor to be raised. When the visor is closed the hook springs back to its position and locks the plates together. No. 3 is a catch of the same kind, but is worked by a spring of the same kind as that which locks the " Topf " hook. The pressing of the button A sets back the hook B, which is riveted to the plate at D. No. 4 is a " spring pin," or " federzapfen " as they are called in German and " auberon " in French. The small flange let into the pin is kept pressed outwards by a spring and is pressed back to slip the pauldron, in which is a hole cut for the purpose, over the pin. No. 5 shows a series of turning pins which are riveted to the lower plate in taces, cuisses, tassets, etc., but can be turned at will. The upper plates that are fastened by these pins are pierced with narrow oblong slits through which the flat head of the pin can be passed ; a turn at right angles locks the two plates closely. No. 6 is an ingenious contrivance found on 1086, Wallace Collection. The armour plate is bossed upwards to form a covering for the free end of the strap when buckled, to prevent the chance of this loose piece of leather being cut off or of hindering the wearer in any way.

On Fig. 34 is shown the support for the jousting-sallad, without which it was always liable to be struck off. It is screwed with wing nuts to the crest of the sallad and to the back of the cuirass. The reinforcing piece for face and breast of the same nature as the mentonnière and grandguard. These various methods of fastening plates together can be only studied to advantage by careful examination of actual suits, and even here there is always the chance that they may be modern restorations. Perhaps the most elaborately contrived suit in existence is that made for Henry VIII for fighting on foot in the lists (Tower, II, 28). This covers the wearer completely with lames back and front, and allows as much movement as is possible in a suit weighing 93 lb. (Plate VIII). It is composed of 235 separate pieces, all of different form. There are similar suits in the Musée d'Artillerie, Paris (G, 178, 179) of a more ornate character. The cuisse of one of these suits is shown on Plate XI and the inside of the cuisse of the Tower suit on Plate IX. While dealing with this question of the pieces that compose a suit, it should be noted that the " Leicester " suit in the Tower (II, 10) is made up of 194 pieces, and a suit at

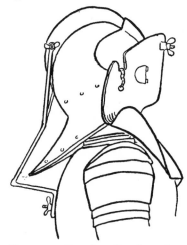

FIG. 34. Bracket for jousting-sallad and reinforcing bevor, Dresden, C, 3, 4.

Madrid (A, 164, the " Muhlberg " suit of Charles V) requires one mounted and six unmounted figures to show it off completely.

THE MAKING OF ARMOUR IN ENGLAND, FROM CONTEMPORARY DOCUMENTS

1321. Edward II sends David le Hope, armour-smith, to Paris to learn the method of making sword-blades for battle.

1322. Regulations concerning the covering of helmets with fabric and the selling of old and broken helmets. *Arm. Co., Lond.* (see Appendix A).

1347. Regulations of the Heaumers' Co. *City of London Letter Book, F, fol. cxlii* (see Appendix B).

1355. The Mayor and Sheriffs of London ordered to appraise the armour in the armourers' shops. *Rymer, III, v, 817.*

1365. The armourers of London are in full work, but the results are not satisfactory. The King (Edward III) insists on proof or trade marks. " Certa signa sua super omnibus operationibus suis ponant." *Rymer, III, 772.*

1386. Armourers are forbidden to increase the prices of their wares. *Rymer, III, 546.*

1408. Oct. 12. Petition to the Mayor and Aldermen of London against foreign importers who use marks similar to English marks, and praying to keep the price fixed and regulated by the masters of the cutlers and bladesmiths jointly. Agreed to by the Mayor. *City of London Letter Books, I, fol. lxxi.*

1434. This is very similar to the Ordinances of the Hastings MS. noticed in *Archæologia*, LVII. It is given here in full, as it is the only literary effort of an armourer that is known in England. *Treatise on Worship in Arms*, by Johan Hill, armourer (Bod. Lib. Ash., 856) (see Appendix C).

1436. Proclamation forbidding the armourers to increase their prices. *Fædera*, Rymer, X, 647.

1509. Sir Nicholas Vaux, Lieutenant at Guisnes, orders all the garrison to be English except gunners, crossbow-makers, spies, beer-brewers, armourers, and smiths. *Cal. State Papers, Hen. VIII, Vol. I.*

1511. Payments made for a forge for Milanese armourers at Greenwich.

1514. The armourers from Brussels are installed by Henry VIII at Greenwich.

1515. Almain or German armourers mentioned as King's servants.

1544. A complete account of the charges of the King's Armoury, with wages of the workmen. *Brit. Mus., Cott. App. XXVIII*, 75 (see Appendix F).

1556. Sir John Mason reports to the Council that he has obtained 50 fardels of plate for harness provided by the Schorers from Augsburg. In *Considerations delivered to Parliament in 1559* it is suggested " that iron mills be banished out of the realme, where wood was formerly 1d. the load at the stalk now by reason of the iron mills it is 2/- the load. Formerly Spanish iron was sold for 5 marks the ton now there are iron mills English iron is sold at 9/-." This may be the key to the question of importation of armour ready made. Evidently the use of wood in iron-smelting presented a serious difficulty. As may be seen in the chapter on Iron (p. 40), the use of wood in the furnaces was considered a grave danger, as it took material which should have been used for shipbuilding. The English forests were limited and had not the vast acreage of the German woods, so that the deforestation was merely a question of time.

1578. Inquiry as to a dispute between the armourers and blacksmiths as to right of search for armour, etc. The judges state that " the Armourers did show us that King Edward the Second did grant to the Lord Maior and his bretheren the searche with the armourers." *Records Arm. Co., London.*

1580. Sir Henry Lee made Master of the Armouries.

1590. Petition of the armourers of London to Queen Elizabeth against the importation of foreign armour and workmen. *Lansdowne MS., 63, 5* (see Appendix G).

1611. Survey and inventory of all armour, etc., in the armouries of the Tower, Greenwich, and Windsor in the late custody of Sir Henry Lee, deceased, and now of Sir Thos. Monson, Master of the Armoury. *State Papers Domestic, Jac. I, lxiv, June 8.*

1614. Warrant to pay to Wm. Pickering, Master of the Armoury at Greenwich, £200, balance of £340, for armour gilt and graven for the late Prince. *Sign. Man., Vol. IV, 29.*

This suit, made for Henry, Prince of Wales, is now in the Royal Collection at Windsor (see Plate XX).

1618. Undertaking of the Armourers' Company to make certain armours every six months and the prices of the same. *Records of the Armourers' Company of London* (see Appendix H).

1619. Proclamation against the excessive use of gold and silver foliate except for armour and ensigns of honour. *S.P.D. Jac. I, cv, Feb., Proclamations, 65* (see Appendix I).

1621. Gild of Armourers and Smiths incorporated at Shrewsbury by James I. The "Arbor" of the Gild existed at Kingsland in 1862. The Gild carried a figure of Vulcan dressed in black armour in their processions. Their motto was "With hammer and hand all hearts do stand." The armour is in the Museum at Shrewsbury. *Reliquary, Vol. III.*

1624. Erection of plating-mills at Erith by Capt. John Martin. *S.P.D. Jac. I, clxxx, 71* (see Appendix J).

1625. Falkner asks for an inquiry as to the condition of the Royal Armouries. *S.P.D. Car. I, xiii, 96.*

1627. Report of George, Earl of Totnes, on Falkner's petition advising John Cooper, Keeper of the King's Brigandines, to surrender his patent. *S.P.D. Car. I, liv, 1.*

Cooper refuses to surrender unless his arrears of 16d. a day for a year and a half are paid. *S.P.D. Car. I, lv, 70.*

1627. Petition of Falkner (Fawcknor) as to the condition of the armouries. *S.P.D. Car. I, lxxxiv, 5.*

1628. Order to gun-makers, saddlers, and cutlers to bring patterns of their wares. *S.P.D. Car. I, xcv, March 10.*

1628. Whetstone's project to make armour lighter and as good as proof. *S.P.D. Car. I, lxxxix, 23.* No details as to the process are given in this entry.

1630. Inquiry into the work done in the State armouries of the Tower, Greenwich, etc., with lists of the Remaines, moved by Roger Falkenor. *S.P.D., clxxix*, 65. The whole of this document is given in *Antient Armour*, Sir S. Meyrick, III, 78.

1631. Regulations respecting the use of a hall-mark by the Armourers' Company. *Rymer, XIX*, 309 (see Appendix K).

1635. Petition of the Workmen Armourers of London who are now old and out of work. *S.P.D. Car. I, cclxxxix*, 93 (see Appendix L).

1636. Benjamin Stone, blade-maker, of Hounslow Heath, states that he has, at his own charge of £6000, perfected the art of blade-making, and that he can make "as good as any that are made in the Christian world." *S.P.D. Car. I, cccxli*, 132.

1660. A survey of the Tower Armoury and the Remaines contained therein. This was taken after the Civil War and shows that much of the working plant had been scattered. *Harl. MS.* 7457 (see Appendix M).

1666. "Armour of the Toyras provision with headpeeces whereof made in England to be worn with the said armes." *Tower Inv. sub ann.* Meyrick considers that this was made at Tours, but brings no evidence to support his statement. It may have been part of the equipment of the infantry under Marechal de Toiras, who assisted Charles I against the Huguenots in La Rochelle in 1625. Several breastplates in the Tower are stamped "Toiras."

1666. Col. Wm. Legge appointed Master of the Armoury. Legge was Governor of Chester in 1644, Governor of Oxford in 1645, was offered and declined an earldom by Charles II, and died in 1672. His eldest son was created Baron Dartmouth.

1685. An ordinance of James II that all edged tools, armour, and all copper and brass made with the hammer in the city of London should be approved by the Armourers' Company. *Records of the Company.*

There are no details relating to the lives of any of the known English armourers that are worth recording. Pickering, the pupil of Topf, was the most celebrated, and the record of his position of Master of the Armourers' Company will be found under that heading. John Blewbery, whose name occurs in several entries in the Letters and Papers Foreign and Domestic, seems to have been merely the master-workman, and we have no evidence that he attained to a higher position. His name does not appear in the existing records of the Armourers' Company. Asamus or Erasmus Kyrkenor first appears in a list of payments in 1518.

ALEGORIA DEL TACTO, BY JAN BRUEGHEL, CIRC. 1600

PRADO, MADRID

PLATE XV

1. VENETIAN SALLAD COVERED WITH VELVET, XVI CENT.
2. BACK PLATE OF BRIGANDINE COVERED WITH FABRIC, 1470
3. MORION WITH COVER, XVI—XVII CENT.
4. SURCOAT OF THE BLACK PRINCE

PLATE XVI

He was employed to make candlesticks and for " garnishing books " with clasps, etc., in 1529, when presumably there was a slack time in the armouries.   There are further entries of this nature in 1530, 1531, and 1532, in which year he " garnished " eighty-six books.   In 1538 he was made Brigandarius to the King, vice John Gurre, deceased ; but we find no details as to the duties of this office, which was continued to the reign of Charles I, when it became the subject of a complaint from Roger Falknor (Appendix J).   In 1547 we find Erasmus in charge of the Greenwich Armoury, and in 1593 a note of the will of Wm. and Robt. Mighill states that they were the grandsons of Erasmus Kirkenor, deceased.

A list of English armourers is given on page 126.

THE PROOF OF ARMOUR

AS soon as the armed man realized that iron and steel were the best defences for his body, he would naturally insist that some sort of a guarantee should be given him of the efficacy of the goods supplied by his armourer. This system of proving armour would be effected by using those weapons most commonly in use, and these, in the early times, were the sword, the axe, the lance, the bow, and the crossbow. The latter seems to have been the more common form of proof, though as late as the seventeenth century we have evidence that armour was proved with the " estramaçon " or sword blow.[1]

In considering the proof of mail we are met with certain terms which are somewhat difficult of explanation, but which evidently are intended to convey the fact that the mail mentioned was of especially good quality. These terms are " haute cloueur," " demi-cloueur," " botte cassée," and "botte."

M. Charles Buttin,[2] in his studies on the arms used for proving armour, considers that " botte " is here used to denote a blow in the sense that it is used in fencing for a thrust or a lunge (It. botta). The word " cassée " he takes to be derived also from the Italian " casso," vain or empty.

The term "haute" or "demi-cloueurs" seems rather to suggest the single or double riveting of each link of mail. Ordinary mail is either welded or joined with one rivet, but in some cases, as in III, 339, Tower, two rivets are used to obtain increased strength for the fabric (see also page 44).

Mail seems to have been proof against arrows at a very early period, for we find in the *Chronicon Colmariense*, under the year 1398, the statement that the men-at-arms wore " camisiam ferream, ex circulis ferreis contextam, per quae nulla sagitta arcus poterat hominem vulnerare." The earliest entry of this mail of proof is found in the Inventory

---

[1] Gaya, *op. cit.*   [2] *Revue Savoisienne*, 1906, fasc. 4.

62

of Louis X (le Hutin) of France, which is here given together with other entries of the different expressions used with regard to proof of this nature.

> 1316. *Inventory of Louis le Hutin. Bib. Richel., MS. fr., 7855.*
>
>> Item uns pans[1] et uns bras de roondes mailles de haute cloueur.
>> Uns de meme d'acier plus fors.
>> Item uns couverture a cheval . . . de jaseran de fer, uns de mailes rondes demy clouees.

In this entry there is evidently a variety of mail which is even stronger than that of "haute cloueur," but this may possibly be of stouter or better-tempered metal. The horse-armour would not need to be of such high proof as that of the man, because from its form it would be more or less in folds when the horse was in action and would therefore present double thicknesses to the weapon. An illustration of the mail-clad horse is given in the present writer's *Armour and Weapons*, and also in *Monumenta Vetusta*, Vol. VI.

> 1390. *Archives Camerales de Turin Comptes Tres. gen. de Savoie, No. 38, fol. 62v.*
>
>> Achettez de Simond Brufaler armeur, de mons . . . per le pris de un auberjon d'acier de toute botte.

This expression "de toute botte" suggests that the armour was proof against all blows, that is from the sword, the axe—the "estramaçon" above alluded to—and also against the bow and the crossbow. In 1612 Sturtevant in his *Metallica* writes on page 62 that the iron-worker should "make things stronger than the Exact strength which the thing is to have," and we find this borne out in an extract from the Armerie di Roma, Arch. Stat. c. 150, of the date 1627, which mentions old armour "a botta" which had been proved with "due e tre colpi dell' arma alla quale dovevano resistere."[2]

The proof by the crossbow is mentioned by Angellucci in a note, quoting from the *Arch. Gonz. Copialett.*, T. II, c. 65: "et si te manderemo doi veretoni di nostri saldi, como i quali tu farai aprovare la ditta coraza como uno bono balestro di cidello."[2] The last-mentioned weapon is the "arbalest à tour" or windlass crossbow. It would seem from M. Buttin's researches that the armour "à toute épreuve" was proved by

---

[1] Panzer, body-armour.   [2] *Cat. Armeria Reale Turin*, 129.

crossbow and sword, and that "à demi épreuve" by the smaller lever crossbow or by the javelin thrown by hand. These varieties of proof were indicated by the marks stamped upon them, one mark for the single and two for the double (see page 65). In some documents we have definite entries of arrows used for proof, which would naturally have exceptionally well-tempered points :—

> 1378. *Reg. de la Cloison d'Angers, No. 6.*
> Pour deux milliers de fer pour viretons partie d'espreuve et autre partie de fer commun.

The "vireton" was a crossbow-bolt which had spiral wings of metal or wood so fitted that it revolved in its course.

> 1416. *Compt de Gilet Baudry, Arch. Mun. Orleans.*
> Fléches à arc empannées a cire et ferres de fers d'espreuve.

Here the "feathering" of the arrow with copper is specified, for it was this metal wing which, acting like the propeller of a boat, caused the arrow to revolve with increased velocity.

These arrows of proof cost double the price of ordinary arrows, for we have entries of such projectiles in the year 1419 costing 8s. the dozen, while the ordinary quality cost but 4s. the dozen.[1]

Details of the regulations of setting proof marks upon armour will be found in Appendices B, E, K.

The proving of brigandines was most carefully carried out, for in some instances every separate plate was stamped with the proof mark. In the Paris Collection double proof marks are found on the brigandine G, 206, and a similar double mark appears stamped on the Missaglia suit G, 3, but of a different design. The helmet of Henry VIII on II, 29 (Tower) also bears the double proof mark of one of the Missaglia family (Plate X). It would be tedious and unnecessary to give a list of those armours which bear these proof marks, for they are to be found in every armoury of note in Europe ; but it will be of some profit to quote various extracts showing the reason and the effects of proofs or trials of armour.

In the sixteenth century the firearm had become a serious factor in warfare, therefore the proof was decided by submitting the armour to pistol or musket shot.

---

[1] *Rev. Savoisienne*, 1906, fasc. 4, p. 3.

1347. *Regulations of the Heaumers of London* (original in Norman-French), *City of London Letter Book, F, fol. cxlii.*

> Also that helmetry and other arms forged by the hammer . . . shall not from henceforth in any way be offered for sale privily or openly until they have been properly assayed by the aforesaid Wardens and marked with their marks (see Appendix B).

1448. *Statutes des Armuriers Fourbisseurs d'Angers.*

> It. les quels maisters desd. mestiers seront tenus besoigner et faire ouvrage et bonnes étoffes, c'est assavoir pour tant que touche les armuriers, ils feront harnois blancs pour hommes d'armes, de toute épreuve qui est à dire d'arbalestes à tilloles et à coursel à tout le moins demie espreuve . . . marquées de 2 marques . . . et d'espreuve d'arbaleste à crocq et traict d'archier, marquées d'une marque (see Appendix E).

The "arbaleste à tilloles" was the large bow bent with a windlass, the "arbaleste à crocq" was smaller and was bent with a hook fastened to the waist of the archer (see Payne Gallwey, *The Crossbow*).

1537. *Discipline Militaire*, Langey, I, chap. xxii, pp. 79, 80.

> . . . les Harnois soient trop foibles pour résister à l'Artillerie ou à l'Escopeterie, néantmoins ils defendent la personne des coups de Pique de Hallebarde, d'Epée, du Trait, des Pierres, des Arbalestes, et des Arcs. . . . Et par fois une Harquebuze sera si mal chargée ou si fort eschauffée ou pourra tirer de si loin, que le Harnois pour peu qu'il soit bon sauvera la vie d'un homme.

The above writer considers, and with reason, that when the uncertainty of firearms was taken into consideration defensive armour was of much practical use ; and this theory was held as late as the eighteenth century, for Marshal Saxe in his *Les Rêveries*[1] warmly recommends the use of defensive armour, especially for cavalry, as he considers that a large proportion of wounds were caused by sword, lance, or spent bullets. It was evidently from reasons such as the above that a reliable proof by pistol or musket shot was insisted upon, for the armour of the Duc de Guise in the Musée d'Artillerie (G, 80) is of great thickness and weighs 42 kilos. It has either been tested by the maker or has seen service, for there are three bullet marks on the breastplate, neither of which has penetrated.[2]

[1] Edit. 1756, p. 58.
[2] A half-suit in the possession of H. Moffat, Esq., Goodrich Court, formerly the property of New College, Oxford, has a heavy " plastron " or reinforcing piece. The bullet has dented this and also the cuirass underneath. The head-piece and back-plate are pierced by bullets.

1569. *Arch. cur. de Nantes*, I, col. 305.

> 612 corps de cuyrace . . . garnis de haulzecou . . . desquelz le devant sera a l'espreuve d'arquebuse et le derrière de pistol.

The terms "high proof," "caliver proof," and "musket proof" often occur in writings of this period and onwards up to the time when armour was discarded; but it is difficult to get any definite information as to how the proof was made. In the above entry there are two kinds of proof, which show that the back-plate was thinner than the breastplate, the resisting power being obtained not only by temper of metal, but also by its thickness.

1568. *Les Armuriers français et étrangers*, Giraud, pp. 191, 192.

> Ung corps de cuirasse lequel sera a l'espreuve de la pistolle, ung habillement de teste a l'esprouve de la pistolle, brassartz . . . a l'esprove de la pistolle, tassettes courtes a l'esprouve de la pistolle.

Here is evidently a necessary definition of each piece. Probably on some former occasion the armourer had classed the whole suit as of proof when such a description might only be honestly given to the cuirass. Accounts of actual trials are rare, but the following extract is of interest as showing the methods employed in England. It is given in full, with many valuable extracts bearing on the craft of the armourer, by Viscount Dillon, in *Archæologia*, Vol. LI. The extract is taken from a letter from Sir Henry Lee, Master of the Armoury in 1580, to Lord Burghley, and bears the date Oct. 12, 1590.

The first part of the letter states that a gentleman of Shropshire was anxious that the metal mined in his county should be used for armour instead of the German iron which at this time was considered to be the best in the market. Sir Henry writes: "To give the more credyte to that stuffe to the armourers of London and to Jacobi the Mr. workman of Grenewhyche, the Counsell apoynt in there presence that Sr. Robarte Constable and my cossyn John Lee shoulde see a proofe made wh. by tryall proved most usefull." The "Shropshire gentleman" sent Sir Henry "a new brest beyng sent owt of the country of gret litenes and strengthe as he was made beleve," and entrusted him to "cause another of the very same wayght to be made in her Matys office of Greenwhyche, wh. I presently performed." Pistols were then loaded with equal charges and fired at the two breastplates, with the result that "that made in the

Offyce and of the metall of Houngere[1] helde out and more than a littel dent of the pellet nothinge perced, the other clene shotte thereowe and much tare the overpart of a beme the brest studde upon as longe as my fyngeers.   Thus muche for the Ynglyshe metall."

From time to time, as has been noticed before, there had been efforts to wrest the monopoly of the supply of metal for armour from the foreigner, but here was a very tangible proof of the superiority of the alien material.   It is true that the Shropshire breastplate appears to have been sent from that county for the test, while the foreign metal was made up by the highly skilled workmen in the Royal Armoury at Greenwich under the eye of Jacobi (Topf), a master-craftsman who can have had but few rivals at that time.   Possibly he may have possessed some secrets of tempering and hardening his metal which were unknown to less experienced smiths, and so have obtained the award of superiority for the metal of his own country.   Topf had migrated to England from Innsbruck and must certainly have had friends among the iron-merchants of that locality.   So his interests were obviously on the side of the foreign metal.

It may be only romance or it may be fact, but certainly Oliver de la Marche,[2] writing about the year 1450, describes some such process of tempering armour after it was made.   " Boniface avoit trempe son harnois d'une eau qui le tenoit si bon que fer ne povoit prendre sus." It is not to be suggested that it was a special kind of water that was used for this, but rather that it was some method of heating and cooling the metal which was employed.   Angellucci, in the *Catalogue of the Armeria Reale, Turin* (p. 129), quotes, from documents of the sixteenth century, the account of a breastplate made by Colombo, an armourer of Brescia, being spoiled because he had used excessive charges for his pistol or musket.

1602. *Milice français*, Montgomery, Pt. II, p. 187.

Les chevau-légers estoient armez d'armes complètes d'une cuirasse à l'épreuve.   Le reste estoit à la légère.

The last detail shows that the back-pieces were much lighter than the proof breastplates, and this is borne out by other similar entries during the century.   Evidently the efficacy of the musket had increased in the first

---

[1] Hungarian or Innsbruck iron.   [2] *Memories*, I, xxi (edit. 1884).

years of the seventeenth century and with it the weight of the proved armour. In later entries we find that pistol proof is of more frequent occurrence, and from this we may gather that the weight of metal was a serious hindrance to the soldier and that he preferred the risk of a bullet.

Still there are cases to be found of complete proof, for in 1605 even the brayette was of proof (*Arch. Gov. Brescia Privil.*, R. 7, *V*, p. 10),[1] and if this small, in fact the smallest, portion of the armour was proved, we may be sure that the whole suit was tested equally.

In 1628–9 we learn from the State Papers Domestic, lxxxix, 23, that one Whetstone had a project for making light armour as good as proof, but there are no details of his methods. It is quite probable, in most cases, that when one piece of the armour was proved the rest were made of similar material and tempered in the same way, and that actual proof was not expected or given. An interesting extract from the *Memorials of the Verney Family*, IV, 30, gives us some information as regards the proof of armour :—

> 1667, Feb. Richard Hals is choosing some armour for his cousin in London : he has tested it with as much powder as will cover the bullet in the palme of his hand.

This rough-and-ready method of estimating the charge is borne out in Gaya's *Traité des Armes*, p. 30 (Reprint 1911, Clarendon Press).

The Verney extract goes on to say that Verney wished to have the armour tested again, but the armourer refused, for by this time it was finished, and he said that "it is not the custom of workmen to try their armour after it is faced and filed."

This suit cost £14 2s. 8d., and when it was delivered Verney was by no means pleased, as it did not fit.[2] A clear proof that armour was tested before it was finished is to be found on the suit made by Garbagnus of Brescia for Louis XIV of France, now in the Musée d'Artillerie (G, 125). M. Buttin[3] in noticing this suit describes it as "La magnifique armure offerte à Louis XIV par la République de Venise," but in this we must certainly hold a different opinion, for the production, although elaborately engraved, is perhaps the best example of the decadence of the craft of the armourer, so graceless and clumsy are its lines

---

[1] *Cat. Armeria Reale Turin*, p. 73 note.   [2] See page 105.   [3] *Rev. Savoisienne*, 1901, fasc. 2 and 3.

CAST OF IVORY CHESSMAN, XIV CENT.

IVORY MIRROR CASE, XIV CENT.

PLATE XVII

PORTRAITS BY MORONI

NATIONAL GALLERY, LONDON

PLATE XVIII

and proportions. The proof mark is upon the left of the breastplate, at the point where the lower edge of the pauldron ends. It has been made the centre of a double-petalled rose, showing plainly that the bullet mark was there before the engraver began his work. A similar mark at the back is made the centre of a flower (Fig. 35). The document

Fig. 35. Detail showing proof mark on breast of suit of
Louis XIV, Mus. d'Art, Paris, G, 125.

relating to the "proof mark" of the Armourers' Company of London will be found in Appendix K.

Gaya in his *Traité des Armes*, 1678, referred to above, states on page 53 that the casque and front of the cuirass should be of musket proof, but the other parts need only be of pistol or carbine proof. In speaking of head-pieces he states, on the same page, that the heavier kinds were proved with musket-shot, but the light varieties were only tested with "estramaçon" or sword-cut ; and he adds that for armour to be good it must be beaten and worked cold and not hot.

We have seen how armour was proved and how the proof mark of crossbow-bolt or bullet is often found as a witness to the fact. In addition to this we frequently find the mark or poinçon of the armourer, which invariably means that the piece is of good workmanship and worthy of notice.

Like all the other craft gilds, that of the armourer was very jealous of the reputation of its members. The tapestry weavers of Flanders were obliged to mark, in some cases, every yard of their production ; and so in fine suits of armour we find many of the individual pieces that go to make up the suit stamped with the maker's mark and also with the stamp of the town. These town stamps are mostly found in German work from Nuremberg, Augsburg, etc. We find the name Arbois used on some Burgundian armour, but never are the names of Italian or French towns stamped. With the sword this rule does not hold good, for the Spanish, Italian, and German makers frequently used the town of origin as a mark in addition to their own. Toledo, Passau, Ferara, Solingen are all found upon swords, and are very often stamped upon blades of an entirely different nationality. This forgery of the stamp may have been perpetrated with the intent to defraud, or it may simply have been used as a mark of excellence, like " Paris fashions " or " Sheffield steel " at the present day. The forgery of marks on suits of armour is very seldom met with and where it exists it is obviously done for ulterior reasons.

The stamps take the form of signs such as the trefoil of Treytz, the monogram such as the "M Y" of the Missaglias, and the crowned "A" of the Armourers' Company of London; the rebus, as for example the helm used by the Colman (Helmschmied) family, or a combination of two or more of the above variety.

About the year 1390 we have the following entry :—

Achettez de Symond Brufaler armeur . . . 1 auberion d'acier de botte cassé duquel toutes les mailes sunt seignier du seignet du maistre.[1]

This shows that in some cases every link of mail was stamped with the armourer's mark. In Oriental mail letters and sometimes words

---

[1] Arch. Cam. de Turin, Compte des Trés. gén. de Savoie, Vol. XXXIX, f. 163.

from the Koran are stamped on each link, but we have no examples extant of European mail stamped with the maker's mark on each link.

On May 11, 1513, Richard Thyrkyll writes to Henry VIII from Antwerp saying that he can find no "harness of the fleur de lys" in any part of Brabant (Brit. Mus. Galba, B, III, 85).

This probably refers to a trade-mark or poinçon well known as denoting metal of high temper. A brigandine in the Museum at Darmstadt bears this mark repeated twice on each plate, showing that it was proof against the large crossbow (Fig. 36). Demmin (*Guide des Amateurs d'Armes*) gives a mark of a lion rampant as stamped on the plates of a brigandine in his collection, and an example in the Musée d'Artillerie has the Nuremberg mark on each of the plates.

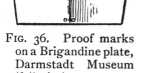

FIG. 36. Proof marks on a Brigandine plate, Darmstadt Museum (full size).

In the case of mail a small label is sometimes found, riveted on to the fabric, on which is the maker's stamp; an example of this is the eagle which is stamped on a label attached to the mail skirt G, 86, in the Armeria Reale, Turin (see Table of Marks, 59). In brigandines we sometimes find each of the small plates stamped with the maker's mark, which is held to be evidence of "proof."

As we have seen from the entry under the date 1448, on page 65, the single stamp signified proof against the small crossbow and the double stamp proof against the heavy windlass-bow.

As has been noticed above, the forgery or imitation of marks is more common on sword-blades than on defensive armour, and of these the wolf, dog, or fox of Passau is most frequently imitated. In some instances the representation is more or less life-like, but in others there is simply a crude arrangement of straight lines that suggest the head, legs, body, and tail of the animal.

Stamping of armour was practised early in the middle of the fourteenth century, as will be seen in the Regulations of the Company of Heaumers transcribed in Appendix B.

In Rymer's *Fœdera* (XIX, p. 312) we find accounts for repairing and remodelling armour in the year 1631, and at the end of the list comes the entry " For stamping every harness fit to be allowed

£o o o ", which shows that even armour that was remade from old material was subjected to tests, and also that these tests were recorded by a gratuitous stamp of the craftsman or of the company to which he belonged.

The only entry extant which actually refers to the making of these stamps for armourers is given in the *Mem. de la Soc. Arch. de Touraine, T. XX, pp.* 268–9 (*Arch. de Tours, Grandmaison*).

> 1470. A Pierre Lambert orfèvre, la somme de 55 s. t. . . . pour avoir fait et gravé 6 poinsons de fer acérez pour marquer les harnois blancs et brigandines qui seroient faiz et délivrez en lad. ville, de la façon que le roy l'avait ordonné, et pour avoir retaillé et ressué 2 desd. poinsons qui estoient fenduz en marquant les harnois.
>
> A Jehan Harane orfèvre, pour avoir gravé les armes de la ville en 2 poinsons de fer pour marquer les harnois et brigandines vendues en lad. ville 30 s.

The number of armourers' marks known at present amounts to several hundred, but of the majority nothing is known as to ownership and history. A few of the principal marks in English and Continental collections are given on page 148.

THE DECORATION OF ARMOUR

FROM the earliest times defensive armour has been more or less decorated and ornamented with more or less elaborate detail as the armourer became skilled in his craft and as the patron indulged in vanity or caprice. Perhaps the most astonishing work in this direction is the shoulder-piece of a cuirass known as the Siris bronze in the British Museum, which is of such elaborate repoussé work that it is difficult to see how the tool can have been used from the back. It is not, however, the intention of this work to deal with Greek or Roman armour, or indeed with armour previous to the eleventh century; otherwise its limits would have to be considerably enlarged. The ornamentation of early armour, the employment of brass or latten rings, which formed patterns on the hauberk, called for no special skill on the part of the craftsman, and it is only when we come to the thirteenth century that we find traces of actual decoration on the pieces of plate which composed the suit.

And here it should be remembered that the axiom of suitability was, in later years, forgotten, and the ever-important "glancing surface" was destroyed by designs in high relief, which not only retained the full shock of the opposing weapon, but also hindered the free movement of the several plates one over the other. The word "decoration" in itself suggests a "decorous" or suitable adornment, and this suitability was not always considered by the sixteenth and seventeenth century armourers.

The use of jewels was always favoured among the nobility, and we find in the inventory of the effects of Piers Gaveston[1] plates ornamented with gold and silver and ailettes "frettez de perles." In 1352 King John of France and the Dauphin had elaborate head-pieces ornamented with jewels, and in 1385 the King of Castile wore a helmet at the battle of Aljubertota which was enriched with gold and valued at 20,000 francs.[2]

---

[1] *New Fœdera*, II, 203.　　[2] Froissart (Johnes' trans.), II, 124.

The well-known brass of Sir John d'Aubernon, 1277, shows the first traces of the actual ornamentation of armour, which culminated in the work of Piccinino and Peffenhauser in the sixteenth century. Similar

ornamentation is found on the brass of Sir Robert de Bures, 1302 (Fig. 37). It is possible that the poleynes shown on this brass and also the beinbergs on the figure of Guigliemo Berardi in the Cloisters of the Annunziata at Florence (Fig. 38) were made of cuir-bouilli and not metal, for there is not much incised or engraved iron found in domestic objects of this period (Fig. 37). But when we reach the end of the century we find a richly decorated suit of complete plate shown on the brass of an unknown knight of about the year 1400 which in no way suggests any material but iron or steel (Fig. 39).

FIG. 37. Poleynes on the brass of Sir Robert de Bures, Acton, Suffolk, 1302.

This engraving of armour, either by the burin or by etching with acid, was employed with more or less intricacy of detail from the beginning of the fifteenth century up to the period when armour was discarded; for the suits of Charles I (Tower, II, 19) and of Louis XIV of France (Musée d'Artillerie, G, 125) are almost entirely covered with fine engraving. The tradition is well known that the art of engraving and printing the results on paper was discovered by the Florentine metal-workers of the fifteenth century, who employed this expedient for proving their ornamental work upon various metals. In some cases the engraving of armour was merely the first process of the niello-work, in which the lines and spaces cut out were filled in with a black compound. Neither the engraving alone nor the niello-work in any way interfered with the utility of the armour, for the surface was still capable of a high polish and would still deflect the weapon. No better example of this could be found than the ' Engraved Suit" made for Henry VIII by Conrad Seusenhofer (Tower, II, 5). Here the entire surface is covered with fine engraving of scenes from the lives of SS. George and Barbara, and of decorative designs of the royal badges—the

FIG. 38. Beinbergs on the statue of Guigliemo Berardi, Florence, 1289.

Rose, the Portcullis, and the Pomegranate. Originally the whole suit was washed with silver, of which traces remain, but there was no attempt to destroy the utility of the armour. Indeed, it would have been a daring armourer who would have essayed such decoration when making a suit which was to be a present from Maximilian to Henry VIII, both of whom were among the most practised jousters in Europe (Plate XII). It was only when work in high relief was produced that this utility was destroyed. While condemning the neglect of true craft principles in this respect, we cannot but give our unstinted admiration for the skill in which this embossed armour was produced. The Negrolis, the Colmans, Campi, Lucio Piccinino, Peffenhauser, and Knopf were all masters of this form of applied art; but the admiration which their work compels is that which we have for the work of a gold or silver smith, and not for that of the armourer. In some cases, it is true, there is some definite idea in the craftsman's mind of a subject, as for example the parade suit of Christian II (Johanneum, Dresden, E, 7), in which the artist, who is generally considered to have been Heinrich Knopf, embossed scenes from the labours of Hercules on the horse-armour. As a rule, however, the ornamentation is merely fantastic and meaningless, and consists for the most part of arabesques, masks, and amorini based upon classical models of the worst period and style. For sheer incoherence of design, and at the same time for technique which could hardly be surpassed, we have no better example in any of the applied arts than the parade suit made for King Sebastian of Portugal by Anton Peffenhauser of Augsburg in the second half of the sixteenth century (Real Armeria, Madrid, A, 290). Here we have tritons, nereids, dolphins and sea-horses, combats of classical warriors, elephants, allegorical figures of Justice, Strength, and Victory,

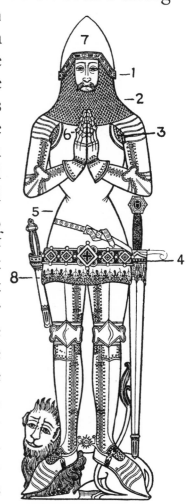

FIG. 39. Brass of an unknown knight at Laughton, Lincs, 1400.

1. Vervelles.
2. Camail.
3. "Vif de l'harnois," "défaut de la cuirasse."
4. Baldrick.
5. Jupon.
6. Gadlings or gauntlets.
7. Bascinet.
8. Edge of hauberk.

gods, goddesses, heroes, virtues, and symbolic figures spread broadcast among a wealth of arabesques and foliation which leaves the beholder breathless at the thought that this was simply produced for parade purposes, when but little of the detail could be seen and none of it could be adequately studied or admired. In fact the whole equipment may be described in a sentence originally used in far different circumstances: "C'est magnifique, mais ce n'est pas la guerre" (Plate XIV).

Much of this embossed work was blackened or oxidized so that the full value of the relief-work could be appreciated. Gilding and gold inlay were also in high favour, but the latter art never reached the high pitch of excellence which we find in Oriental weapons, though the arrogant Cellini asserted that he could damascene swords as well as any Oriental craftsman, and better. That the art was not seriously attempted we gather from Cellini's own words, for he says that it " differed from any he had as yet practised."[1]

In all this ostentatious riot of ornament we in England preserved a dignified reticence. It is true that the City of London commissioned Petit of Blois to make the cumbersome gilded and engraved suit for Charles I, but we have in our national collections no specimens of elaborately embossed parade armour which were made for kings, princes, or nobles in England.

The master-craftsman Jacobi Topf and his pupil William Pickering both produced suits of great richness and beauty, but they were always eminently practical, and their utility and convenience were never hampered or destroyed. Where there is embossing it is shallow, and as the relief is not sharp there is no edge which might catch the lance-point or sword. Much of the work of Topf was russeted and gilt, a method which produced a highly ornate and yet never a trivial or confused effect.

The parade suit by Bartolomeo Campi, made for Charles V (Real Armeria, Madrid, A, 125), is so obviously a fantastic costume for masque or pageant that it can hardly be criticized as armour. It is based upon a classical model, for the cuirass is moulded to the torse after the manner of the armour of the late Roman Empire. As metalwork it will rank with the finest specimens extant, but as armour it completely fails to satisfy (see page 132 and Plate XIV).

---

[1] *Life of Benvenuto Cellini*, 1910 edition, I, 112.

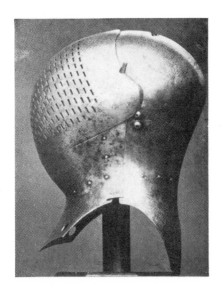

HELM OF SIR GILES CAPEL.   XVI CENT.

ARMING FOR COMBAT IN THE LISTS
FROM THE HASTINGS MS., XV CENT.

PLATE XIX

ARMOUR OF HENRY, PRINCE OF WALES, BY WILLIAM PICKERING, 1591-1630

PLATE XX

Although not in any way decorative, the " puffed and slashed " armour copied from the civilian dress of the sixteenth century is an example of the armourer making use of embossing apart from the actual requirements of the constructive side of his craft. Radiating lines of repoussé work, simple, fine, and delicate, had been introduced into the later forms of Gothic armour, the pauldrons had been fluted like the cockle-shell, and these flutings had been made of practical use in Maximilian armour, giving increased rigidity without weight, a factor which is found in modern corrugated iron.

The imitation of fabrics in steel is, however, unpardonable, and has not even the richness or minute technique of the parade suits mentioned above. It is true that the embossing gives greater rigidity to the metal, but we can have none of the admiration for these unnatural forms of armour that we have for those in which the goldsmith and armourer worked together. The style of dress which was imitated was in itself designed to create a false impression, for the slashings were intended to convey the idea that the wearer was a swashbuckler, fresh from the wars. We can only, therefore, regard it as an absurdity to represent fabrics, which were supposed to have been frayed and cut by weapons, in weapon-proof steel. That the fashion was popular we know from the number of suits extant, and even Conrad Seusenhofer himself did not disdain to produce them. The vogue did not endure for more than about twenty years, for as soon as the fashion in civilian dress changed the armour became simpler and the imitation ceased (Plate XXI).

THE CLEANING OF ARMOUR

AN important part of the work of the armourer was the cleaning and keeping in repair his master's effects. This was especially the case with mail, which from its nature is peculiarly susceptible to the action of rust. It is to this cause and to the incessant remaking of armour that we owe the loss of all authentic mail armour of the twelfth and thirteenth centuries. A good example of this may be cited in the hoard of plate armour and helmets, of which last nearly a hundred were collected, found in a cistern in the castle of Chalcis, in Eubœa, in the year 1840.[1] They had lain there since the year 1470, when the castle was taken by the Turks, and are in many instances in excellent preservation considering the condition in which they were found. The collection was brought to light and catalogued in a very unscientific manner by the historian Buchon, but there is no trace of mail of any kind except one link attached to a helmet.

In the early part of the fifteenth century mail was used extensively both for complete defence and for protecting vital parts not covered by plate, of which details will be found on page 109; therefore it is most improbable that a large collection such as this should have been left with no vestiges of mail. It is obvious, therefore, that the delicate fabric was attacked and destroyed by rust long before the same agent could make any effect on the solid plate. The following extracts will give in chronological order the various entries which concern the cleaning and repairing of armour :—

1250 (?). *The Avowynge of King Arthur, stanza* 39.

> Gay gownus of grene
> To hold thayre armur clene
> And were[2] hitte fro the wette.

Here we find the reason, or at any rate one of the reasons, for wearing the surcoat. Some writers have suggested that it was worn to protect

---

[1] Charles ffoulkes, " Italian Armour at Chalcis," *Archæologia,* LXII.   [2] Protect.

the Crusader from the sun in his Oriental campaigns, but the quotation given definitely asserts that it was to keep off the rain.   This is certainly a practical reason, for, as has been stated before in this chapter, the intricate fabric of mail was peculiarly susceptible to damp.

1296. 23-24 *Edw. I (Duchy of Lancaster Accounts)*.
Itm. xx s. xj d. in duobus saccis de coreo pro armatura comitis.

This refers to leather sacks used either for keeping the armour in or for cleaning it by shaking it with sand and vinegar.

1344. *Inventory of Dover Castle* (see also page 25).
i barrele pro armaturis rollandis.

The barrel was here used in the same way.   The mail was placed inside with sand and vinegar and rolled and shaken.   The same method is still practised in some districts for cleaning barrels for cider or ale. Chains are placed in the barrel with sand to obtain the same result.   On Plate XV a barrel is shown on the extreme left of the picture with a mail shirt hanging over the edge.

1364. *Inventory of the donjon of Vostieza.*[1]
i barellum ad forbiendum malliam.

1369. *Prologue, Canterbury Tales*, Chaucer.
Of fustyan he wered a gipoun
Alle sysmoterud with his haburgeoun.

This extract shows clearly the need for the barrel and sand.   The mail had evidently rusted with rain and perspiration, and left stains and marks on the quilted undergarment.   We find the term " rokked " used in the poem of *Syr Gawayn*, which means cleaned by rolling.

1372. Froissart *uses the expression*
a rouler leurs cottes de fer.

1417. *Inventory of Winchester College*.
i barelle pro loricis purgandis.

1423. *Roll of Executors of Henry Bowet, Archbishop of York*, Oct. 20.
j barrelle cum suis pertinentiis ad purgandos loricas et alia arma de mayle.

1467. *Howard Household Book (Dom. Expenses in England, 416)*.
9d. to an armerer at Pawles Cheyne for an harneys barelle.

[1] *Arch. Journ.*, LX, 106.

1513. *Earl of Northumberland's Equipage* (see also page 30).
a paommyshe.
Eight yards of white blaunkett for trussing of my Lord's harnes in.

The pumice was for cleaning off the rust, and the blanket was used for packing the armour when in store or on a journey.

1515. *King's Book of Payments, Record Office, under various payments to armourers.*
Oct. 11. Payment to Adrian Brand for hire of his mill house for cleaning the king's harness, 26s. 8d. the month.

1517. April. Wm. Gurre, armourer, making clean of certain harness, bockeling & ledering of 400 Almain rivets for the Armoury at Eltham £24 7 8.

The "bockeling & ledering" of course refers to the fitting of new leather straps and buckles. The Almain rivet was the half-suit of the foot-soldier and has been explained on page 52.

1520. April. William Gurre for scouring 1000 pr. of Almain rivets at 12d. a pair.

1530. Hans Clerc armorer for furbishing and keeping clean the king's armour in the armoury in the Tilt yard at Greenwich which John Diconson late had at 6d. a day.
Thos. Wollwarde for keeping & making the king's harnes att Windsor & York Place 30s. 5d.

1567. *S.P.D. Eliz.*, *Addenda xiii*, 101.
Payments are made in this entry to paint black various corselets which had become "fowle and rustie" and had "taken salt water in the sea" at a charge of 5d. each.

Froissart describes the champion Dimeth, at the coronation of Henry IV, as being "tout couvert de mailles de vermeil, chevalier et cheval."[1] This painting of armour was frequently indulged in both for the above practical reason and also for personal adornment. Tinning was also used for protecting armour from wet (*vide* page 33 *sub ann.* 1622). Armour in the Dresden Armoury and elsewhere is painted black. Hall in his Chronicles in the account of the funeral of Henry V states that men-at-arms in black armour rode in the procession. The armour in the seventeenth century was often blacked or russeted. Suits of this kind are to be seen in the Gun Wharf Museum at Portsmouth and else-

---

[1] Vol. IV, c. 114. This detail is not given either in Johnes' or Lord Berners' translation.

where. Haselrigg's "lobsters" were so called, according to Clarendon,[1] because of their "bright shells." It is quite possible that their armour was blacked. In the Lansdowne MS. 73, William Poore suggested a remedy for " preserving armour from pewtrifying, kankering or rusting," but there are no details given of the method he employed; it was probably some kind of lacquer or varnish. Among the Archives of the Compte du tresor de Savoie (63 f. 157) is mentioned a payment to Jehan de Saisseau " por vernicier une cotte d'aciel," and in one of the Tower inventories (Harl. MS. 1419) of the year 1547 "a buckler of steel painted " occurs.[2]

> 1567. *S.P.D. Eliz., Add. xiii*, 104.
>> Sundry payments for cleaning and repairing armour at the Tower, Hampton Court, and Greenwich at 10d. the day.
>
> 1580. *S.P.D. Eliz., cxli*, 42.
>> A document written on the death of Sir George Howard ordering the cleaning and putting in order of the arms and armour at the Tower.
>
> 1628. *S.P.D. Car. I, xciii*, 61.
>> Capt. John Heydon to Wm. Boswell, Clerk to the Council, for the new russeting of a corslet, 5sh.
>
> 1603. *Inventory of the Armoury at Hengrave.*
>> Item one barrel to make clean the shirt of maile & gorgets.
>
> 1671. *Patent* applied for by Wolfen Miller (John Caspar Wolfen, and John Miller), for twenty-one years, " for a certain oyle to keep armour and armes from rust and kanker " for £10 per annum.
>
> 1647 (*circ.*). *Laws and Ordinances of Warr, Bod. Lib., Goodwin Pamphlets, cxvii*, 14.[3]
>> Of a Souldiers duty touching his Arms.
>> II. Slovenly Armour.—None shall presume to appear with their Armes unfixt or indecently kept upon pain of Arbitrary correction.

With regard to the keeping of armour in store two instances have been mentioned above under the dates 1296 and 1513. In addition to these we find that in 1470 in the *Chronique de Troyes*, the French soldiers were forbidden to carry their arms and armour in " paniers," which, from the statement, was evidently a practice.

---

[1] *Rebellion*, VII, 104.   [2] *Archæologia*, LI.   [3] *Cromwell's Army*, Firth, 413.

In the Wardrobe Account of Edward I, 1281, published by the Society of Antiquaries, we find payments to Robinet, the King's tailor, for coffers, sacks, boxes, and cases to contain the different parts of the armour.

In the Wardrobe Expenses of Bolingbroke, Earl of Derby (Camden Soc.), 1393, are found the following entries :—

fol. 32.   pro j cofre . . . ad imponendum scuta domini.   xvij scot.
fol. 33.   pro j house[1] pro scuto domini   ix scot. xij d.
fol. 40.   pro i breastplate domini purgando ibidem iij li. vij s.

The " buckler of steel painted " mentioned above is scheduled as being in "a case of leather."   In an engraving of Charles I by W. Hole, in the British Museum, a box is shown for holding the breast and back plates.[2]

[1] Cover.   [2] *Arch. Journ.*, LX.

THE USE OF FABRICS AND LINEN

AN important variety of defensive armour, which has not hitherto received the notice which it deserves, is the padded and quilted armour of linen, which was always popular with the foot-soldier on account of its cheapness, and was in the thirteenth century held in high esteem by the wealthier knight. In the case of crushing blows it would of course protect the body from breaking of the skin, but would not be of such use as the more rigid defence of plate. It was, however, very effectual against cutting blows, and had the advantage of being more easily put on and off, and, although hot, was less oppressive than metal in long marches. In miniatures of the fourteenth century we frequently find parts of the armour coloured in such a way as to suggest that it is either not metal or else metal covered with fabric. Where there was no metal and where the wearer depended entirely on the fabric for protection it was heavily quilted and padded, or else several thicknesses of the material were used (Fig. 40). Where metal was used the defence was the ordinary plate armour covered with fabric, or the metal was inserted in small plates as is the case in the brigandine.

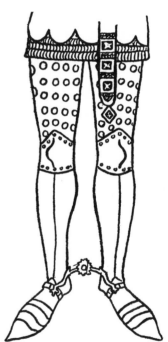

FIG. 40. Pourpointed cuisses from the brass of Sir John de Argentine, Horseheath, Cambs, 1360.

It is not the intention of the present section to deal with the various details of defensive armour except only as far as those details bear directly on the employment of fabrics, therefore the construction of the brigandine, which is well known to all students of the subject of armour and weapons, will be found under the heading of the Craft of the Armourer on page 49. The same may be said of the horn and metal jacks which were a humbler form of the brigandine. The most concise descriptions of such armour will be found in the Catalogue of Helmets and Mail by de Cosson and Burgess (*Arch. Journ.*, XXXVII). Guiart in his Chronicles, written in the early part of the fourteenth century, speaks of "cotes faitices de coton a pointz entailliez." These were probably common doublets, quilted or laced like the jack.

Few of these defences of fabric have survived, owing to the ravages of moth and damp.

In the Pitt-Rivers Museum, Oxford, are a pair of culottes or drawers lined with thin busks of steel, and also two sets of rose-pink silk doublets, breast, back, and fald padded with cotton, both presumably of the late sixteenth century ; they are noticed in *Arms and Armour at Oxford*, by the present writer, but no definite history is known of either of the specimens. Doublets and "coats of fence" of this nature occur frequently in inventories and other documents, but the following extracts give certain definite details which bear directly on the subject.

> 1150–1200 (?). *Speculum Regale, Kongs-Skugg-Sio*, edit. 1768, pp. 405–6 (actual date unknown).
>
> > For the rider the following accoutrements are necessary : coverings for the legs, made of well-blacked soft linen sewed, which should extend to the kneeband of his chaucons or breeches ; over these steel shin-pieces so high as to be fastened with a double band. The horseman to put on linen drawers, such as I have pointed out.
> >
> > (Of the horse) let his head, bridle, and neck, quite to the saddle, be rolled up in linen armour, that no one may fraudulently seize the bridle or the horse.

There is a doubt as to the actual date of this manuscript. In the edition from which the above translation is taken it is described as of Icelandic origin about the year 1150, but it may be possibly as late as the beginning of the thirteenth century. The details of the dress worn under the armour may be compared on the one hand with the leggings shown on the Bayeux tapestry and on the other hand with those mentioned in the Hastings MS. of the fifteenth century (*Archæologia*, LVII), which gives the details of undergarments worn by the armed man at this date (page 107). The horse-armour is the "couverture" or trapper so frequently mentioned in inventories, which was often decorated with fine embroidery. Even altar-hangings were used for this purpose, as was the case in the sack of Rome in 1527. Padded horse-armour was

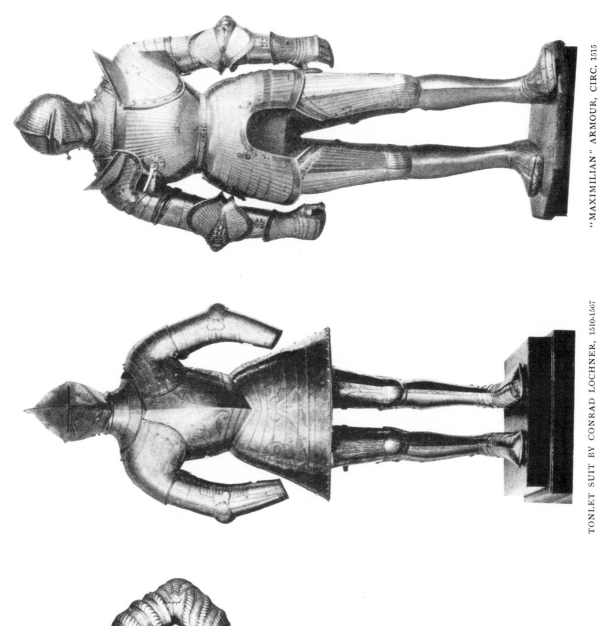

"MAXIMILIAN" ARMOUR, CIRC. 1515

TONLET SUIT BY CONRAD LOCHNER, 1510-1567

HALF ARMOUR, CIRC. 1520

PLATE XXI

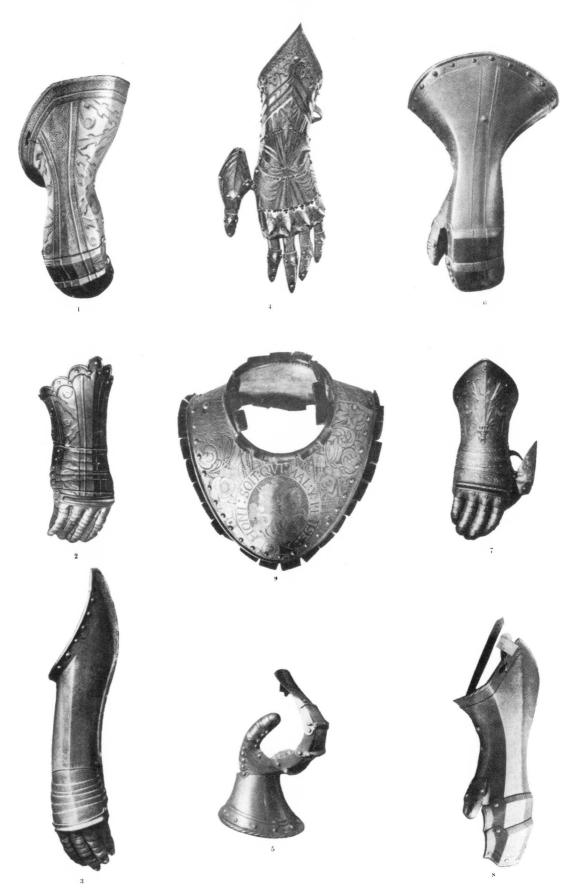

GAUNTLETS AND GORGET

1. BRIDLE GAUNTLET. 2. RIGHT HAND GAUNTLET BY JACOB TOPF, PART OF THE "LEICESTER" SUIT.
3. BRIDLE GAUNTLET OF JAMES I. 4. XV CENT. GAUNTLET WITH "GADLINGS" ON THE KNUCKLES.
5. LOCKING GAUNTLET, XVI CENT. 6. BRIDLE GAUNTLET, XVI CENT.
7. PARADE GAUNTLET BY HEINRICK KNOPF, 1590. 8. GAUNTLET FOR FIGHTING AT BARRIERS, XVI CENT.
9. GORGET BY JACOP JORINGK, 1669

PLATE XXII

used in the fifteenth and early sixteenth centuries for tournaments, minute regulations for which are found in the *Traité d'un Tournoi* by King René of Anjou, which will be referred to farther on in this chapter.

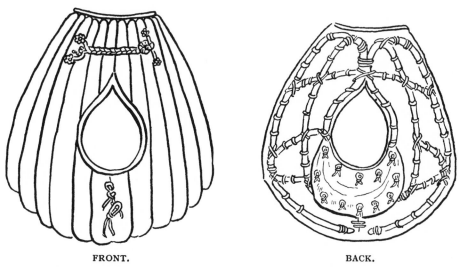

FRONT.   BACK.

FIG. 41.   Padded Horse-armour for the Tourney (from King René's *Traité d'un Tournoi*).

1286. *Comptus Ballivorum Franciæ.*[1]

Expense pro cendatis, bourra ad gambesones, tapetis.

This item is evidently for stuffing gambesons with cendal[2] and tow. Cendal is somewhat of a mystery as to its exact nature. Like all fabrics of past ages, we can but guess at its nature. It has been discussed under its name in Gay's *Glossaire Archæologic.*

1296. *Ordonnances des Métiers de Paris*, p. 371.

Que nus (armuriers) ne puisse fère cote ne gamboison de tèle dont l'envers et l'endroit ne soit de tèle noeve, et dedenz de coton et de plois de toiles, et einsi que est qu'il soient dedenz d'escros.

It. Si l'en fait cote ne gamboison dont l'endroit soit de cendal et l'envers soit de tèle, si veulent il que ele soit noeve et se il i a ploit dedenz de tèle ne de cendal, que le plus cort ploit soit de demie aune et de demi quartier de lonc au meins devant, et autant derrières, et les autres plois lons ensuians. Et si il i a borre de soie qui le lit de la bourre soit de demi aune et demy quartier au meins devant et autant derrières et se il i a coton, que le coton vienge tout contreval jusques au piez.

The first of these regulations concerns the materials used, and is

[1] Meyrick, *Antient Armour*, I, 139.
[2] Cf. jupon of Black Prince at Canterbury, wadded with cotton.

very similar to that of the Armourers' Company of London made in 1322, which is given in full in Appendix A. So much of the work of the padding and lining was hidden from sight that these regulations were most necessary to prevent the use of old rags and bad materials. The second entry seems to refer to the manner in which canvas and cendal were to be used and in what proportions. It should be noticed that at this period the surcoat, in England at any rate, was being gradually shortened. The regulation above quoted, however, suggests in the last sentence that in France it was still worn long.

> 1311. *From the same source as the above.*
>
> > Que nules d'ores en avant ne puisse faire cote gamboisée où il n'ait 3 livres de coton tout neit, se elles ne sont faites en sicines et au dessous soient faites entre mains que il y ait un pli de viel linge emprès l'endroit de demi aune et demi quartier devant et autant derrière.

Here the quantity of cotton is given and it is ordered to be new. It seems to have been allowed to put old linen, but this may possibly only mean seasoned linen, between the folds.

> 1322. *Chamber of Accounts, Paris.*
>
> > Item Adae armentario 40 sol 4 d. pro factoris gambesonorum.

The name "Ada" of the armentarius rather suggests that it might be a female who provided these gambesons.

> 1383. *Chronique de Bertrand du Guesclin (T. II, p. 95, 235.)*
> > Ainsois l'ala d'une lance tranchant
> > L'escu li a rompu et le bon jaserant
> > Mais l'auqueton fu fort qui fu de bougeran
> >
> > .   .   .   .   .
> >
> > Et prendre auquetons de soie ou de bougerans.

From the context of the first extract this haketon of buckram would appear to be a very serviceable defence, for the lance which had penetrated the shield and the jaserant, or coat of plate, had not penetrated the undergarment of buckram. Like all other fabrics mentioned in medieval writings, we cannot definitely say of what material this buckram was composed, but from the second extract it seems to have been used equally with silk for the haketon.

1450. *Ordinance of Louis XI of France, Chambres des Compts, Paris.*[1]

> . . . l'abillement de jacques leur soit bien proufitable et avantageux pour faire la guerre, veu qui sont gens de pié, et que en ayant les brigandines il leur faut porter beaucoup de choses que en homme seul et à pied ne peut faire. Et premièrement leur faut des dits jacques trente toilles, ou de vingt-cinq, à un cuir de cerf a tout le moins : et si sont de trente-un cuirs de cerf ils sont des bons. Les toiles usees et déliées moyennement sont les meilleures ; et doivent estre les jacques a quartre quartiers, et faut que manches soient fortes comme le corps, réservé le cuir. Et doit estre l'assiette pregne pres du collet, non pas sur l'os de l'épaule, qui soit large dessoulz l'assielle et plantureux dessoulz les bras, assez faulce et large sur les costez bas, le collet fort comme le demourant des jacques ; et que le collet ne soit bas trop hault derrière pour l'amour de salade. Il faut que ledit jacque soit lasse devant et qu'il ait dessoulz une porte pièce de la force dudit jacque. Ainsi sera seur ledii jacques et aise moienant qu'il ait un pourpoint sans manches ne collet, de deux toiles seulement, qui naura que quatre doys de large seur lespaulle ; auquel pourpoint il attachera ses chausses. Ainsi flottera dedens son jacques et sera à son aise. Car il ne vit oncques tuer de coups-de-main, ne de flèches dedens lesdits jacques ses hommes.

These very minute regulations show that the "jack" was considered a most serviceable defence in the fifteenth century. At the same time it must have been a hot and uncomfortable garment, for twenty-nine or thirty thicknesses of linen with a deerskin on the top, or worse still thirty-one thicknesses of deerskin, would make a thick, unventilated defence which would be almost as insupportable as plate armour. The last item may be a clerical error, and indeed from the context it would appear to be thirty thicknesses of linen with one of deerskin, for the leather would be far more costly to work up than the linen. The extract has been given in full because it is so rare to come across practical details of construction of this nature.

1470. *Harl. MS. 4780. Inventory of Edward IV.*

> Item a doublet of crimson velvet lined with Hollande cloth and interlined with busk.

This may be only an ordinary doublet, or it may be some kind of "coat of fence" or "privy coat" lined with plates of steel, horn, or whalebone. These "busks" of steel are found as late as the seventeenth century,

---

[1] See also Du Cange, *Glossaire*, under "Jacque."

for Gustavus Adolphus had a coat lined with them (Lifrustkammer, Stockholm) and Bradshaw's hat (Ashmolean Mus., Oxford) is strengthened with steel strips.   (Fig. 50.)

1450 (*circ.*). *Traité d'un Tournoi*, King René.

> . . . que ledit harnoys soit si large et si ample que on puisse vestir et mettre dessoulz ung porpoint ou courset ; et fault que le porpoint soit faultre de trys dois d'espez sur les espaules, et au long des bras jusques au col.

> .   .   .   .   .   .

> En Brabant, Flandre et Haynault et en ce pays-la vers les Almaignes, ont acoustome d'eulx armer de la personne autrement au tournoy : car ils prennent ung demy porpoint de deux toilles . . . de quatre dois d'espez et remplis de couton.

It would seem from the above that in France the garment worn under the tourney-armour was folded till it was three fingers thick on the shoulders.   In the Low Countries, however, the pourpoint was of a different fashion, for there they made the garment of two thicknesses and stuffed this with cotton-waste to the thickness of four fingers.   The difference of thickness can be accounted for by the fact that folded linen would not compress so much as cotton-waste.   It should be noted in the extract from the Ordinances of Louis XI that old material is advised as being more pliable and softer.   At the same time we may be sure that it was carefully chosen.   It is interesting to note that in 1322 the material is ordered to be new, but in 1450 old linen is recommended.

Besides the making of undergarments or complete defences of linen overgarments, pourpoints, the Linen Armourers, as we find them called in the City of London Records, made linings for helmets.   This was a most important detail in the equipment of a man, for the helm or helmet was worse than useless if it did not fit securely and if the head was not adequately padded to take off the shock of the blow.   In the Sloane MS. 6400, we find among the retinue of Henry V at Agincourt, "Nicholas Brampton, a stuffer of bacynets," and in the Oxford City Records under the date 1369 are the entries "Bacynet 1 3/4, stuffing for ditto 3/4." In the Hastings MS. (*Archæologia*, LVII), among the items given as the "Abilment for the Justus of the Pees," the first on the list is "a helme well stuffyd."   This stuffing consisted of a thickly padded cap or lining tied to the head-piece with strings, which are clearly shown in the well-known engraving of Albert Dürer, of a man and a woman supporting a shield on which is a skull (Fig. 42, 2). There are some of these caps in the Waffensammlung, Vienna, which have been noticed in Vol. II of the *Zeitschrift fur Historische Waffenkunde*.

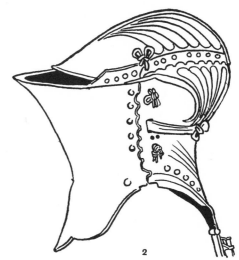

FIG. 42.
1. Padded " harnisch-kappe," Vienna.
2. Helm showing attachment of cap and lining (after Dürer).

The original lining of Sir Henry Lee's helmet (Plate XIII) is still *in situ*; this, however, is riveted to the helmet and follows the shape of the head. In this respect it is different from the helmet-cap, which was

FIG. 43. Sallad-cap (from a picture by Paolo Morando, 1486 – 1522, No. 571, Uffizi, Florence).

FIG. 44. Helmet-cap (from a sixteenth-century engraving of Iacob Fugger).

padded. A padded cap was worn independently of the lining of the helmet. These are shown on Figs. 43, 44. Similar caps are shown on the following works of Dürer: S. George on foot, S. George (Stephan Baumgartner) and Felix Hungersbourg.

1586. *Chronicles*, Raphael Holinshed (edit. 1807, II, xvi, 333).

> Our armour differeth not from that of other nations, and therefore consisteth of corselets, almaine riuets, shirts of maile, iackes quilted and couered ouer with leather, fustian, or canuas, ouer thicke plates of iron that are sowed in the same, & of which there is no towne or village that hath not hir conuenient furniture.

These defences are of the same nature as the jack shown on Figs. 24, 25. The brigandine was more elaborate and costly, for it was composed of small plates riveted to the foundation and covering of fabric and was therefore the work of a skilled artificer. The jack, on the other hand, was more easily put together and could be done by the wearer himself or by his wife. An interesting example of one of these village armouries mentioned above is to be found at Mendlesham Church, Suffolk, in the strong-room of which are portions of suits and half-suits dating from the late fifteenth to the middle of the seventeenth century. The church also preserves the records of the upkeep of the equipment, one of the last entries being in 1613, a payment of 1s. 4d. to an armourer for " varnishinge the town head-piece and the corslitt and for setting on leathers and rivettes."

1591-5. *Instructions, Observations and Orders Militarie*, p. 185, Sir John Smith.

> Archers should weare either Ilet holed doublets that will resist the thrust of a sword or a dagger and covered with some trim and gallant kinde of coloured cloth to the liking of the Captain. . . . or else Iackes of maile quilted upon fustian.

From the nature of their composition these " eyelet doublets " are rarely to be met with. They were made of twine or thread knitted all over in eyelets or button-holes. The appearance is much the same as modern "tatting" and macramé work. The best-known examples are in the Musée Porte de Hal, Brussels (II, 81), in the Cluny Museum, and in the Musée d'Artillerie, G, 210 (Fig. 45).

1662. *Decades of Epistles of War*, Gervase Markham.

> The shot should have on his head a good and sufficient Spanish morian well lined in the head with a quilted cap of strong linen and bound with lined ear plates.

1643. *Souldier's Accidence*, Gervase Markham.

> . . . the shot should have good comb caps well lined with quilted caps.

It will be obvious that the maker of linings and undergarments for the soldier had to be in constant touch with the armourer, for he had to make allowances for the style and cut of the armour.

In the Wardrobe Accounts of Edward I quoted on page 79 there are entries of payments to Robinet, the King's tailor, for armour, banners,

FIG. 45. Details of Eyelet Coats.
1. Musée d'Artillerie, Paris, G, 210.   2. Musée de Cluny, Paris.

crests, helmets, and robes for the King, his son, and John of Lancaster. At the end of this chapter we shall notice this combining of the crafts of the armourer and tailor when dealing with the linen armourers.

It was obviously important that the tailor should be in touch with the armourer and suit his material and cut to the equipment worn over them.

1591-5. *Instructions and Orders Militarie, p.* 185, Sir John Smith.[1]

> No armed man should weare any cut doublets, as well in respect that the wearing of armour doth quicklie fret them out and also by reason that the corners and edges of the lames and jointes of the armours doo take such holde upon such cuttes as they do hinder the quicke and sudden arming of men.

All parts of the suit were lined, for in spite of the padded undergarment there was bound to be a certain amount of chafing which, if the armour was unlined, would in time rub through the undergarment. In many portraits, especially those of the late sixteenth century, the linings are shown projecting below the edges of the various pieces of the suit. The edges of these linings are generally scalloped.

---

[1] Cousin of Edward VI, and knighted by Elizabeth in 1576. His free criticism on military matters led to the suppression of his " Discourses on the form and effects of divers sorts of weapons," and he was committed to the Tower.

In the picture by Breughel on the frontispiece a cuisse is shown, immediately beneath the basket of glass bottles in the centre of the picture, which clearly has a padded lining. In a list of payments for work done to Henry VIII's armour we find " 9 yards of Cheshire cotton at 7d. for lining the king's pasguard grandguard great mayn de fer." A similar charge is made in 1521 for two yards of yellow satin at 7/4 for lining two head-pieces, two pair of tasses, a pasguard, and two maynd fers. In 1510 we find an entry of payment of 25 fl. 29 kr. to Walter Zeller of Innsbruck for lining armour with black velvet and silk.[1] Frequently the padding is shown in miniatures, especially on the inside of shields and bucklers. The Highland targes are generally padded on the inside with straw to take some of the shock of a blow from the arm. The lining of such pieces as the taces and pauldrons was added to prevent the metal over which they worked from being scratched, and also to lessen the metallic noise, which would be a serious factor in night attacks. Horse-armour, of course, needed heavy lining, but little of this remains. An excellent reconstruction of lined horse-armour is to be found on No. 620, Wallace Collection.

The stuffing of these padded garments was not always of cotton. In the inventory of the goods of Sir John Falstoffe, 1459 (*Archæologia*, XXI), we find " i. jack of black linen stuffed with mail and vi. jacks stuffed with horne, xxiiij. cappes stuffed with horne and mayle, vj. payre of glovys of mayle of shepys skynne." Under the heading " Gambeson," Du Cange[2] states that the gambeson was stuffed with wool soaked with vinegar, to resist iron, and he gives a reference to Pliny, Bk. VIII, c. 48, as bearing on this statement. This was probably done to keep out vermin, a serious factor when long marches with bad camping arrangements were undertaken.

In all the defences which were mainly composed of fabrics, the object seems to have been to provide a substance which would resist cut or thrust and at the same time would offer a certain resiliency to the blow. A practical experiment upon thick leather and upon folded or padded cloth will prove this. Till recent years the Japanese made much of their armour of quilted fabrics, the chief drawback to which was its heat and want of ventilation.

[1] *Jahrbuch des Kunsthist. Sammlungen*, II, 995.   [2] Johnes' edit., I, 131.

MAN AT ARMS. MIDDLE OF XV CENT.

PLATE XXIII

*

PARADE SHIELD BY DESIDERIUS COLMAN, 1554

* THE DETAIL IS GIVEN ON PAGE 135

PLATE XXIV

This linen armour or linen and fabric covering for armour was a distinct craft in itself, and was practised by the linen armourers, who had the sole right to cover armour or to make such defences as have been enumerated above.   That they were also tailors we know from their subsequent incorporation with the Merchant Tailors and also from the Wardrobe Accounts[1] of Edward I, in which Robinet, the King's tailor, is mentioned as making robes and armours and banners.

Besides the lining of armour and the provision of padded defences of fabric, there was a large field of employment in the covering of armour.   As may be noticed in Appendix A, this covering of helmets seems to have been common in the first years of the fourteenth century. There were three reasons for covering the steel head-piece with fabric. Firstly, as Chaucer writes with regard to the mail hauberk (page 78), to keep it from wet, the enemy of all iron and steel work ; secondly, as Roger Ascham writes of the peacock-wing for arrows, "for gayness"; and thirdly, to prevent the glitter of metal attracting attention.[2]   In the *Treatise* of Johan Hill, written in 1434 (Appendix C, page 173), the covering of the armour, especially for the legs, is ordered to be of scarlet "because his adversarie shall not lightly espye his blode."   Helmet-bags are mentioned in inventories, etc.

In 1578 we find "steel caps with covers" noticed in more than one will,[3] and in the Lieutenancy Accounts for Lancashire, *temp.* Elizabeth, the archer's dress includes a "scull and Scottish cap to cover the same" (Fig. 46).   Several helmets in the Waffensammlungen at Vienna still show the silk and satin coverings, and in Munich a triple-crowned burgonet has a black velvet cover.   The highly ornate Venetian

FIG. 46. Sallad with cover, from a sixteenth-century engraving.

sallads, covered with crimson velvet, over which is set a gilt open-work decoration of metal, are fairly common in collections (Plate XVI).

---

[1] *Lib. Gardrobæ,* 28 Ed. I, 1300. Soc. of Antiq.
[2] *Vide* modern War Office regulations of the present day as to scabbards of swords, Highland kilts, etc.
[3] *Arch. Journ.,* LX, "Armour Notes."

The surcoat and tabard hardly come within the province of the armourer, for they were quite distinct from the armour. They were, however, in fashion in various forms till the middle of the reign of Henry VIII, who landed in France, according to Hall, in 1514 with a garment of " white cloth of gold bearing a red cross." Padded and quilted defences appear to have been worn in the early seventeenth century, for the Hon. Roger North in his *Examen* writes that " there was great abundance of silk armour," which in many cases was said to be of pistol proof. Some of these backs, breasts, and taces, wadded with cotton and covered with salmon-coloured silk, are preserved in the Pitt-Rivers Museum, Oxford.

THE LINEN ARMOURERS

As we have seen on page 91, in the thirteenth and fourteenth centuries the tailor was often also a purveyor of armour. M. Buttin[1] quotes several extracts from documents of the fourteenth century in which different names of craftsmen appear classed as " Brodeurs et Armuriers." It may not be out of place to notice here that the " milliner " of the present day was originally the Milaner or Milanese pedlar, who purveyed armour, weapons, and clothing of all sorts.

The Linen Armourers, as they were called, were a gild distinct from the Armourers, for in 1272 they were instituted as " The Fraternity of Tailors and Linen Armourers of Linen Armour of S. John the Baptist in the City of London." Edward III was an honorary member of the gild, and Richard II also became a member when he confirmed their charter. Their first patent of arms was granted by Edward IV in the year 1466, and in this document the society is called " Gilda Armorarii."[2] This naturally causes some confusion with the Armourers' Company, and in many documents it is uncertain which gild is referred to. The first master was Henry de Ryall, who was called the Pilgrim or Traveller. As has been stated above, their first charter was from Edward III. Richard II confirmed by " inspeximus " this charter. Henry IV also confirmed the charter, and Henry VI granted right of search, which allowed the gild to inspect shops and workshops and

---

[1] *Le Guet de Genève*, Geneva, 1910.
[2] *Hist of 12 Livery Co.'s of London*, Herbert, 1836.

confiscate any work which did not come up to their standard. It is doubtful whether the document given in Appendix A refers to this gild or to that of the Armourers, for it contains regulations which would affect both gilds. It gives details as to that " right of search " which was an important part of the duties of the gilds.

In the reign of Edward IV the gild was incorporated, and under Henry VII it became the Merchant Tailors' Company, with the charter which is held by that company at the present day. This charter was confirmed by Henry VIII, Edward VI, Philip and Mary, Elizabeth, and James I.

THE USE OF LEATHER

FROM the earliest times leather has been a favourite material for defensive armour. The shield of Ajax was fashioned of seven bulls' hides, and the soldiers of the King and of the Parliament in the Civil War favoured the buff coat. Between these periods leather was utilized in many ways, and when specially treated was a most serviceable protection which had the merit of being lighter and less costly than metal. The word "cuirass" itself is derived from the body-defence of leather (cuir).

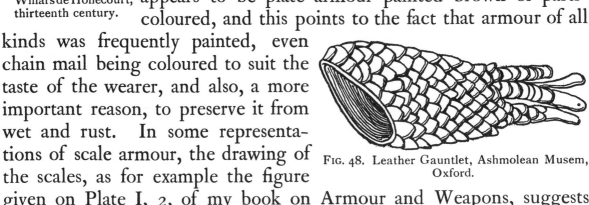

FIG. 47. Cuirass from the sketch-book of Willars de Honecourt, thirteenth century.

The Hon. Robert Curzon, writing in 1869, mentions a cuirass of three thicknesses of leather found in a stone coffin of the thirteenth century (*Arch. Journ.*, XXII, p. 6).

At a time when the weaving of fabrics was in a more or less primitive state, the skins of beasts were used either as the sole defence of the warrior or were reinforced with plates of metal applied over the most vital parts of the body (Figs. 47, 48).

It is always a matter of some difficulty, especially in the earlier examples, to tell what materials are intended in illuminated miniatures, for we find what appears to be plate armour painted brown or particoloured, and this points to the fact that armour of all kinds was frequently painted, even chain mail being coloured to suit the taste of the wearer, and also, a more important reason, to preserve it from wet and rust. In some representations of scale armour, the drawing of the scales, as for example the figure given on Plate I, 2, of my book on Armour and Weapons, suggests

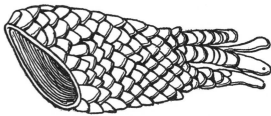

FIG. 48. Leather Gauntlet, Ashmolean Musem, Oxford.

leather rather than metal, and certainly the much-debated-upon "banded mail" must have been a mixture of leather and metal.

Towards the end of the twelfth century we find the material known as "cuir-bouilli" or "cuerbully" mentioned as being used for the armour of man and horse. The hide of the animal was cut thick, boiled in oil or in water, and, when soft, moulded to the required shape. When cold it became exceedingly hard and would withstand nearly as much battle-wear as metal.

It had the advantage of being easily procured, easily worked, and also of being much lighter than the metal. For this reason it was used largely for jousts and tourneys, which up to the fifteenth century were more of the nature of mimic fights than was the case at a later date, when the onset was more earnest and the armour was made correspondingly heavy to withstand it.

The best leather seems to have come from Spain and especially from Cordova. Among the *Ordonnances des rois* in the Bib. Nat. Français (T. II, 357) we find it distinctly stated that Cordova leather was far better than that of France or Flanders. This may have been due to the breed of horses or cattle found there, but it is more likely that the tanners of that town had made a speciality of treating the hides.

On the sculptured effigies and monumental brasses of the fourteenth century we find the jambs and poleynes often richly decorated and moulded with more skill than the other parts of the armour,[1] and these were probably of cuir-bouilli.

The d'Aubernon, Setvans, and Gorleston brasses are good examples of this. Chaucer in his *Rime of Sir Thopas* mentions jambs of cuir-bouilli as being part of the ordinary equipment of the knight (see page 100).

Both King Rene and Antoine de la Salle prescribe cuir-bouilli as the material for the brassards used in the tourney (Fig. 49), and this fashion seems to have lasted

FIG. 49. Brassard of leather and cord for the tourney (from René's *Traité d'un Tournoi*).

from the last quarter of the thirteenth century, at which date we have cuir-bouilli armour mentioned in the roll of purchases for the tournament

---

[1] The Pembridge effigy in Hereford Cathedral has thigh-pieces which apparently represent leather laced on the inside.

at Windsor Park, held by Edward I, down to the last quarter of the fifteenth century. Oliver de la Marche, writing at the end of the same century, describes the armour of Mahiot and Jacotin Plouvier fighting in a duel as being of cuir-bouilli sewn on the body, legs, and arms.[1] In his *Advis de gaige de battaile* the same author mentions leather armour as being only fit for the man who is " point gentilhomme."

As late as the year 1500 cuir-bouilli was much used for horse-armour on account of its lightness. Of this we have two specimens remaining to us in the full suit at Turin (G, 2) and the crupper at the Tower (VI, 89). The horse on Plate XVII is apparently armed with mail which is covered with trappers of leather. The original, which was an ivory chessman in the possession of Rev. Eagles, has disappeared. It was figured by Hewitt in *Ancient Armour*, Vol. I, and was cast. The photograph given here is from the cast. Among the few specimens of leather armour for the man may be noted a morion in the Zeughaus, Berlin (60*b*), and a pair of seventeenth-century leather "lobster-tail" cuisses at Goodrich Court, Herefordshire.

The reason for this dearth of examples of leather armour in collections at the present day is twofold. Much of the discarded armour of this nature would be used for various domestic purposes, such as jugs, horse-furniture, and such-like uses, and also much would be thrown away as useless, for leather unless carefully kept and oiled tends to crack and warp out of shape.

The above-mentioned bards for horses appear frequently in paintings of the early sixteenth century. The picture of the battle of Pavia in the Ashmolean Museum, Oxford,[2] shows many of these brilliantly painted with armorial and fancy designs, and the absence of rivet-heads points to the fact that they are not of metal.

The painting of bards seems to have been a distinct trade, for we find in the Statuto de' pittori Fiorentini rubr. 79 (*Carteggio ined. d'artisti*, T. II, p. 40) regulations forbidding any but the registered bard-painters to undertake such work.

That cuir-bouilli was not proof against firearms we learn from Jean de Troyes (page 260), who writes: "Si y eut un cheval tout barde de cuir bouilli qui fut tue d'un coup de coulverine." This refers to

---

[1] *Memoirs*, Vol. I, ch. 33.   [2] *Arms and Armour at Oxford*, C. ffoulkes.

the date 1465, when firearms were but primitive weapons. Dressed leather, however, in the form of the buff coat was used up to the middle of the seventeenth century, when the penetrating power of the bullet was greater. At the same time we should remember, as Marshal Saxe very truly points out in his advocacy of plate armour (*Rêveries*, p. 58), that many wounds at this time were caused by sword, lance, and spent bullet, all of which might have been avoided by the use of some thick material. The Marshal suggests sheet-iron sewn upon a buff coat, but the buff coat itself, $\frac{3}{8}$ in. thick, would be a very adequate, though hot and heavy, protection without the addition of metal.

The leather guns of Gustavus Adolphus will be found mentioned in the following pages, but these were only covered with leather, presumably to protect them from wet, and were not made entirely of this material. We have no record of cuir-bouilli being employed to make artillery, and of course the chief reason against its use would be the weakness of the seam or join.

The only use of leather or cuir-bouilli for defensive armour found at the present day is found in the small bucklers of the hill tribes of India. These are often so skilfully treated that the leather is transparent and is almost impervious to a sword-cut, forming a very fair defence against the bullet from the primitive flintlocks in use among those tribes.

FIG. 50. Hat of Bradshaw the regicide, of leather and steel. Ashmolean Mus., Oxford.

The leather hat reinforced with steel plates given at Fig. 50 was worn by the regicide Bradshaw at the trial of Charles I.[1]

[1] *Arms and Armour at Oxford*, C. ffoulkes.

REFERENCES TO LEATHER AND CUIR-BOUILLI FROM CONTEMPORARY DOCUMENTS

1185. *Chanson d'Antioche.*

> Moult fu riches qu'il li a chief mi
> Son poitrail lui laca qui fu de cuir bolis.

The " poitrail " in this extract is the breastplate of the knight and not of the horse.

1278. *Roll of Purchases for the Tournament at Windsor Park.*

> De Milon le Cuireur xxxviij quiret : p'c pec iij s.
> Itm. ij Crest & j Blazon & una galea cor & j ensis de Balon
> de Rob'o Brunnler xxxviij galee de cor p'c galee xiv.

This tournament seems to have been more of a pageant than a serious contest like those of the fifteenth century. No armour of metal is mentioned among the purchases and the weapons are of whalebone, a material which was used also for gauntlets, as we know from Froissart's[1] description of the equipment of the troops of Philip von Artevelde at the battle of Rosebecque in 1382. Whalebone was also employed for " privy coats " or brigandines, in which it was inserted between the lining and the cover. Buckram is also mentioned as being used for body-armour, which material will be found alluded to in the section devoted to the Linen Armourers.

1345. *Les Livres de Comptes des Freres Bonis, I.* 174, Forestie.

> Item deu per un brasalot. . . de cuer negre.

1351. *Ordonnances du roi Jean IV,* 69.

> Ordenons que l'arbalestrier . . . sera arme de plates . . . et de
> harnois de bras de fer et de cuir.

These brassards of cuir-bouilli seem to have been common in the fourteenth century ; their popularity being doubtless due to their lightness and cheapness as compared with metal. M. Buttin in his interesting pamphlet *Le Guet de Genève*[2] gives several extracts from inventories and other documents which bear out this statement.

1350. *Rime of Sir Thopas,* Chaucer.

> His jambeux were of curebully.

---

[1] Johnes' trans., I, 739.   [2] Kündig, Geneva, 1910.

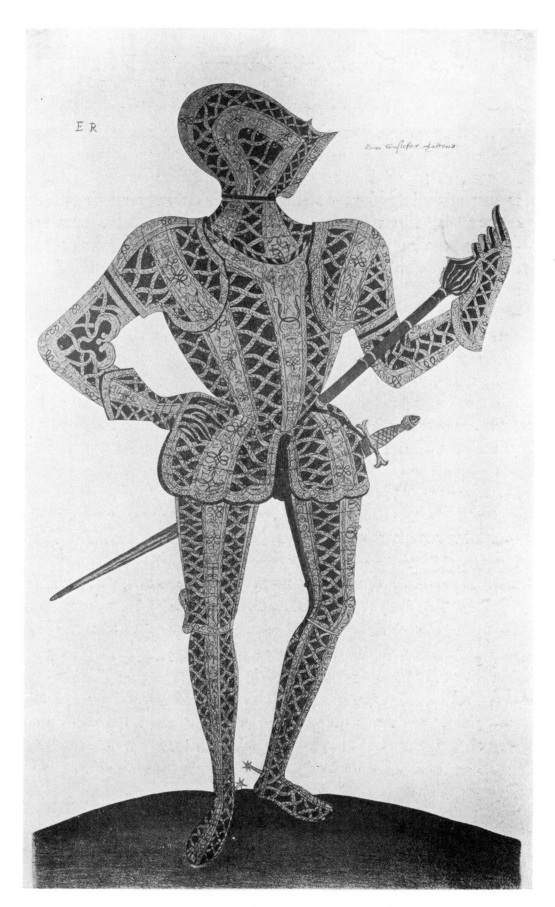

ER

DRAWING BY JACOB TOPF, 1530-1597
FROM THE "ARMOURER'S ALBUM," VICTORIA AND ALBERT MUSEUM

PLATE XXV

ARMOUR OF SIR CHRISTOPHER HATTON, BY JACOB TOPF

PLATE XXVI

The skilfully modelled jambs and poleynes which appear on many brasses and effigies of the fourteenth century rather suggest that leather was used and not metal, as the rest of the armour does not show such skill of forging. These leg-pieces are nearly always shown as richly engraved, which also points to the suggestion that they were of cuir-bouilli, which would be an easier material to decorate with painting or modelling than metal.

> 1411. *Inventorie de l'ecurie du roi, f.* 108 *vo.*
>
> Une armure de cuir de Surie pour armer l'homme et le cheval.

> 1450. *Traité d'un Tournoi*, Roi René.
>
> En Brebant, Flandres et Haynault at en ces pays la vers Almaignes . . . mettant unes bracieres grosses de 4 dois d'espez et remplies de cotton sur quoys ils arment les avant bras et les garde-bras de cuir bouilly.

This entry may be compared with that of the Windsor Park Tournament quoted above. King René's book has the advantage of being illustrated with drawings of these and all the other details mentioned in his regulations for a tourney. The brassards shown in the drawing have cords fixed lengthways so as to provide an extra protection against the blow of the mace or wooden sword which René describes as the weapons to be used. Brassards of a similar kind are mentioned in Antoine de la Salle's *Des anciens tournois et Faictz d'Armes* (edit. B. Prost., p. 120).

> 1471. *Inv. du Roi Rene à Angers, fo.* 3 *vo.*
>
> Quatre targetes de cuir bouilly a la facon de Tunes.

These targets, made after an Oriental model, would probably resemble those which are frequently seen in India and Persia at the present day, in which the leather is hard and often highly polished and decorated with painting and gilding. The Highland targe is fashioned differently, for the foundation is of wood and the skin or hide stretched over it.

> 1480. *L'Artillerie des Ducs de Bourogne, Garnier, appendix, p.* 230.
>
> Onze gands et huit brasselets de cuir pour archiers.

Here the " brasselets " are not arm-defences, but are simply the "bracer" or arm-guard which protected the wrist of the archer from the string of his own bow when released.

1493. *L'advis de gaige de battaille*, O. de la Marche.

> S'il n'est point gentilhomme il peut combattre selon l'ancienne coustume armé de cuir bouilly.

This evidently refers to the regulations laid down by King René in 1450, and suggests that by the end of the fifteenth century they had become obsolete and that full plate armour was the only equipment for the joust or tourney.

1500. *Inv. de Francois Ier. de Luxembourg, p. 6.*

> Plusiers bardes de chevaux de cuyr de cartes ou cartons.

The last-named materials were obviously only employed for parade or masque. They would be early forms of papier-maché, but were probably more like the modern cardboard than the hard papier-maché now in use.

1559. *Notes sur Dioscoride, II, chap.* 21, Matthée.

> Le cheval marin une beste du Nil [the hippopotamus] de la peau l'on en fait des écus, animes et rondelles ; aussi n'y ha il armes ny poinctures quelles qu'elles soyent qui la puissent transpercer, si premièrement elle n'est baignée.

This entry shows clearly that even the hide of the hippopotamus was not held to be weapon-proof till it had been soaked (in water or oil). One of these leather bards exists in the Armeria Reale, Turin, B, 2. It is catalogued as being of hippopotamus hide. A crupper of cuir-bouilli (VI, 89) is the only specimen of leather armour in the Tower.

1630 (*circ.*). *Hist. of London, p.* 26, Pennant (1790).

> Robert Scot . . . was the inventor of leather artillery which he introduced into the army of Gustvus Adolphus.

1644. *Military Memoirs of the Great Civil War, p.* 42, Gwynne.

> At Crobredery Bridge (Cropredy) we overtook Waller's army which we engaged and beat, took Wemes General of their army prisoner and withal took his leather guns which proved serviceable to the King.

These leather guns were formed of a cylinder of copper round which was twisted thick hempen cord and the whole enveloped in a leather jacket. An example which is traditionally stated to be one of Scot's guns used by Gustavus Adolphus, is exhibited in the Rotunda Museum, Woolwich (II, 173). The dolphins on this specimen are fashioned to the letter "G" placed horizontally. There are two similar guns in the Musée d'Artillerie.

THE USE OF LEATHER

1678. *Traité des Armes, p. 55*, Gaya.

> Quoy que les Bufles ne soient proprement que les habillemens de Cavaliers, nous pouvons neanmoins les mettre au nombre de leurs armes deffensives, plus qu'ils peuvent aisement resister à l'Epée lors qu'ils sont d'une peau bien choissie.
>
> Les Bufles . . . sont faits en forme de Juste-au-corps à quatre basques qui descend jusqu'aux genoux.
>
> Il n'y a pas un Cavalier dans les trouppes de France qui n'ait un habillement de Bufle.

The buff coat of leather or "cuir de bœuf" was a part of the military equipment as early as 1585 and was in common use during the Civil War. It was worn by the Life Guards at the Coronation of James II in 1685 and by a detachment of the Artillery Company at the entry of George I in 1714. It ceased to be worn as part of the uniform in the following reign.[1]

1591-5. *Instructions, Observations and Orders Militarie, p.* 185, Sir John Smith.

> . . . halbadiers . . . armed with burganets and with short skirted Ierkins of buffe with a double buffe on their breasts and the sleeves of their doublets with stripes of maile or serecloth aforesaide.

Here we find a return to the primitive defence of the eleventh century, due to the increased weight of armour which was necessary against the improved firearms which were by this time a serious factor in war. The serecloth recommended was probably a stout waxed or oiled canvas. In recommending sleeves of mail, which are shown on Plate XVIII, Sir John Smith considers that they are more convenient for the handling of the halberdier's weapon than the more rigid brassards worn by the cavalry. These strips of chain are shown on one of the figures painted by Memling for the "Chasse of S. Ursula" at Bruges, 1486, which is given on Fig. 24 of this work. They have been re-introduced as shoulder-straps for heavy cavalry at the present day.

[1] Cannon, *Historical Records of the Life Guards*, p. 74.

THE WEARING OF ARMOUR

THOUGH perhaps the wearing and putting on of armour was not directly part of the craft of the armourer, it was certainly a part of his duties to be present during the process and be ready to carry out any small alterations which might be needed on the spot.

As has been noticed in a preceding chapter, as late as 1625 we find this insisted upon by de Pluvinel (see page 115). Shakespeare describes the armourers as busy "accomplishing the knights" before Agincourt (page 33), and the fact that the travelling knight took his armourer with him shows that he was indispensable during the operation of dressing for war or joust.

Armour of the best kind was made to measure, and for ordinary purposes a mould or "dobble" was kept on which to make the ordinary harness for the man-at-arms (page 28). The following extracts show the methods employed for sending measurements, which were often obtained by submitting the clothes of the patron to the armourer :—

1406. In the will of Sir Ralph Bulmer, "armatura mea corpori talliata."[1]

1470. *Archives de Bruxelles.*[2]

Baltazar du Cornet, armourer at Bruges, delivers for the Duke of Burgundy "2 cuiraches complettes faites a la mesure de Monseigneur."
Lazarus de St. Augustin delivers "un harnais complet fait naguere a la mesure de Monseigneur et pour son corps."

1512. A jacket and hose of Prince Charles (afterwards Charles V) are sent to Conrad Seusenhofer.[3]

1520. *Brit. Mus., Calig. D, VIII*, 181.

16 March. Francis I asks for an "arming doublet" of Henry VIII that he may have made a new kind of cuirass which he will send him as a present.

---

[1] *Arch. Journ.*, LX.   [2] *Archives de Bruxelles*, Cat. Mus. Porte de Hal, 1885.
[3] *Jahrbuch des Kunsthist. Sammlungen*, II, 1032.

DRAWING BY JACOB TOPF, 1530-1597

FROM THE "ARMOURER'S ALBUM," VICTORIA AND ALBERT MUSEUM

PLATE XXVII

ARMOUR OF SIR JOHN SMITH, BY JACOB TOPF

PLATE XXVIII

1564. *S.P.D. Elizabeth, Jan.* 30.

> Warrant to the Master of the Armoury. To cause to be made one armour complete fit for the body of our well beloved servant Christopher Hatton, one of our Gentlemen Pensioners, he paying according to the just value thereof.

1667. *Verney Memoirs, IV,* 301. Rich. Hals to Edmond Verney.

> The armour fits well enough only the man did cut away to much just under the arme pit both of back and breast, but for the head piece it is something heavy, yet I think it well enough if it did not come downe so low upon my forhead as to cover all my eyes and offend my nose when I put my head backwards to look upwards.

In the preceding chapter some notice was taken of the part which the linen armourer played in the equipment of the armed man, and it was to him that the clothing which was worn under the armour was entrusted. Under the heading of the "Cleaning of Armour" mention has been made of Chaucer's knight whose "gipoun" was "besmoturyd with his haubergeon," but this garment was an outer garment or surcoat. In the age of plate armour a complete dress was worn for legs, arms, body,

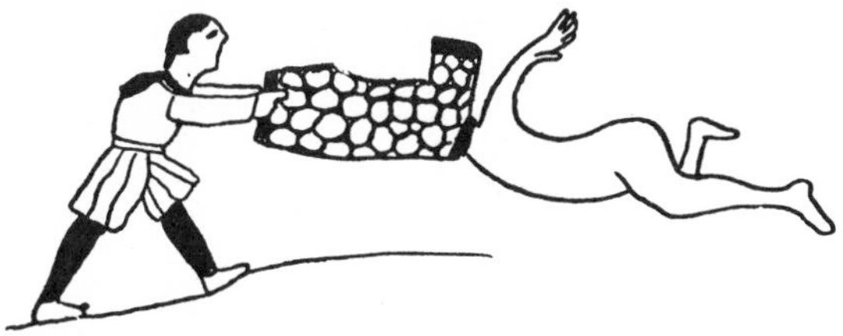

FIG. 51. Stripping the dead (Bayeux Tapestry).

and head to prevent the chafing of the armour, which in spite of its own lining of silk, velvet, cloth, leather, or other fabric would cause grave inconvenience, if not danger to the wearer. Besides this reason there was also a question of warmth, which was of importance, for in long marches and expeditions there was no warmth in a suit of plate, in fact there was an added cold which had to be counteracted by warm garments worn underneath.

FIG. 52. Knight arming (from *Livre des Nobles Femmes*, Bib. Nat., Paris, fourteenth century).

In the eleventh and twelfth centuries we have not much in the way of documentary evidence which will help us as to the clothes worn under the armour. The Bayeux Tapestry shows us the wounded and dead being stripped of their hauberks, under which nothing was apparently worn (Fig. 51). It should be remembered, however, that these hauberks were probably of quilted fabric, which therefore did not gall the body of the wearer. The drawing from a fourteenth-century manuscript on Fig. 52 gives some hint at the arming-doublet, which will be noted farther on in this chapter, and shows also the laces or points that held up the hose. Towards the end of the fourteenth century, however, we find on the incised brasses, which are such valuable records of the military equipment of the period, very distinct garments represented. On the brass to Sir John de Creke at Westley Waterless, Cambs, 1325, we see the "cyclas" or outer surcoat, the "upper pour-point," of fabric, studded with metal, "the hauberk," and under all the "haketon" or "gambeson" (Fig. 53). According to William de Guilleville, in the *Pelerinage de l'Ame*, written in the fourteenth century, the "pour-point" was so called because of its quiltings :—

FIG. 53. Brass of Sir John de Creke, Westley Waterless, Cambs, 1325.
1. Bascinet.
2. Vervelles and camail.
3. Cyclas or surcoat.
4. Upper pourpoint.
5. Hauberk.
6. Gambeson or haketon.
7. Poleynes.
8. Beinbergs or jambs.

De pontures de gambison
Pourquoi pourpoint l'appelle-t-on.

The gambeson continued in use up to the seventeenth century under the name of "arming-doublet," with but little change except in shape and form, as the style of armour required. Of the undergarments of the early fifteenth century we have little or nothing to guide us, and we are often at a loss to know even what armour was worn under the tight-fitting, small-waisted jupon or surcoat which distinguishes the end of the fourteenth and the beginning of the fifteenth century. We have, however, a valuable record under this head in the monument at Ash, which shows "splinted armour" of lames worn instead of a cuirass.

The illustration on Plate IV is from a wood-carving in the church of S. William, Strasburg. It represents the travelling armourer riveting what appear to be bands of iron on arms and legs. Whether these are some contrivance used in arming in the fifteenth century, or whether they are some instrument of torture used upon the saint, Duke William of Acquitaine, it is impossible to discover, as no other instances of the kind can be found.

For full details of the equipment of the latter half of the fifteenth century we cannot do better than refer to the Hastings MS. of the fifteenth century, which has been discussed by the late Albert Way,[1] and more fully by Viscount Dillon.[2] Under the heading of "The Abilment for the Justes of Pees" we find much that is of value in this respect. On page 122*b* of the manuscript we find the following minute directions for dressing a man for the joust, which should be compared with those given in Appendix C, page 173.

How a man schall be armyd at his ese when he schal fighte on foote :

He schal have noo schirte up on him but a dowbelet of ffustean lyned with satene cutte full of hoolis. the dowbelet must be strongeli boude there the pointis muste be sette aboute the greet [bend] of the arm. and the b ste [*sic*] before and behynde and the gussetis of mayle muste be sowid un to the dowbelet in the bought of the arme. and undir the arme the armynge poyntis muste ba made of fyne twyne suche as men make stryngys for crossebowes and they muste be trussid small and poyntid as poyntis. Also they muste be wexid with cordeweneris coode. and than they will neyther recche nor breke Also a payr hosyn of stamyn sengill and a payre of shorte bulwerkis of thynne blanket to put aboute his kneys for chawfynge of his lighernes Also a payre of shone of thikke Cordwene and they muste be frette with smal whipcorde thre knottis up on a corde and thre cordis muste be faste swoid on to the hele of the shoo and fyne cordis in the mydill of the soole of the same shoo and that ther be betwene the frettis of the hele and the frettis of the mydill of the shoo the space of three fvngris.

To arme a man

ffirste ye muste sette on Sabatones and tye them up on the shoo with smale poyntes that wol breke And then griffus [greaves] & then quisses & he the breeche of mayle And the tonletis And

---

[1] *Arch. Journ.*, IV.   [2] *Archæologia*, LVII.

the brest And h̄e vambras And h̄e rerebras And then glovys
And then hange his daggere upon his right side And then his
shorte swered upon the lyfte side in a rounde rynge all nakid to
pull it oute lightlie. And then putte his cote upon his back And
then his basinet pynid up on two greet staplis before the breste
with a dowbill bokill behynde up on the bak for to make the
bassinet sitte juste. And then his long swerde in his hande. And
then his pensil in his hande peyntid of seynt George or of oure
lady to blesse him with as he goeth towards the felde and in the
felde.

From the above extract it will be seen that the undergarments consisted of a thick doublet lined with silk, but with no shirt underneath;
the reason for this being one that we at the present day can well appre-
ciate, for when the body is hot from exertion and exercise a shirt is apt

FIG. 54. Arming-points (from the portrait
of a Navigator, Ashmolean Mus.,
Oxford).

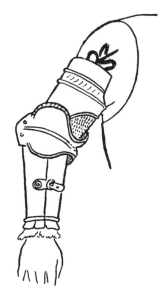

FIG. 55. Attachment of
brassard by points (from
the portrait of the Duc de
Nevers, Hampton Court).

to " ruck up," and it would be impossible to readjust it when fully
armed. In the *Paston Letters* we have the following request from
Edward IV :—

> Item I praye you to send me a newe vestmente off whyght damaske
> ffor a Dekyn, whyche is among myn other geer, I will make an armyng
> Doublet off it.

ARMET, MIDDLE OF XVI CENT.

ARMET ENGRAVED AND GILT, END OF XVI CENT.

HELM OF SIR RICHARD PEMBRIDGE, CIRC. 1360

PARADE CASQUE, AFTER NEGROLI,
MIDDLE OF XVI CENT.

SALLAD BY ONE OF THE NEGROLIS, END OF XV CENT.

PLATE XXIX

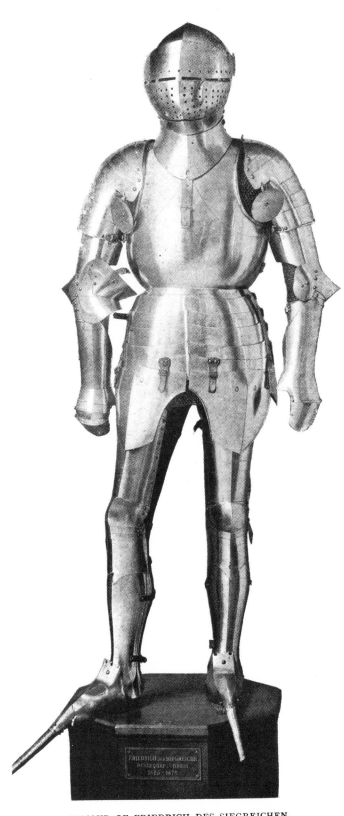

ARMOUR OF THE MIDDLE XV CENT.

ARMOUR OF FRIEDRICH DES SIEGREICHEN,
BY TOMASO DA MISSAGLIA, 1460

PLATE XXX

The gussets and, in the sixteenth century, the sleeves of mail protected the bend of the arm and armpit, and sometimes the bend of the knee, which were not adequately covered with plate. The two portraits of unknown noblemen by Moroni (National Gallery) show these details of the equipment very clearly (Plate XVIII). The arming-points or "tresses" were used in civilian as well as in military attire and joined the hose to the doublet, laced sleeves, and held coats together, much as laces are used in ladies' dresses at the present day (Figs. 54–57). They are also shown tying up the hose on Fig. 52 and the brayette on Plate VIII.

FIG. 56. Moton attached by points (from Harl. MS. 4826).

Lord Dillon explains the hose of "stamyn sengill" as being a worsted cloth made in Norfolk. The "bulwerkis" were pads of blanketing fastened over the hose at the knees to prevent the chafing of the knee-cop, and the shoes were of Cordova leather fastened with laces. A complete under-dress of this kind, with quilted doublet and hose with gussets of mail at the knees, is to be found in the Museum at Munich. The arming of a man began at the feet, and as far as was possible each piece put on overlapped that beneath it, to ensure that glancing surface upon the utility of which such stress has been laid in the first chapter of this book.

FIG. 57. Arming-points on the foot (from the picture of S. Demetrius, by Ortolano, Nat. Gall.).

The arming of a man, therefore, was carried out in the following order and his equipment put on in the following order : Sollerets or sabatons, jambs, knee-cops, cuisses, skirt of mail, gorget, breast and back plates, brassards with elbow-cops, pauldrons, gauntlets, sword-belt, and helmet (Fig. 58).

The "tonlet" would appear to be a bell-shaped skirt of plate or deep taces such as is shown on Plate XXI, and is another example of the use of the "glancing surface," especially in combats with axe and sword at barriers, for in these jousts the legs were often unarmed and were not attacked. The rerebrace, elbow-cop, and vambrace are usually joined by rivets in which there is a certain amount of play. Where this was not the case, each piece was separately strapped to the arm, as may be seen in the brasses of Sir John de Creke, 1325 (Fig. 53), and

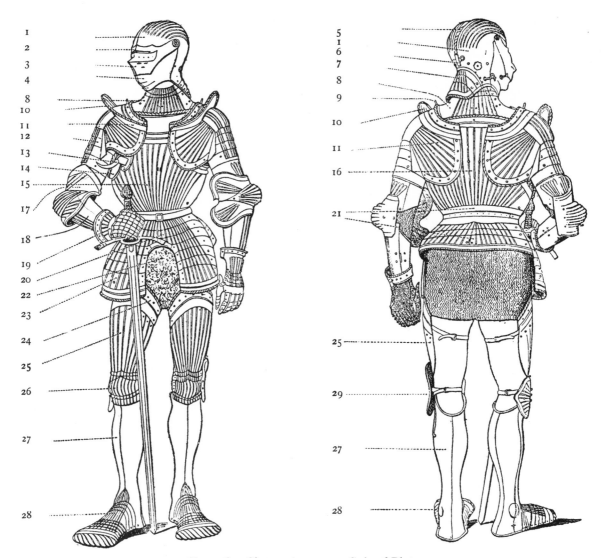

Fig. 58.   Sixteenth-century Suit of Plate.

	English	French	German	Italian	Spanish
1.	scull	timbre	scheitelstück	coppo	calva
2.	visor	visière	visier	visiera	vista
3.	ventail	ventail	schembart	ventaglio	ventalle
4.	bevor	{ bavière { mentonnière	} kinreff	baviera	barbote
5.	crest	crête	kamm	cresta	cresteria
6.	plume-holder	{ porte-plume { porte-panache	}	pennachiera	penacho
7.	nape-guard	couvre-nuque	nackenschirm	gronda	cubrenuca
8.	gorget	colletin	kragen	goletta	gorjal
9.	spring-pin	piton à ressort	federzapfen		
10.	neck-guard	garde-collet	brechränder	guarda-goletta	bufeta
11.	pauldron	épaulière	achseln	spallaccio	guardabrazo
12.	rerebrace	arrière-bras	oberarmzeug	bracciali	brazali
13.	lance-rest	faucre	rüsthaken	resta	restra de muelle
14.	rondel or besague	} rondelle	achselhöhlscheibe	{ rotellino da bracciale	} luneta

	ENGLISH	FRENCH	GERMAN	ITALIAN	SPANISH
15.	breast	plastron	brust	petto	peto
16.	back	dossière	rücken	schiena	dos
17.	elbow-cop or coude	coudière	armkasheln	cubitiera	codales
18.	vambrace	avant-bras	unterarmzeug	bracciali	brazali
19.	gauntlet	gantelet	handschuhe	mittene	manopla
20.	taces	bracconière	bauchreisen	panziera	faldaje
21.	loin-guard	garde-reins	gesassreifen	falda	,,
22.	fald or skirt of mail	brayette	stahlmaschen- unterschutz	braghetta	
23.	tasset	tassette	beintaschen	fiancale	escarcela
24.	upper cuishe	cuissard	oberdiechlinge	cosciali	quijotes
25.	cuishe	,,	unterdiechlinge	,,	,,
26.	knee-cop	genouillère	kniebuckel	ginocchielli	guarda o rodillera
27.	jamb or greave	jambière, grêve	beinröhen	gambiera	greba
28.	solleret or sabbaton	soleret	schuhe	scarpe	escarpe
29.	fan-plate	ailerons			

of Sir Hugh Hastings, 1347. When the three pieces, called collectively the Brassard, were joined together, they were kept in place on the arm by arming-points fastened to the "haustement" or doublet just below the shoulder. The operation of tying on the brassard is shown on the portrait now labelled the "Duc de Nevers" at Hampton Court (Fig. 55). In the list of the equipment taken by the Earl of Northumberland to France in 1513[1] we find mention of arming-pateletts of white satin quilted, for wearing under the armour, trussing-bolsters to wear round the waist to keep the weight of the cuirass from the shoulders, arming-hose, arming-doublets, arming-shoes, garters to wear under the armour, and coffers in which to keep the armour.

There is no mention of the pauldron in the Hastings MS., but when this was worn it was strapped to the neck-opening of the cuirass or hung from spring-pins which project from the shoulder-plate of the cuirass.

The staples mentioned in the Hastings MS. are often very elaborate contrivances, especially in jousting-armour, and the foremost fastening was called the "charnel." Fig. 59 shows the methods of attaching jousting-helms to the cuirass. No. 1 shows the adjustable plate which fixes the front of the helm of the suit of Philip II (Madrid, A, 16). A similar contrivance was used with the "Brocas" helm (Fig. 12). No. 2 is the front of a helm (Mus. d'Art, Paris, G, 163) in which

[1] *Antiquarian Repertory*, IV.

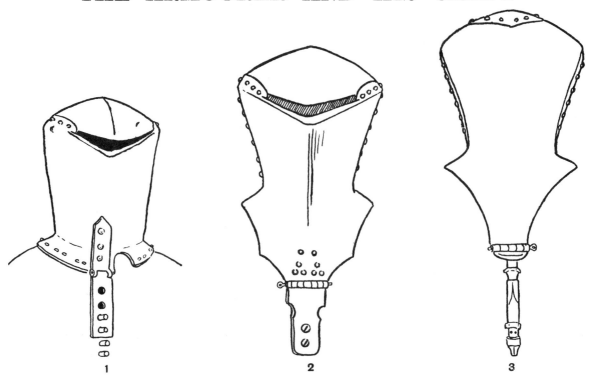

FIG. 59.   Attachment of jousting-helms to the cuirass.

FIG. 60.
Side view
of attach-
ment on
Fig. 59, 3.

the lower plate is bolted to the breast and can be released from the helm by withdrawing the hinge-pin.   No. 3 shows the back of the same helm.   Fig. 60 is a larger sketch of the fixing-hook of this helm.   A is the back-plate of the helm, E the pillar hinged at D and hooked into a lug on the back of the cuirass.   B is a solid block of steel of circular section pierced with holes and connected to a screw in E.   B can be turned by inserting a pin in the holes and the screw tightened or loosened.   Minute details as to the fastenings of the helm will be found in Appendix D, page 178.

It can therefore be easily imagined that the work of arming a man was a serious business, and it was necessary that the armourer or an expert assistant should be present in case some portion of the suit or its fastenings gave way.

Details of the different parts that went to make up the complete suit, with the thickness of each plate, the laces or points, and various fastenings and methods of attachment, will be found in the fifteenth-century Treatise on Military Costume of which a portion is given in Appendix D.

The Marquis de Belleval published an interesting monograph on this manuscript in 1866, which is now scarce and difficult to obtain.

In the illustration on Plate XVII the squires are shown arming their masters from horseback, which appears to involve some gymnastic exercises.

That such agility of the armed man was by no means an artistic licence we may gather from the fact that Froissart[1] mentions Sir John Assueton leaping fully armed behind his page on to his war-horse. Again, Shakespeare makes Henry V (Act V, Sc. 2) say, " If I could win a lady at leapfrog or by vaulting into my saddle with my armour on my back," and Oliver de la Marche states that Galliot de Balthasin in 1446 leaped fully armed out of the saddle as though he had on a pourpoint only. That this was no mere figure of speech we may judge from a little book entitled *The Vaulting Master*, written by W. Stokes, an Oxford riding-master, in 1641.

FIG. 61. Armourer in the lists (Heralds' Coll., MS. M, 6, f. 56).

In the preface he writes : " In war the nimble avoydance of a man's horse if wounded or killed under him, and in like manner the ready ascent into his enemies saddle if it be his hap to unhorse him, and much more which the experienced souldier shall find."

There is an engraving on Plate I of the work showing a cuirassier in half-armour about to vault into the saddle without stirrups. Stokes occasionally breaks out into verse as follows :—

> Here's that will make a stubborne armour weare
> Gentle as Persian silks and light as air,

which refers to the ease of mounting which his prescribed exercises ensured.

On the subject of the wearing of armour we have much valuable information from the works of the great military reformer of the sixteenth century, Sir John Smith, who, as has been stated previously, suffered imprisonment for his opinions. In his *Instructions and Observations and Orders Militarie*, 1591–5, he writes :—

[1] Johnes' edition, I, 449.

Page 183. "No man can be conveniently armed unless he be first fitly apparelled." He states that at Tilbury he saw " but very few of that army that had any convenience of apparel and chieflie of doublets to arme upon, whereof it came to passe that the most of them did weare their armors verie uncomelie and uneasilie. . . . But because the collars of their armours doe beare the chief waight of all the rest of the armour, I would wish that the souldiers . . . should have under Collars of Fustian convenientlie bombasted to defend the heveth weight, and poise of their armours from the paining or hurting of their shouldiers."

On page 193 he writes : " Also I would have them to have pouldrons of a good compasse and size, and vambraces both joined together, and not asunder, because that the poise of the pouldrons and vambraces, hanging upon the pinnes and springes of their collars, they doe not weigh so much, nor are not so wearisome as when they are separated ; and that they weare their vambraces tied with points to their doublets under their pouldrons." Here the author, who was pre-eminently a practical soldier, saw the discomfort and inconvenience caused by the drag of the arming-point on the sleeve and wisely considered that the whole arm-defence should hang from a pin or strap from the gorget or cuirass, so that the weight might be on the shoulders and not on the arms.

The armour for the joust in the sixteenth and seventeenth centuries was far too heavy to allow of such vagaries. Pluvinel in his *Maneige Royale*, 1625, gives an imaginary conversation between himself and the King which bears upon the subject :—

The King.

It seems to me that such a man would have difficulty in getting on his horse and being on to help himself.

Pluvinel.

It would be very difficult, but with this armament the case has been provided for. In this way, at triumphs and tourneys where lances are broken, there must be at the two ends of the lists a small scaffold the height of the stirrup, on which two or three persons can stand ; that is to say, the rider, an armourer to arm him, and one other to help him, as it is necessary in these dangerous encounters that an armourer should always be at hand and that all should be ready. Then the rider being armed, and the horse brought near to the stand, he easily mounts him . . . for this reason the horses must be steady.

A little pen-drawing of the sixteenth century in a manuscript dealing with jousts (Heralds' Coll., M, 6, 56) shows the armourer on one of these scaffolds at the end of the lists (Fig. 61).

In the chapter on the Proving of Armour the question of disuse on account of weight was considered. From the sixteenth century and even earlier we have records of the discarding of armour because it hampered the wearer or for some equally cogent reason. The following extracts bear upon the subject :—

1383. *Chroniques de Dugesclin*, line 5973 (edit. 1839).

> Leurs cuissieres osterent tres tous communement
> Par coi aler peussent trop plus legierement.

This refers to the action of Sir Hugh Calverly at the battle of Mont Auray, who ordered his men to take off their cuisses in order to move more easily.

1590. *Discourses*, p. 4, Sir John Smith.

> But that which is more strange, these our such new fantasied men of warre doe despise and scorne our auncient arming of ourselves both on horseback and on foote saying that wee armed ourselves in times past with too much armour, or peces of yron as they terme it. And therefore their footmen piquers they doo allow for verie well armed when they weare their burganets, their collars, their cuirasses, and their backs, without either pouldrons, vambraces, gauntlets or tasses.

Sir John Smith goes on to say that it was the discarding of his cuisses that cost Sir Philip Sidney his life, for he received a wound from a spent bullet which his armour might have deflected.

1619. *The Art of Warre*, Edward Davies.

[the arquebusiers were loaded] with a heavie shirt of male and a burganet, by the time they have marched in the heat of summer or deepe of winter ten or twelve English miles they are more apt to rest than readie to fight.

1625. *Souldiers' Accidence*, Markham.

As for the pouldron or the vant-brace they must be spared because they are but cumbersome.

Against these extracts we must place the opinions of military leaders who deplored the disuse of armour :—

1632. *Militarie Instructions for the Cavallrie*, Cruso.

Captain Bingham in his Low Countrie exercise appointeth him [the harquebusier] a cuirass pistoll proofe which condemneth the late practice of our trained Harquebusiers to be erroneous which have wholly left off their arms and think themselves safe enough in a calf's skin coat.

1756. *Réveries*, Marshal Maurice of Saxe, p. 56.

Je ne sais pourquoi on a quitte les Armures, car rien n'est si beau ni si avantageux. L'on dira peut-etre que c'est l'usage de la poudre qui les a abolis ; mais point du tout car du tems de Henri IV. et depuis jusq'en l'annee 1667 on en a porter, et il y avoit deja bien longtems que la poudre etoit en usage : mais vous verrez que c'est la chere commodite qui les a fait quitter.

Marshal Saxe further suggests that the large proportion of wounds are received from sword, lance, or spent bullet, and that all these might be guarded against by wearing armour or a buff coat of his own invention which when reinforced with steel plates weighed 30 lb.

THE WEIGHT OF ARMOUR

We have but few records in contemporary documents of the actual weight of the different parts of the suit of armour, but we can obtain these from examples of the sixteenth century onwards from specimens in the different museums and collections.

PORTRAIT MEDAL OF COLOMAN, COLMAN, 1470-1532

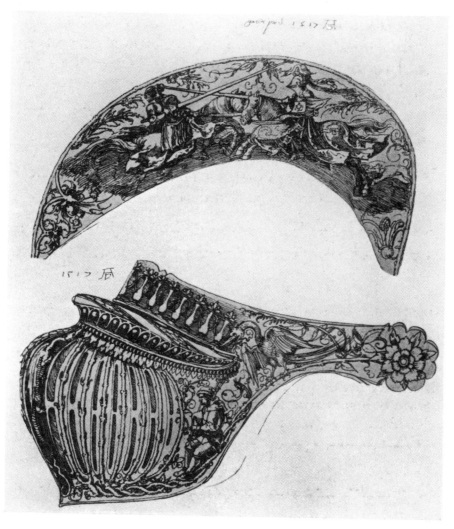

DESIGNS FOR ARMOUR BY ALBERT DÜRER, 1517

PLATE XXXI

That armour had become burdensome in the extreme owing to the necessity of subjecting it to pistol and musket proof we know from various writers on the subject.

La Noue in his *Discours Politiques et Militaires*, translated by " E. A." 1587, writes on page 185 : " For where they had some reason in respect of the violence of harquebuzes and dagges [muskets and pistols] to make their armor thicker and of better proofe than before, they have now so farre exceeded, that most of thē have laden themselves with stithies [anvils] in view of clothing their bodies with armour . . . neither was their armour so heavie but that they might wel bear it 24 hours, where those that are now worne are so waightie that the peiz [weight] of them will benumme a Gentleman's shoulders of 35 yeres of age."

On page 196 of Sir John Smith's *Instructions, Observations, and Orders Militarie*, the author strongly objects to the discarding of the arm and leg defences which was advised by other authorities. He insists that these limbs are as important as the " breste, belly, and backe," and should be adequately protected. His opinions are also held by Marshal Maurice of Saxe in his *Rêveries*, quoted above.

Edward Ludlow, at the battle of Edgehill, 1642,[1] was dismounted in getting through a hedge, and says : " I could not without great difficulty recover on horse-back again being loaded with cuirassiers arms as the rest of the guard were also."

It would be superfluous to mention the different occasions on which unhorsed knights were captured or killed through their inability to remount in battle. Froissart in describing the battle of Poitiers says that when once dismounted men could not get up again, and other historians bear equal witness of the disadvantage of armour when unmounted ; and the Sieur de Gaya, who has been so often referred to in these pages, writing in 1678, says in his *Traité des Armes*, page 60 : " Ils n'avoient trop de tort à mon avis d'équiper ainsi leurs chevaux parce qu'un Cavalier armé n'est plus propre à rien quand il est demonté."

Although this may be taken as a reason put forward by the writer for more armour for man and horse, it shows at the same time that the fully armed man was considered to be comparatively useless when un-

---

[1] *Ludlow's Memoirs*, Firth, I, 44.

horsed, as the Spanish proverb ran: "Muerto el Cavallo, perdido el hombre d'armas."

It may be somewhat of a surprise to learn that the present-day equipment is but little lighter than that of the fifteenth century. The Under Secretary for War, speaking in the House of Commons on November 28th, 1911, stated that the infantry soldier marched on an average thirty miles a day during the manœuvres, carrying 59 lb. 11 oz. of equipment and kit. Against this we may place the weight of some suits of foot-soldiers' armour of the sixteenth century, which weigh with the helmet at the outside 25 lb.; leaving therefore a wide margin for underclothes and weapons. And this comparison of weight carried is even more interesting when considering the cavalry equipment, as will be seen from the annexed table on the opposite page.

Of course all these figures represent "dead weight"; and here we are brought back to one of those fundamental rules of good craftsmanship—the recognition of "Convenience in Use."

Even in the Golden Age of armour, the fifteenth century, the armourer was hampered by material and by methods of construction which even the most expert craftsman could not overcome; but when we reach the period of decadence in the seventeenth century, the excellence of craftsmanship had deteriorated to an alarming extent and these difficulties were still greater. The secret therefore of the weight-carrying powers of man and horse at the present day is greater convenience in carrying, the scientific distribution of weight, and a more adaptable material, which when taken together give greater freedom and greater mobility, even though the actual weight be the same as the equipment of steel.

The following table gives the weights of typical suits from the fifteenth century onwards:—

ARMOUR FOR THE JOUST

XV–XVI.—HELMS (ENGLISH).

		lb.	oz.
	Barendyne, Great Haseley, Oxon	13	8
	Wallace Collection, No. 78	17	0
	Westminster Abbey	17	12
	Brocas, Rotunda, Woolwich	17	12
	Dawtrey, Petworth, Sussex	21	8
	Captain Lindsay, Sutton Courtenay, Berks	24	14
1518.	Madrid, A, 37	41	9

SUITS.

		lb.	oz.
1520.	Tower, II, 28, for fighting on foot	93	0
1530 (*circ.*).	Madrid, A, 26 { man	79	0
	{ horse	79	0
1590.	Tower, II, 9, man	103	0

WAR HARNESS

		lb.	oz.
1439.	Musée d'Artillerie, Paris, G, 1, man and horse	163	0
1514.	Tower, II, 5 { man	64	13
	{ horse	69	3
1588.	Musée d'Artillerie, G, 80, man	92	6
1590.	Tower, II, 10	79	0
1590.	Tower, II, 12	55	8
1612.	Tower, II, 18	77	14

CAVALRY

	1450	1875	1909
G, 1, Musée d'Artillerie, Paris. *Man, about 140 lb.* *Armour for man and horse, 163 lb.[1]* *Arms, clothes, saddlery, etc., about 30 lb.*	333 lb.		
British Household Cavalry		308 lb.	
„ Heavy „		280 lb.	
„ Medium „		266 lb.	246 lb.[3]
„ Light „		259 lb.[2]	
German Cuirassier			334 lb.
All the above are Service equipment, including rider and saddlery.			

INFANTRY

	1550	1875	1911
106–8, Rotunda, Woolwich, Maltese Suits. *Half-armour and helmet, 25 lb.* *Clothes and arms, about 15 lb.*	40 lb.		
British Infantry. *Service equipment, including arms*		52 lb.[2]	59 lb. 11 oz.[4]

[1] Catalogue of the Museum.
[2] Sir G. P. Colley, K.S.I., *Encyc. Brit.*, 1875.
[3] Col. F. N. Maude, *Encyc. Brit.*, 1910.
[4] *Morning Post*, December 9, 1911.

THE ARMOURERS' COMPANY OF THE CITY OF LONDON, ARMOURERS' HALL, COLEMAN STREET, E.C.

AT the present day this Company is combined with that of the Braziers, but this combination only dates from the beginning of the eighteenth century, when it had ceased to deal with the making of armour and was more concerned with other branches of the craft of the metal-worker. The objects of the craft-gild of the armourers were the same as all those of like nature in the Middle Ages.

FIG. 62.   Arms of the Armourers' Company of London.

Members were protected from outside piracy of methods and trade-marks, they were cared for in body when ill or incapable of working, and in soul by masses and religious exercises.

An important detail in the organization of these craft-gilds and one sadly lacking in modern trade combinations was the examination and approval of the members' work by the gild-masters. In this way was the craftsman encouraged to produce good work, and also the purchaser was protected against inferior workmanship. A reference to the Appendices B, K will exemplify this, for in these two instances alone we find that careless work is condemned by the Company. In the document of the reign of Edward II it is noted that " old bascute broken and false now newly covered by men that nothing understood of ye mystery wh. be put in pryvie places and borne out into ye contrye out of ye said Citye to sell and in ye same citie of wh. men may not gaine knowledge whether they be good or ill of ye wh. thinge great yill might fall to ye king and his people."

Again, under Charles I, in the appeal of the Company to the Crown, leave to use the mark is requested " because divers cutlers,

120

smythes, tynkers & other botchers of arms by their unskillfulness have utterly spoiled many armes, armours, &c."

The Company seems to have existed during the reign of Edward II, but was not then incorporated, and with the exception of the document transcribed in Appendix A, there is but little evidence of their existence before the date of 31st Henry VI, in which year a Charter of Incorporation was granted. This deals mostly with questions relating to religious observances, the gild-chapel and like matters. A report to the Court of Aldermen, dated 20th Eliz. (1578), as to right of search for armour, etc., states that " the Armourers did shewe us that in Kinge Edward the Second his time, the Lord Maior and his bretheren did then graunte the serche unto the Armourers."

As has been noticed before, the fact that armour plates were expensive and difficult to forge will account for the scarcity of examples of the defensive equipment up to the sixteenth century. Either the suit was remade or, having been cast aside, it was utilized by the common soldier as well as might be. It was only when the age of the firearm was reached that armour was left in its perfect state and was not improved upon. We have therefore but little to show whether the English armourers of the fourteenth and fifteenth centuries were more or less expert than their foreign rivals, but, from other examples of metal-work that remain to us, we are forced to the conclusion that the foreigner was our superior. At the same time we find on more than one occasion that the English armourer claims to equal his foreign rival ; but whether these claims were ever proved we are unable to decide without actual examples of the craft work or documentary evidence. In Appendix J is printed an appeal from Capt. John Martin in 1624 for leave to import German "platers" to teach English armourers, with the hope that this will establish a home trade and will stop the import of foreign work. At the same time the very fact of this request shows that the craft in England in the reign of James I was not in a very flourishing condition. On the other hand, in 1590 the Armourers of London petitioned Queen Elizabeth to purchase only home products, because they can furnish her with " farre better armors than that wch cometh from beyond the seas."

In the year 1580 the Armourers' Company endeavoured to obtain an Act of Parliament to protect and encourage the craft of the Armourer, but with no result owing to the opposition of other Companies.   In the minutes of the Company detailing this effort occurs the following passage, which is of interest as bearing upon the skill of English workmen at that date : " It was the Master's chance to speak with Sir Walter's[1] honor again, Dr. Doull, one of the Masters of Requests, being with him, praying him to have the Armourers' Bill in remembrance.   'What,' said Mr. Doctor, 'there is none of your

Company that can make an armor.'   'Yes, sir,' said the Master, 'that there is verily good workmen, and skilful as needeth to be.'   'Tell me not that,' saith he, 'for I will hould you a hundred pounds that there is none in England that can "trampe" an armor for " the Cappe to the Soul of the foot." '   'I will lay with your worship afore Sir Walter's honor if you will give me leave that we have in England that shall work with any in the world from the toe to the crown of the head from 100 to 1000 '; and then he made as though he would have laid it.   'No,' saith Sir Walter, 'ye shall not lay, for he will win of you, for

Fig. 63. Design on manifer of suit made for Henry, Prince of Wales, by Pickering, *circ.* 1611.   Windsor Castle. Half-size (from a rubbing).

they have very good workmen, and I know of the workmanship myself. "

This skill in craftsmanship was doubtless attained under the tutelage of the Almaine armourers that have been referred to before who were brought over by Henry VIII to Greenwich. As an example of this we may notice the work of Pickering,[2] to whom is attributed the suit made

---

[1] Sir Walter Mildmay, Chancellor of the Exchequer.
[2] William Pickering was Master of the Company 1608–9

for Henry, Prince of Wales, now at Windsor Castle, which bears a strong resemblance to the work of Jacob Topf, who was Master Armourer at Greenwich in 1590 (Fig. 63).

In 1595 a Court of the Armourers' Company was held to examine targets and other pieces of armour, and the decision arrived at was that it was "not of the proportion that cometh from beyond the seas, the Breast and Back Plates were too short and too narrow everywhere." Again in the year 1620 at a Court it was certified that a Sussex smith "did alter old Armour, persuading the Countrey that they were workmanly done, which notwithstanding were utterly unserviceable." This matter was reported to the Justices at Guildford to be dealt with by them. From these entries it will be seen that the control of the Company was very real and that in the main the English craftsman was of not much account until he had learned his trade from foreign experts.

It was doubtless due to the instruction given by the foreigner that the Company possessed skilled hammermen. Under Elizabeth in 1560 these hammermen were employed to assist in the process of coin-striking and were sent, two to the Clothworkers' Hall, two to the Sessions Hall, Southwark, and two to the Merchant Taylors' Hall, to strike and stamp "with portcullis and greyhound the several pieces of money called ' Testons,' there to continue until the end of fourteen days from the date of precept."[1]

Many of the foreign immigrants took out letters of naturalization and became members of the Company, but none of these seem to have been craftsmen of note, for the expert workmen were generally recalled to the German Court after some time, where there was a wider scope and, possibly, higher remuneration for their services.

The Company, like other Corporations, suffered severely during the Reformation. Religious observances were so much a part of the gild life that the members soon fell under suspicion as practising superstitious rites. Heavy fines were enacted, and it was only by the generosity of John Richmond, a member of the Company, who bought part of the corporate property of the Farringdon estate for £120 and left it back to the Company in his will, that the fine was paid.

---

[1] In September, 1575, " Hopkins, a maker of coining irons in the Mint, has also been making calivers and great iron pieces."—State Papers, *sub ann.*

Informers, of whom Tipper and Dawe were the chief, levied black-mail on the Company up to the end of the reign of Elizabeth, and continued to suggest that superstitious practices were indulged in till their demands were met at heavy expense.

The Armourers had, in 1515, absorbed the whole craft of the Blade-smiths, which seems to have caused much friction with the Cutlers. The books of the Company are full of appeals and negotiations before the Court of Aldermen on the question of search for unlicensed crafts-men and faulty goods, which was one of the important duties of the Company. These were finally arranged by a joint search being made by the two Companies. The Company was from the beginning dedicated to S. George, who was the patron of armourers all over Europe. His statue by Donatello, formerly outside the gild-church of Or San Michele in Florence, is well known. The figure of S. George appears on the charter granted by Henry VI in 1453, and also upon the matrix of a seal of about the same date. The registered mark of the Company was " A," surmounted by a crown, and this was ordered to be stamped upon all weapons, armours, and guns supplied by the Company when tested and approved.

There are many interesting details dealing with the apprentices of the Company which, although they do not bear directly upon the craft of the armourer, are nevertheless worth recording as typical of the craft laws and regulations as practised in England.

In most craft-gilds it was considered sufficient for an apprentice to serve for seven years before he was free of the gild ; but in the Armourers' Company we frequently find entries of apprentice bonds for nine years, and in some instances ten and fourteen. There are records of misbehaviour of one of the apprentices, who is ordered " honest correction as that a Servant shall be used." This correction was some-times administered in the Hall before the Gild-Court, and is described as being " indifferently well " carried out. The case of the Sussex smith who produced unworkmanly armour has been referred to above. In a letter from the Lord Mayor in 1560 we read that the apprentices are not to use " swearing and blaspheming, haunting evil women or Schools of Fence, Dancing, Carding, Dicing, Bowling, Tennis play, using of Ruffs in their shirts, Tavern haunting or Banqueting, and if any shall be found faulty the same be forwith punished by whipping openly in your Hall in the sight of other Apprentices, and ye shall give in charge that the said Masters shall not permit nor suffer any of their Apprentices to wear in their hosen any cloth of other colours than are here expressed, that is to say, White, Russet, Blue, Watchet, and the said Hosen to be made without great Breeches in most plain manner without stitching of Silk or any mannar of Cuts."

The most valuable of the possessions of the Armourers' Company from the technical point of view is the suit of armour made by Jacobe, who is now considered to be the same as Jacob Topf, an Innsbruck craftsman who was Master Armourer at Greenwich in 1590. The design for this suit appears in the *Almain Armourer's Album*, which is noticed under the heading of German Armourers. There is also a "locking-gauntlet," which is sometimes erroneously called the "forbidden gauntlet," by the same craftsman (Fig. 32).

The Company at one time possessed a model suit of armour made in 1567 by John Kelk, a naturalized German member, which, when completed, was brought into the Hall with much ceremony and laid upon the high table. It was intended to be a pattern of the armour made by the Company. There are various entries in the Company's Records of payments for repairing and keeping up this "Mannakine," as it was called. It has since disappeared; but Hewitt, the noted authority on medieval armour, seemed to think that it was in the Tower in 1855 (II, 52).

LISTS OF EUROPEAN ARMOURERS

THE following short notices give what details are known of some of the more important armourers. In many instances they are only known by their works, and no details are forthcoming about their private or professional lives. The dates given are those of the earliest and latest mention of the individual in contemporary chronicles.

ENGLAND

(K.A., Q.A. = KING'S OR QUEEN'S ARMOURER)

Albert, Hans. 1515.
Ashton, John. 1633. K.A. and Armourers' Co.
Aynesley, Edward. 1633. K.A. and Armourers' Co.
Baker, Thomas.[1] 1547. Armourers' Co.
Basyn, John. 1524–44. (Naturalized Norman.)
Bawdesonne, Alen. 1547. King's Armourer, Westminster.
Blewbery, John. 1511–16. (Yeoman of the Armoury at Greenwich, 1515.)
Boreman, W., also called Alias Hynde. 1599–1609. (Appointed armourer at Greenwich, 1599. Will dated 1645.)
Brande, Rauffe.[2] 1520.
Baltesar Bullato. 1532. Milanese, King's Armourer.
Carter, William. 1534. Ludlow.
Clere, Hans. 1530. K.A., Greenwich.
Clynkerdager, Hans. 1542–4. K.A., Greenwich.
Clynkerdager, John. 1525.
Copeland. 1529. London.
Cooper, John. 1627–9. Keeper of the King's Brigandines.
Cowper, Thomas. 1559. K.A., Greenwich.
Coxe, Wm. 1633. K.A. and Armourers' Co.
Croche, Francis. 1528–9. K.A., Greenwich.

---

[1] At funeral of Henry VIII.
[2] Sent to Flanders in this year to provide armour, etc., for the Field of the Cloth of Gold.

Crochet, John.   1515–20.   K.A., Greenwich.

Crompton, John.   1544.   Southwark.

Crouche, Wm.   1633.   K.A. and Armourers' Co.

Cutler, Richard.[1]   1520.

Dael, Thomas.   1515.   K.A., Greenwich.

Daniele, Edmond.[2]   1547.

Daniele, John.[2]   1547.

Darwin, William.   1613.   Yeoman of the Armoury at Greenwich.

Dawson.   1515.   K.A., Greenwich.

Dedikes, Dirike.   1530.   Yeoman of the Armoury at Greenwich.

Dericke or Diricke, Mathew.   1559–74.   K.A., Greenwich.

Dericke or Diricke, Robert.   1524.

Diconson, John.   1528.   K.A., Greenwich.

Faulkenor, Roger.[3]   1625–31.

Fevers, Peter.   1512–18.   K.A., Greenwich.

Foster, Rowland.   1633.   K.A. and Armourers' Co.

Franklin, John.   1633.   K.A. and Armourers' Co.

Fuller, James.   1559.   Yeoman of the Armoury, Greenwich.

Garret, John.   1559–1601 (date of will).   Q.A., Greenwich.

Gurre, Wm.   1511–38.   Brigandarius.

Halder, Jacob.   1574.   Q.A., Greenwich.

Halore (?), Jacob.   1559.   Q.A., Greenwich.   (Possibly the same as Halder.)

Harford, Richard.   1590.   London.

Herste, Martyn.   1574.   Q.A., Greenwich.

Hill, Johan.   1434.   Armourer to Henry VI.   See page 173.

Horne, Geofrey.   1516–18.

Hotton, Richard.   1592.

Hunter, Hans.[2]   1547.   Westminster.

Jacobi or Jacobe.[4]   1530-90.   Master Armourer, Greenwich.

Kelte, John.   1559–74.   Q.A., Greenwich.

Kemp, Jasper.   1544.   K.A., Greenwich.

Keymer, Roger.   1571.   Q.A., Greenwich.

Kirke, John.   1577.   Master Armourer at Greenwich.

---

[1] Sent to Flanders in this year to provide armour, etc., for the Field of the Cloth of Gold.
[2] At funeral of Henry VIII.
[3] Made sundry petitions for inquiry as to the state of the Armouries, S.P.D. Car. I, xiii, 96, etc.
[4] Now considered to be the same as Topf.   Only mention as armourer in England, 1590.

Kirkener, Erasmus or Asamus. 1519–93. Brigandarius, 1538 ; Chief Armourer, 1544.

Kornelys. 1515. K.A., Greenwich.

Lasy, John. 1533. Nottingham.

Lincoln, Thomas. 1604–8. Yeoman of the Armoury at Greenwich.

Mare de la, Will. K.A., 1672.

Marshall, Nicholas. 1533. K.A. and Armourers' Co.

Martyn, "Old." 1544. K.A., Greenwich.

Mightner, Hans. 1559–74. Q.A., Greenwich.

Oliver, Jermyn. 1514–44. (Naturalized Norman.)

Pellande, Richard. 1520.

Pellysonne, Frances. 1524–44. (Naturalized "from the domains of the Emperor.")

Pickering, William. 1591–1630. Master Armourer at Greenwich, 1604–14.

Pipe, Nighel. 1559. Q.A., Greenwich.

Pitwell, Giles. 1516–44. (Naturalized Gascon.)

Polston, John. 1552. K.A., Greenwich.

Pounde, John de. 1520.

Poyes, Francis. 1525–44. (Naturalized Norman.)

Purday, John. 1562.

Sewell, John. 1590–1.

Sherman, Nicolas. 1629. Chief Armourer at Greenwich.

Spirarde, Carries or Tarys. 1574. Q.A., Greenwich.

Spyltherup or Speldrup, Francis.[1] 1532.

Stephens, Thos. 1626. K.A. and Armourers' Co.

Stile, John.[2] 1524. K.A., Greenwich.

Stone, Benjamin. 1636. Sword-smith, Hounslow.

Ureland, Peter van. 1515. Gilder and Graver, Greenwich.

Watt Copyn Jacob de. 1512–26. K.A., Greenwich.

Whetstone. 1628.

White, Thomas. 1416. Master Armourer.

Wolf, John. 1538–42. K.A., Greenwich.

Wollwarde, Thomas. 1530–41. K.A., Greenwich.

Woode, Richard. 1590. London.

---

[1] Appropriated gold intended to gild armour, also clipped money.   [2] Died by burning in this year.

GERMAN ARMOURERS

Aldegraver, Heinrich. 1502–58.

Brabenter, Wilhelm, Solingen. Sixteenth century.

Colman, Coloman. 1470–1532. Augsburg. Mark No. 40. See page 133.

Colman (Helmschmied), Desiderius. 1552. Mark No. 40. See page 134.

Colman (Helmschmied), Lorenz. 1490–1516. Mark Nos. 2, 23, 41. See page 133.

Frauenpreis, Matthaias. 1549. Mark No. 38. See page 135.

Frauenpreis, Matthaias, the younger. See page 135.

Grofsschedl, Franz. Landshut. 1568. Mark No. 39.

Grünewald, Hans. Nuremberg. 1503. Mark No. 54. See page 135.

Hopfer, Daniel. 1566. See page 136.

Jövingk, Jakob. Dresden. 1650–9.

Knopf, Heinrich. 1604.

Lochner, Conrad. Nuremberg. 1567. Mark No. 46. See page 136.

Obresch, Heinrich. Grätz. 1590. Mark No. 47.

Peffenhauser, Anton. Augsburg. 1566–94. Mark No. 48.

Ringler, Hans. Nuremberg. 1560. Mark No. 49.

Rockenberger or Rosenberger, Hans. 1543–70. Dresden.

Rockenburger, Sigmund. 1554–72. Mark No. 79.

Rotschmied. Nuremberg. 1597. Mark No. 6.

Seusenhofer, Conrad. Innsbruck. 1502–18. Mark No. 7. See page 141.

Seusenhofer, Jorg. Innsbruck. 1558. Mark No. 8. See page 141.

Seusenhofer, Wilhelm. Augsburg. 1547.

Siebenburger, Valentine. Nuremberg. 1547. Mark Nos. 20, 74.

Sigman, George. 1560. Mark No. 76.

Speyer, Peter. Dresden. 1560. Mark No. 60.

Speyer, Wolf. Dresden. 1580.

Topf, Jacob. Innsbruck. 1530–90. See page 143.

Treytz, Adrian. Innsbruck. 1469–1517. Mark No. 15.

Veit. Nuremberg. Sixteenth century. Mark No. 16.

Wolf, Sigismond.   Landshut.   1554.
Worms, Wilhelm (father and son).   Nuremberg.   1539.   Mark No. 17.

FRANCE

Petit, M.   Seventeenth century.   Mark No. 83.

NETHERLANDS

Merate, Gabriel and Francesco.   Arbois.   1495.   Mark Nos. 18, 51, 53.
    See page 136.
Voys, Jacques.   Brussels.   Fifteenth to sixteenth century.   Mark
    No. 56.

ITALY

Campi, Bartolomeo.   Milan.   1573.   See page 132.
Camelio, Victor.   Brescia.   1500.   See page 131.
Cantoni, Bernardino.   Milan.   1500.   See page 133.
Chiesa, Pompeo della.   Milan.   1590.
Missaglia, Antonio.   1492.   Mark Nos. 24, 25, 26.   See page 138.
Missaglia, Petrajolo.   Milan.   1390.   Mark Nos. 27, 78.
Missaglia, Tomaso.   Milan.   1468.   Mark Nos. 27, 78.   See page 137.
Mola, Gesparo.   Rome.   1640.   See page 139.
Negroli, Philip and Jacopo.   Milan.   1530–90.   Mark Nos. 42, 43,
    44.   See page 140.
Piccinino, Lucio.   Milan.   1550–70.   See page 140.

SHORT BIOGRAPHIES OF NOTABLE ARMOURERS

Hans Burgmair,
Augsburg, 1473–1531.
This celebrated engraver was the son of Hans Burgmair or Burgkmair. There is some confusion between the father and son, but the former seems to have worked either as a maker or a decorator of armour. The family were neighbours of the famous Colmans, the armourers, who lived in the Lange Schmiede gasse, while the Burgmairs had a house close by in Mauerburg. In 1526 Coloman Colman left his house to live with Hans Burgmair the elder, while Hans the younger took Colman's house. The two families seem to have been on most intimate terms. S. Quirin. Leitner considered that the bard of A, 149, Madrid, which represents the labours of Hercules and Samson, was designed by Burgmair, and Wendelin Boeheim[1] also inclined to this view. His principal works were the Triumph of Maximilian and the illustrations of the *Weisz Künig*, both of which show such endless varieties of armour and weapons that we cannot but feel that the artist must have had a very practical knowledge of the craft of the armourer.

It would enlarge the present work beyond its original scope if mention were made of all the artists who designed armour and weapons, for in all ages the painter and sculptor have been employed in this direction. It will be sufficient to note that designs of this nature are to be found in the sketch-books of Donatello, Giulio Romano, Holbein, Leonardo da Vinci, Benvenuto Cellini, and Albert Dürer. Reproductions of two drawings by the latter are given on Plate XXXI.

Vittore Camelio,
Venice, *circ.* 1450–1509.
Camelio was born either at Venice or Vincenza. He was a fine engraver and medallist, and is considered by Nägler to have invented the process of striking coins and medals from steel dies. He was especially noted for light steel armour of high temper. He was granted a patent

---

[1] Meister der Waffenschmiedkunst.

or concession for the sole working of his invention by the Senate of Venice from 1509 for five years.

Bartolomeo Campi,
Pesaro, Venice, Paris, 1573.
Campi was born at Pesaro, but the exact date of his birth is unknown. He was a goldsmith, and engraver and maker of arms and armour of such merit that they elicited the highest praise from Pedro Aretino in his letters from Venice to Bartolomeo Egnazio in 1545. About this date he made a magnificent pageant suit of pseudo-Roman armour for Guidobaldo II, Duke of Urbino, who presented it to Charles V. The cuirass is superbly modelled on the human torse and is decorated with a Medusa's head and bands of gold with silver flowers. The shoulder-pieces are of blackened steel in the form of masks with golden eyes, and the lambrequins hanging from the cuirass end in medallions and masks. The helmet is decorated with a crown of golden leaves. On the cuirass is the inscription: "BARTOLOMEVS CAMPI AVRIFEX TOTIVS OPERIS ARTIFEX QVOD ANNO INTEGRO INDIGEBAT PRINCIPIS SVI NVTVI OBTEMPERANS GEMINATO PERFECIT." If this inscription is not an exaggeration, it is little short of miraculous that this suit should have been made in one year. It is now at Madrid (A, 188). In 1547 Campi directed the fêtes held in honour of the marriage of Guidobaldo II and Vittoria Farnese at Pesaro. He was military engineer to the Republic of Siena, to that of Venice, and to the King of France between the years 1554 and 1560. He assisted the Duc de Guise at the siege of Calais in 1562, and in 1568 served with the Duke of Alba in Flanders, where he was given a commission as chief engineer of fortifications at a salary of 500 escudi. The Duke, writing to the King on June 3, 1569, says: "I tell your Majesty that you have a good man in Captain B. Campi, because in truth he is a soldier and has art, although not so well founded as Pachote . . . and he is the best man I have met with since I have known men—I do not say only engineers, but men of any sort—very happy and steady in his work." Campi was killed by an arquebus shot at the siege of Haarlem on March 7th, 1573, to the great grief of the Duke and the whole army. His brother was an armourer about 1555, but we have no records of his work. The magnificent specimen of Bartolomeo's work

at Madrid is the only example of his craft as an armourer that has come down to us (Plate XIV).

Jacopo and Bernardino Cantoni, Milan, 1477–1500. But little definite information is to be obtained respecting the Cantoni family. They worked for Galeazzo Maria Sforza and other princes, and are mentioned as " magistri armorum" in the gild-records of Milan. Bernardino worked for the Emperor Maximilian I and produced the brigandine (Madrid, C, 11) which bears his signature (Fig. 64). This is the only work which can be directly ascribed to this family.

FIG. 64. Cantoni's mark on a brigandine, C, 11, Madrid.

Lorenz Colman, Augsburg, d. 1516. Mark Nos. 23, 41. This armourer is also known as Colman Helmschmied. Little is known of his history except that one of his ancestors was living in Augsburg in 1377. His father George was also an armourer who worked in Augsburg in the Harbruc and in the Luginsland, craft-streets of that city. He died in 1479. The name of his son Lorenz first appears in the civic records in 1467, and his work must have soon attracted attention, for in 1477 we find him making armour for Maximilian I and obtaining the freedom of the city. In 1491 he was created Hof Platner to the Emperor and established himself in a house in Innsbruck. From commissions entrusted to him for buying metal in 1498 he appears to have been still at Innsbruck, and in 1506 the records of Mantua show that he was making armour for that court. After this he seems to have been employed entirely by Maximilian, and in 1508 he received a large contract for armour for his army. His work is marked with a helm surmounted by a cross, and always bears in addition the pine, the Augsburg city stamp. Armour from his hand is to be found at Madrid, A, 44, and Vienna, 62, 1005, 1016, 1023.

Coloman Colman, Augsburg, 1476–1532. Mark No. 40. Coloman was the son of Lorenz, and with the rest of his family took the craft-name of Helmschmied, a fact which makes investigations of records, documents, etc., of some difficulty. This is especially the case

with Coloman, whose name is spelt sometimes with a "C" and sometimes with a "K." The first mention of Coloman in civic documents
is in 1507. In 1512 we find him working for Charles V, and shortly
after he entered the service of Maximilian I. In 1516 a silver suit of
armour (steel plated with silver) was ordered from him by Maximilian,
but in 1519 this suit seems still to have been unfinished, probably
owing to lack of payments, a reason which was and is always being
advanced by craftsmen of all kinds for work delayed at this period.
He employed the two Burgmairs, father and son, to decorate his
armour.

Although Charles V frequently urged him to come to Spain,
his numerous commissions at home prevented him. He seems to have
been prosperous in 1525, for he bought the " Schmied haus in the Karo-
line strasse " from the widow of Thomas Burgmair. Two portrait medals
were struck for him in 1518, 1532. His clientele extended to Italy, and
in 1511 he wrote a letter to the Marchesa Francesco di Mantua describing
a project for completely arming a horse with laminated and jointed
defences of plate covering head, body, and legs. A picture in the Zeughaus at Vienna shows Harnischmeister Albrecht riding a horse armed in
this fashion, and a portion of the leg-piece of such a suit is preserved in
the Musée Porte de Hal, Brussels (see page 9).

The following works bear Coloman Colman's mark or are known
from documentary evidence to be from his hand : Vienna, 175.
Wallace Collection, 402. Madrid, A, 19; A, 37–42; A, 59; A, 93–107
(Tonlet suit "The Chase"); A, 108–11; E, 57; E, 59. Dresden, G, 15.

Desiderius Colman, Desiderius was the son of Coloman Colman.
Augsburg, *circ.* 1532. In 1532 he took over the workshops in the
Marks, the same as No. 40. Mauerburg at Augsburg, which his father had
shared with the Burgmair family. He worked at first with the armourer
Lutzenberger, who married the stepmother of Desiderius in 1545. In
1550 he became a member of the City Council, and in 1556 he was
made Court Armourer to Charles V. This title was afterwards confirmed by Maximilian II. Desiderius seems to have used the same
mark as his father, hence there is some confusion between the two
craftsmen. The suits known to be by him are at Madrid, A, 157, 158,

239, 142—the splendid parade suit made for Philip II, which is signed and dated 1550, and the richly embossed and chased round shield A, 241, which is also signed and dated 15 April, 1552. It is upon this shield that he recorded his rivalry with the Negrolis (Plate XXIV, Fig. 65, also page 16).

FIG. 65.   Detail of Shield by Desiderius Colman (Plate XXIV).

Matthaias Frauenpreis,
Augsburg.
Father, 1529–49.
Son, 1530–1604.
Mark No. 38.

The elder Frauenpreis or Frauenbreis was a pupil of the Colman family (q.v.), and in 1529 married the widow of a helm-smith. He is first heard of as an independent workman in 1530. The following works are ascribed to him or his son :—

Madrid.   A, 198. A brassard forming part of the suit A, 190, made by Desiderius Colman.

D, 68. A shield signed with his name on which the figure of Fortuna is ascribed to Hans Burgmair.

M, 6. A small shield marked with his stamp No. 38.

Vienna.   950. Field suit of Archduke Maximilian.

397. A white and gold suit bearing the mark No. 38.

Dresden.   G, 39. A fine suit of Kurfürst Moritz, bearing the mark No. 38. Illustrated on Plate VII.

Hans Grünewalt,
Nuremberg, 1440–1503.
Mark No. 54.

His grandfather was a bell-founder of Nuremberg, who made the bells for the church of S. Sebald in 1396. In 1465, after his father's death, Hans built a large house and workshop, after much litigation with the city over his glazing or polishing mills. In 1480 he owned many houses in Nuremberg, and built the " Pilatus " house near the Thiergartner-Thor, close to the house of Albert Dürer. He worked for the Emperor Maximilian I, and was the most serious rival of the Missaglia family of Milan, who at this time were the most celebrated armourers of Europe. The mark No. 54 is ascribed by Boeheim to Grunewalt. Works bearing this mark are to be found in the Waffensammlung, Vienna, 66, 995.

Daniel Hopfer,
Augsburg, *circ.* 1495–1566.

Hopfer was in the first instance a painter, a designer and maker of stained glass, and an engraver. He settled in Augsburg in 1495. According to Heller he died in 1549, but this is not borne out by the entries in the account books of Maximilian II, who employed him and his brother. In the Hofzahlantsbuch, under the date 1566, it is stated that Daniel and his brother George, both of Augsburg, were ordered by Maximilian II to make 110 new helmets for the Trabantengarde and to decorate them with engraving. Four were made in March as samples, and the remainder were to be delivered in July at a cost of 397 gulden 42 kreutzer. Much of the work of the brothers Hopfer consisted in decorating armour made by other masters, of whom Coloman Colman was the chief. In Madrid are several examples of the work of Daniel: A, 26 and 65 are horse-armours which are decorated in Hopfer's style, and A, 27, 57 are jousting-shields which are certainly from his hand ; the latter is signed and dated 1536.

Conrad Lochner,
Nuremberg, 1510–67.
Mark No. 46.

In 1544 Conrad, or Kuntz as he is sometimes called, was Hofplatner to Maximilian II with a retaining fee of 14 florins 10 kronen, and in 1547 Maximilian gave him a settled yearly pension. He must have given up his appointment in 1551, for we find Hans Siefert Court Armourer in this year. He was born at Nuremberg in 1510, where his father followed the trade of an armourer, and had two brothers who worked with him, but the names of the Lochners do not often appear in the royal accounts. Like most of his craft, he was frequently in money difficulties, and had great trouble in collecting his debts from the King of Poland. His works are found at Berlin, 116, a horse-armour ; Paris, G, 166, 182, 565, 566 ; Madrid, A, 243 ; Dresden, E, 5 and G, 165 ; Vienna, 334. He frequently used tritons and sea-monsters as a motif for his decorations.

Gabrielle and Francesco Merate,
Milan and Arbois,
circ. 1494–1529.
Marks, possibly 18, 51, 53.

In 1494 the Merate brothers were sent for by Maximilian I and did work for him personally. They also obtained a contract for three years, for which they received 1000 francs and 1000 gulden, under which they pledged themselves to set up a forge, workshops, and mill at Arbois, in Burgundy. Gabrielle was also to receive 100 francs a year and to be free of taxes, an advantage frequently granted to master-armourers. For this he had to deliver annually fifty suits stamped with his mark, each suit costing 40 francs, and one hundred helmets at 10 francs each, one hundred pair of grandgardes at 5 francs, and one hundred pair of garde-bras at 40 francs the pair.

The enumeration of the last two items in pairs is unusual, as they were defences only worn on the left shoulder and arm and would not be sold in pairs. At the same time we should remember that the terms used for different portions of the suit are often confused, and a word which now has a certain definite meaning in collections was often used in a totally different sense. The Merates were bound by this contract to work only for the Emperor. Their stamp is generally supposed to be a crown and the word " Arbois," but it is uncertain as to what actual specimens now in existence are by their hands. Possibly the " Burgundian Bard " (II, 3) in the Tower was made by them. It bears a crescent and the letter "M," and is decorated with the cross ragule and the flint and steel, the Burgundian badges which were brought to Maximilian by his wife, Mary of Burgundy. Their names are mentioned in the list of tax-payers in the parish of S. Maria Beltrade, the church of the Swordsmiths' Gild, at Milan under the date 1524–9, and they are also mentioned in a letter from Maximilian to Ludovico il Moro in 1495 as excellent armourers. They took their name from the village of Merate, which is near Missaglia, a township which was the birthplace of the famous Missaglia family.

Work stamped with the word "Arbois" and the crown is found at Vienna, 917, 948, and the " M " with the crescent is marked on the bard of A, 3 at Madrid, on II, 3 and II, 5, Tower of London.

Thomaso Missaglia,
Milan, *circ.* 1415–1468.
Marks 27, 78.

The family name of Thomaso and his descendants was Negroni, as is proved by a tombstone formerly in the church of San Satiro at Milan on which the two names appear. They came from the township of Missalia, near Ello, on the lake of Como. Petrajolo, the father of Thomaso, was also an armourer, and worked about the year 1390, but we have little knowledge of his history. The house occupied by the Missaglias was in the Via degli Spadari, Milan, and was decorated with the family badges and monograms (Fig. 66). It was demolished in 1901 in the course of street improvements, but was first carefully drawn

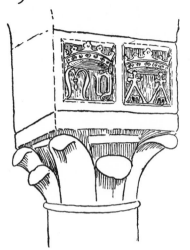

and described by Sigs. Gelli and Morretti in their monograph on the Milanese armourers. The heavy work of the armourers was carried out at a mill near the Porta Romana, for which the Missaglias paid a rent of one sallad a year to the Duke of Milan. Thomaso da Missaglia was ennobled in 1435 by Philip Maria Visconti and was made free of taxes in 1450. There are many records of commissions to him and of taxes and other municipal matters connected with the family in the Archives of Milan. He died in 1469 and was buried in the church of S. Maria Beltrade, Milan. The only known

FIG. 66. Capital formerly in the Via degli Spadari, Milan.

work by this master is No. 2 in the Vienna Collection (Plate XXX). Baron de Cosson[1] has pointed out the strong resemblance between this suit, the effigy of Richard Beauchamp, Earl of Warwick, in S. Mary's Church, Warwick, and the picture of S. George by Mantegna in the Accademia, Venice.

Antonio Missaglia,
Milan, *circ.* 1430–92.
Marks 24, 25, 26.

Antonio was the son of Thomaso Missaglia, and was one of the foremost of the Milanese armourers. As has been noticed in the Introduction, the style of armour which was evolved by him and his father seems to have been adopted by German craftsmen. There are numerous records of payments and letters connected with Antonio in the Archives of Milan from the year 1450 onwards. He worked for Galeazzo Maria Visconti and for Bona di Savoia and after the death of the former became Ducal Armourer. In 1456 he made armour for the Papal troops, and about this time he enlarged the workshops of the family in the Via degli Spadari. In 1469 the Duke of Milan gave him a mill near the S. Angelo Canal. In 1470 he received a lease of iron-mines near the forest of Canzo, near the Lago del Segrino, from the Ducal Chamber, and in 1472, in recognition of his services to the State, he was allowed to purchase the property.

[1] *Arch. Journ.,* XLVIII.

The last entry in the Milanese Archives relating to Antonio refers to his mines and furnaces in a letter to Bona di Savoia, April 20th, 1480. In the MSS. Lib., Trivulziano, is a report of the Venetian Embassy which came to Milan on its way to Germany, written by Andrea de Francesca. This report states that Antonio's workshops were visited and armour was seen there to the value of 1000 ducats. He seems to have had a son Scabrino, but there are no records of him as an armourer. Antonio died at the end of the fifteenth century and is the last of the family who used the name of Missaglia. His successors reverted to the family name of Negroni or Negroli. The suit No. 3 in the Vienna Collection is stamped with his mark (Plate II), and many helmets of the sallad type and various pieces of armour bear a similar stamp in other armouries, such as the Wallace Collection, the Porte de Hal, Brussels, etc. etc. The close helmet on the "Tonlet suit" in the Tower, II, 29 (Plate X), is engraved with the Collar of the Garter and bears the Missaglia stamp, and a suit in the Musée d'Artillerie, G, 3, bears the same mark.

Gasparo Mola,
Rome, *circ.* 1590–1640.

Mola is the only armourer whom we can identify as having worked in Rome. He was born about the year 1590 at Breglio, where his father was an architect. He came to Milan at an early age and worked there as a goldsmith. In 1607 he made various objects in gold and silver for the Duke of Savoy. In the same year he was summoned by Duke Ferdinand de Medici to Florence, where he worked for two years. In the years 1613–14 he produced medals for Mantua and Guastalla, and about the same time he executed work for Carlo Emmanuele I of Savoy. He committed suicide in 1640. Though we have no data for the theory, it seems not unlikely that it was the studio of Mola which Breughel has represented in his picture of Venus at the Forge of Vulcan. The ruins in the background certainly suggest some of the buildings in Rome, which might have been used for this purpose. There are also many medals and examples of goldsmith's work shown on this picture in addition to the armour.

He was an expert in enamel-work and made richly decorated pistols, and in 1642 produced a fine helmet and shield which are now in the Bargello Museum, Florence.

Philippo and Jacomo Negroli,
Milan, *circ.* 1521–80.
Marks 42, 43, 44.

Philippo and Jacomo Negroli were sons of Bernardino who worked in Rome. It is uncertain whether their father still kept the name of Missaglia, which was used by Antonio and Thomaso Negroni. The earliest known work by these masters is dated 1532. For some years they were assisted by their brother Francesco, who left them about this date and worked alone for the Mantuan Court. Brantome and Vasari both mention Philip as being a craftsman of very high repute. His armour was always very costly, and Brantome states that a morion made by him would cost 40 thalers and that in sixteen years he had amassed 50,000 thalers. He seems to have been ennobled, for Brantome calls him Seigneur de Negroli. He had a house in the Porta Comassina, the wealthy quarter of Milan. His work is always ornate, but does not transgress the craft-laws to such an extent as did the armour of Peffenhauser and Piccinino (Plate XXIX). Work by the Negrolis is to be found as follows: In Madrid, A, 139–46; D, 13, 30, 64. Vienna, 330. Paris, G, 7, 10, 178.

Anton Peffenhauser,
Augsburg, 1525–1603.

We have no details of the life of this craftsman beyond the dates of his birth and death. He is best known as the maker of elaborately decorated armour. The suit made for King Sebastian of Portugal (Madrid, A, 290) is one of the most ornate suits in existence (Plate XIV, also p. 75). His works are found as follows: Madrid, A, 290. Dresden, C, 10, 13, 15*a*, 20; D, 11; E, 6*a*, 10; G, 146. Vienna, 489, 490.

Lucio Piccinino,
Milan, *circ.* 1590.

Lucio was the son of Antonio Piccinino, the famous sword-smith. It is uncertain whether he actually produced armour himself or whether he was solely concerned with the decoration. Like Peffenhauser he delighted in lavish display of ornament without any consideration to its fitness for armour. His work is extraordinarily minute and the technical skill displayed is extreme. His work is only to be found at Madrid, A, 291–4, and at Vienna, 543.

Pompeo della Chiesa,
Milan, 1590.

The son of a noted craftsman, Pompeo was one of the foremost armourers in the latter years of the sixteenth century. He was Court

Armourer to Philip III of Spain, and to the Archduke of Milan, Alessandro Farnese. His work is found in the Armeria Reale, Turin, C, 21, 70 ; in Vienna, 858, 859.

Conrad, Hans, and Jorg Seusenhofer, 1470–1555. Marks 7, 8. The brothers Conrad and Hans at different periods filled the position of Court Armourer to Maximilian I. Conrad was born between the years 1450 and 1460. He was cousin to Treytz, who produced the *Weisz Künig*, that chronicle of the doings and artistic endeavours of the young Maximilian which, while it is amusing in its sycophantic adulation of the Emperor is, at the same time, an invaluable record of the operations of the applied arts of the period and of costumes and armour then in fashion.

In 1504 Conrad was appointed Court Armourer for a period of six years with a further agreement for a pension of 50 fl. afterwards for life. In the same year he received money for enlarging his workshops, but after much correspondence it was deducted from his salary. The young Emperor had theories about the making of armour as he had about every other art and craft, and working in conjunction with his armourer, and, presumably, taking credit for his craftsman's expert knowledge, evolved the fluted style of plate armour which still bears his name. It was based upon Italian models of the Gothic type which, at the

FIG. 67. Engraving on the left cuisse of Henry VIII's Suit, made by Conrad Seusenhofer (Tower, II, 5).

end of the fifteenth century, was distinguished by certain graceful flutings which Conrad and his master elaborated till they covered the whole surface of the armour.

At this time the craftsmen of Brussels were noted experts in the tempering of steel, and both Maximilian and Henry VIII employed ironworkers from this city in their armouries.

Much of the raw material was drawn from Styria, and was exported in such large quantities to England that the supply was in danger of running short; so a monopoly was established and exportation forbidden. This naturally raised the price, and was one of the many causes which combined to keep up a ceaseless friction between Maximilian, his Diet, and his armourers.

Seusenhofer favoured elaborate ornament on his armour, and this did not please the officials who were responsible for the equipment of the army. He was urged to produce plainer and more serviceable work, a suggestion which Maximilian with his love of pageantry ignored. In 1511 we find Seusenhofer complaining that Kügler, the mine-master, was sending him inferior metal, and as he considered that the use of it would be detrimental to the reputation of Innsbruck as a factory of armour, he suggested that it should be classed as Milanese. In 1511 the famous "Engraved Suit," now in the Tower of London, was put in hand as a present from Maximilian to Henry VIII.

From the State Archives of Innsbruck (Jahrbuch II, reg. 1028) we find that two cuirasses were ready for the King of England, one gilded. There were apparently five others to be made, one of which was to be silvered. This was probably the suit above mentioned.

The whole of the suit is covered with fine engraving representing the stories of S. George and S. Barbara, with foliage and heraldic badges. The designs have been engraved and a detailed description given by Sir S. Meyrick in *Archæologia*, XXII.

The horse-armour is not by the same hand, for the engraving is coarser. It may have been executed in England by German craftsmen to match the rider's armour (see Plates X, XII, Fig. 67).

There were ceaseless troubles over the payment and delivery of work from the royal workshop. Sometimes Seusenhofer would retain work for which the Emperor had pressing need till payment was made, and on one occasion, when speedy delivery was not made, Maximilian ordered the armourers to be placed in the forefront of the battle, with no armour on, to show them what inconvenience their delay was causing! It is needless to say that the armour was delivered at once. So obsessed with the idea of his omniscience was the Emperor that when, in the *Weisz Künig*, Seusenhofer suggests some secret method of working the metal, he replies : "Arm me according to my own wishes, for it is I and not you who will take part in the tournament." Again, Maximilian writes : "If you have forgotten the art which I have taught you let me know and I will instruct you again."

The date of Conrad's death is unknown, but it was, as far as can be ascertained, about the year 1517.

He was succeeded as Court Armourer by his younger brother Hans, and he in turn gave place to his nephew Jorg, who produced the suits which exist at the present day in Paris, G, 41, 117; Vienna, 283, 407. The only authentic work of Conrad is in the Tower of London, II, 5.

Jacob Topf,
Innsbruck, 1530–90.

We have but little information respecting Topf, in spite of the minute researches of the late Dr. Wendelin Boeheim. From civic records at Innsbruck he appears to have been one of three brothers. David, the youngest, was in service with Archduke Ferdinand at Ambras and died in 1594. In 1575 we find Jacob working for the Archduke at Innsbruck. Boeheim discovered in his investigations that Topf was absent from Germany between the years 1562 and 1575 and was probably employed in Italy, England, and elsewhere. There are no records of his employment in England except in a letter written by Sir Henry Lee in 1590, where mention is made of " Master Jacobe,"[1] who is now considered to be Topf. We have, however, a most valuable record of work which was in all probability his in the *Almain Armourer's Album*, now in the Art Library of the Victoria and Albert Museum.

This book consists of large drawings in ink and water-colour (17 in. by $11\frac{1}{2}$ in.), thirty-one in number, which show twenty-nine suits of armour with details of extra pieces for the joust.

On No. 14 is the signature : " These Tilte peces made by me Jacobe," but the name Topf does not occur in the Album.

In the year 1790 the book was in the possession of the Duchess of Portland, at which time Pennant engraved the second suit of Robert Dudley, Earl of Leicester, for his *History of London*. Strutt also engraved the suit of George, Earl of Cumberland, in his *Dresses and Costumes* (II, Plate CVLI). The library of the Duchess of Portland was sold in

[1] See page 66.

1799 and the Album disappeared till the year 1894, when it passed into the Spitzer Collection. At the Spitzer sale it was bought by M. Stein, of Paris, and on the advice and through the personal efforts of Viscount Dillon, the present Curator of the Tower Armouries, it was acquired for the nation.

Several of the drawings have been carefully reproduced by Mr. Griggs in a book, edited by Viscount Dillon, under the title of *An Almain Armourer's Album*, and it is by the courtesy of the editor and publisher that the accompanying illustrations are reproduced in the present work.

The following list gives the complete series of plates in the Album and shows which of the suits illustrated in the original are now in existence.

DRAWINGS	SUITS IN EXISTENCE (None complete in all parts.)
1. The Earle of Rutlande.	
2. The Earle of Bedforde.	
3. The Earle of Lesseter (1st suit).	
4. The Earle of Sussex . . .	The gauntlets were in the Spitzer Collection.
5. Duke John of ffineland Prince of Sweden.	
6. Ser William Sentle.	
7. My Lorde Scrope.	
8. The Earle of Lesseter (2nd suit) .	A portion of a suit in the Tower of London (II, 10) is of very similar design—evidently by the same hand.
9. My Lord Hundson.	
10. Ser George Howarde.	
11. My Lorde Northe.	
12. The Duck of Norfocke.	
13. The Earle of Woster . . .	A portion of this suit in the Tower (II, 9). At Windsor Castle a burgonet, buffe, breast, back, placcate, gorget, bevor, taces, lance-rest, sollerets.
14. Ser Henry Lee (1st suit).	
15. Sur Cristofer Hattone (1st suit) .	Windsor Castle. The gorget is a restoration (Plates XXV, XXVI).

DRAWINGS	SUITS IN EXISTENCE (None complete in all parts.)
16. The Earle of Penbrouke . .	Wilton House.
17. Ser Cristofer Hattone (2nd suit) .	The suit of Prince Henry at Windsor was copied from this and from No. 17 by W. Pickering (see Plate XX).
18. Ser John Smithe	Tower, II, 12. This suit has brassards which are not shown in the sketch in the Album (Plates XXVI, XXVIII).
19. Sr. Henry Lee, Mr. of tharmerie (2nd suit).	Armet in the Tower (IV, 29). Locking-gauntlet in the Hall of the Armourers' and Braziers' Co., London (Plate XIII, Figs. 32, 68). Burgonet, buffe, and leg-armour at Stockholm.
20. The Earle of Cumberlande . .	Appleby Castle.
21. Sr. Cristopher Hatton (3rd suit).	
22. Mr. Macke Williams.	
23. My L. Chancellor [Sir Thomas Bromley].	
24. My L. Cobbon.	
25. Sir Harry Lea Mr. of the Armore (3rd suit).	Hall of the Armourers and Braziers' Company, London. On each side of the breast in the band of engraving are the initials A. V. (Fig. 69), which probably stand for Anne Vavasour, natural daughter of Sir T. Vavasour and Lady of the Bedchamber to Queen Elizabeth. The *Nat. Dict. of Biog.* states that she was Sir Henry Lee's mistress.
26. My Lorde Cumpton . . .	Portions of this and of the next suit were formerly at Home Lacy and are now in the Metropolitan Museum, New York.
27. Mr. Skidmur [John Scudamor].	
28. My Lorde Bucarte . . .	Wallace Collection, 435.
29. Sr. Bale Desena.	

There is also a suit at Vienna (491), made for Archduke Carl of Steiermark, which Boeheim considered to be from Topf's hands.

Fuller details of the above suits will be found in the reproduction of the Album above referred to, and also in *Arch. Journ.*, LI, 113.

FIG. 68.   Gauntlet and armet of Sir Henry Lee (from the *Armourer's Album*, Victoria and Albert Museum).   See also Plate XIII and Fig. 32.

FIG. 69.   Rubbing of design on breast of Sir Henry Lee's suit, Armourers' Hall, London.

LIST OF ARMOURERS' MARKS

THE following have been taken from rubbings, drawings, and prints, and the authorship of the marks is that given in the several catalogues. The nationality of the armour is given first as German, Italian, Spanish, or French; following this is the approximate date; and lastly the Museums in which the mark is found with the catalogue number. The Roman figures denote the century to which the mark is ascribed.

A = Athens, Ethnological Mus.

B = Brussels, Porte de Hal.

Ber = Berlin, Zeughaus.

D = Dresden, Johanneum.

G = Geneva.

L = London, Tower.

M = Madrid, Real Armeria.

N = Nuremberg.

P = Paris, Musée d'Artillerie.

S = Stockholm, Lifrustkammer.

T = Turin, Armeria Reale.

V = Vienna, Waffensammlung.

Ven = Venice, Museo civico and Arsenale.

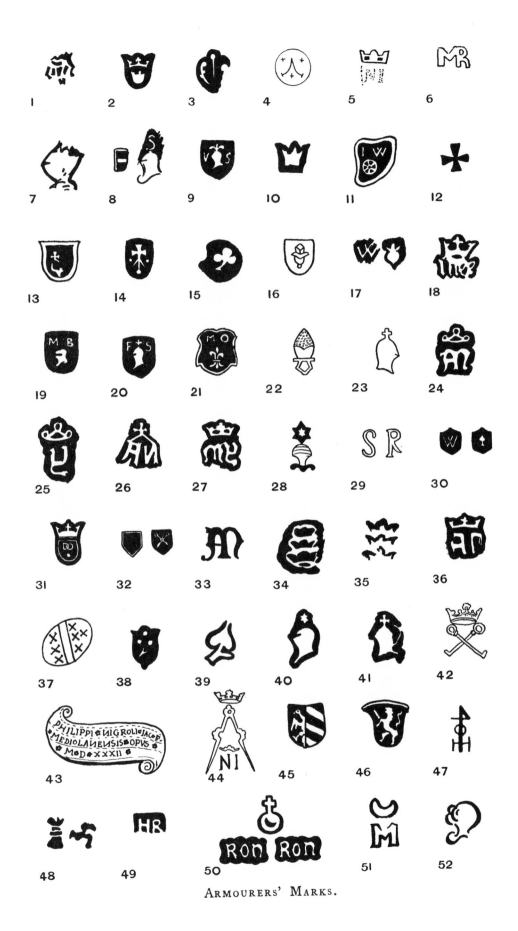

ARMOURERS' MARKS.

1. XIV. **P**, H, 23.
2. XV. **P**, H, 27.
3. XV. **P**, H, 41.
4. Germ., XV. **P**, G, I.
5. XV. **P**, H, 36.
6. Rotschmied, Germ. 1597. **G**.
7. Conrad Seusenhofer, Germ. 1518. **L**, II, 5.
8. Jörg Seusenhofer, Germ. 1558. **V**, 283, 407. **P**, G, 41, 117.
9. Valentine Siebenbürger, Germ. 1531–47. **V**, 226.
10. Germ., XV. **P**, H, 11.
11. Germ., XV–XVI. **P**, H, 42.
12. It., XVI. **P**, H, 55, 305.
13. It., XVI. **P**, H, 54.
14. Germ., XVI. **P**, G, 23.
15. Adrian Treytz, Germ. 1469–1517. **V**, 66, 1018.
16. Veit, Germ., XV–XVI. **N**, **V**.
17. Wilhelm von Worms, Germ., XVI. **V**, 226, 296.
18. Merate brothers, It. 1495. **V**, 917.
19. Germ., XV–XVI. **P**, G, 18.
20. F. Siebenburger, Germ., XVI. **P**, G, 22, 568.
21. Germ., XVI–XVII. **P**, H, 166. **D**, E, 556 (see also 97).
22. City of Augsburg, XV–XVII *passim*.
23. Lorenz Colman or Helmschmied, 1516. **P**, G, 536; **V**, 1005.
24. Antonio da Missaglia, It. 1492 *passim* (see also 36).
25. Antonio da Missaglia.
26. Antonio da Missaglia.
27. Petrajolo and Tomaso da Missaglia. 1400–68. **V**, 2, 3, 897; **P**, H, 29 (see also No. 78).
28. Germ., XVI. **P**, H, 158.
29. Germ., XV–XVI. **P**, G, 382.
30. Sigismund Wolf, Germ. 1554. **P**, G, 63, 64, etc.; **M**, A, 231.
31. It. (?), XVI. **P**, G, 36.
32. Germ., XVI. **P**, G, 147, H, 97.
33. It., XV. **A** (possibly a Missaglia mark, see No. 24).
34. It., XV. **A**.
35. It., XV. **M**, D, 14.
36. Antonio da Missaglia, It., XV–XVI. **P**, H, 29.
37. XVI. **P**, G, 84.
38. Matthaias Fraüenpreis, Germ. 1549–75. **V**, 397, 950; **D**, G, 39.
39. Franz Grofsschedl, Germ. 1568. **V**, 989; **D**, C, 1, 2.
40. Coloman Colman or Helmschmied, Germ. 1470–1532. **V**, 175; **D**, G, 15; **M**, A, 19, 59, 73, etc.
41. Lorenz Colman or Helmschmied, Germ. 1516. **V**, 62 (see also No. 23).
42. Philipp Negroli, It. 1530–90.
43. Philipp and Jacomo Negroli „ } **V**, 330; **M**, A, 139–46; **D**, 13, 30, 64.
44. Philipp and Jacomo Negroli (?). **P**, G, 7, 10, 178.
45. City of Nuremberg, XV–XVII *passim*.
46. Kunz or Conrad Lochner, Germ. 1567. **V**, 334; **P**, G, 182, etc.; **M**, A, 243; **S**, 64.
47. Heinrich Obresch, Germ. 1590.
48. Anton Peffenhauser, Germ. 1566–95. **V**, 489; **M**, A, 290.
49. Hans Ringter, Germ. 1560. **V**.
50. XVI–XVII. **P**, G, 124.
51. Possibly the Merate brothers, It. XV–XVI. **V**, 60; **L**, VI, 28; **M**, A, 3.
52. Germ., XVI. **V**, 9.

ARMOURERS' MARKS.

53. Possibly the Merate brothers, It., XV–XVI. **V**, 948.
54. Possibly Hans Guïnewalt, Germ., XV–XVI. **V**, 66, 995.
55. It., XV. **V**, 5.
56. J. Voys, Netherland, XV–XVI. **B**, II, 39, 40; **M**, A, 11
57. XV. **M**, A, 4.
58. XV. **M**, A, 6.
59. On a mail skirt, XV–XVI. **T**, G, 86.
60. Peter von Speyer, Germ., 1560. **B**er.
61. It., XV. **G**en.
62. It., XV. **G**en.
63. Germ., XV–XVI. **P**, H, 76.
64. It., XV. **G**en.
65. Germ., XVI. **V**, 63.
66. It., XV–XVI. **V**en. Mus. civico.
67. It., XVI. **V**en. Arsenale.
68. On a sallad with Missaglia mark, It., XV. **V**en. Mus. civico.
69. Germ., XVI. **B**, II, 101.
70. Germ., XV–XVI. **V**, 1022.
71. Armourers' Company, London, XVII. **L**.
72. Germ., XV. **D**, A, 75.
73. Netherlands, XV. **D**, A, 75.
74. Siebenburger (?), Germ., XVI. **B**, II, 92.
75. It., XVI. **M**, A, 147.
76. Jorg Sigman, Germ., XVI. **M**, A, 238.
77. It., XV. **A**.
78. T. and P. da Missaglia, It., 1400–1468. **P**, H, 29; **V**, 2, 3; **L**, II, 29 (see Nos. 24–7).
79. Sigmund Rosenburger, Germ. XVI. **D**, C, 3, 4.
80. City of Augsburg (?), XVI. **D**.[1]
81. City of Augsburg (?), XVI *passim*.
82. Germ., XVI. **D**.
83. M. Petit. Fr. XVII. **P**, H, 150; **V**, 711; **M**, A, 379.
84. Sp., XV. **M**, D, 24.
85. It., XV. **A**.
86. It., XV. **A**.
87. XVII. **M**, B, 11; **T**, C, 14.
88. XV. **P**, H, 141.
89. Germ., XV–XVI. **L**, II, 37.
90. XVI. **L**, III, 186.
91. Germ., XVI. **L**, II, 3.
92. Sp., XV. **M**, C, 10.
93. Sp., XV. **M**, C, 10.
94. It., XV. **A**.
95. XV. **M**, D, 18.
96. Germ., XV. **B**, II, 170.
97. Germ., XVI. **B**, II, 182; **D**, E, 556 (see also No. 21); **S**, on a crossbow, 143.
98. Germ., XVI. **B**, II, 30.
99. Germ., XVI. **B**, II, 3.
100. Possibly the city of Wittenburg, XVI. **B**, II, 4, 41.
101. Sp., XV. **M**, C, 10.
102. Sp., XV. **M**, C, 10.
103. It., XV. **A**.
104. Germ. XV. **V**.

[1] A similar mark was used by the Armourers' Company, London, about 1640.

POLYGLOT GLOSSARY OF WORDS DEALING WITH ARMOUR AND WEAPONS

THE meanings of the words in this Glossary are given either from comparison of various scattered entries in contemporary documents or from the following works :—

Boeheim. *Waffenkunde.* 1890.

Cotgrave. *Dictionarie of the French and English Tongues.* 1611. **C.**

Du Cange. *Glossaire Français.* Edit. 1879.

Florio. *A Worlde of Woordes.* 1598. **F.**

Gay. *Glossaire Archéologique*, A–G (never completed). 1887. **G.**

Harford. *English Military Discipline.* 1680. **H.**

Meyrick. *Antient Armour* (glossary). 1842.

Roquefort. *Glossaire de la Langue Romaine.* 1808. **R.**

Valencia *Catalogue of Real Armeria, Madrid.*

Where no reference letter is given the meaning given is that generally accepted at the present day.

The names of the different parts of the suit of plate armour are given in English, French, German, and Italian and Spanish are given on pp. 110, 111.

A

Abzug, Germ. the trigger of a gun.

Achsel, Germ. see pauldron.

Achselhohlscheibe, Germ. see rondel.

Achselschilde, Germ. see ailette.

Acroc, a hook or clasp.

Adargue, a heart-shaped buckler, **G.**

Affust, } gun-carriage.
Afut, }

Agaric, tinder used with flint-lock gun.

Agier, O.F. darts.

Aguinia, machines or engines of war.

Aguzo, It. the point of the spear.

Aiguilettes, tags at the ends of laces for fastening the various pieces of armour.

Ailettes, wing-like pieces of plate or cuir-bouilly worn on the shoulders. Very rare and seldom seen on monuments. XIII–XIV cent.

Aketon, see gambeson.

Alabarda, It. halberd.

Alaguès, Halaguès, O.F. soldiers of fortune, free-lances, **R.**

Alarica, a heavy triangular-pointed spear.

Alberc, Germ. see hauberk.

Alberia, a shield without armorial bearings.

Alborium, a bow of hazel, XI cent.

Alemèle, Fr. the lame or blade of the sword.

Alemella, It. a knife or dagger, XIV cent.

Alfange, Sp. cutlass.

Alferanna, Sp. a banner.

Algier, O.F. dart.

Allecret, a variety of half-armour, end of XVI cent.

Almarada, Sp. a stiletto or dagger.

Almayne rivet, suit of light half-armour, XVI cent.

Almete, Sp. a close, round helmet, armet.

Alzo, It. the " sight " of the firearm.

Amadue, Fr. see agaric.

Ameure, a dagger.

Amorce, priming.

Amorcoir, Fr. powder-flask.

Amussette, Fr. a breech-loading musket, XVIII cent.

Anelace, a broad-bladed dagger, early XIV cent.

Angon, a javelin used in the VI cent. The head was heavy and the top part of the shaft thin, so that it bent on impact and thus hampered the stricken man, **G.**

Animes, a cuirass of horizontal lames, **R.**

Antebrachia, see vambrace.

Antela, see poitrel.

Antia, the handle of a buckler.

Anzerdecke, Germ. see barde.

Appogiar, the cantle of the saddle.

Arbalest, a crossbow.

Arbalest à cric, a heavy crossbow used in sieges.

Arbalest à cranequin, a crossbow drawn with a windlass.

Arbrier, the tiller of a crossbow.

Arcabuz, Sp. see arquebus.

Archet de fer, the moulded ring on the breech of a cannon, base-ring.

Archegaye, a staff sharpened at both ends carried by estradiots, XV cent.

Archibuso, It. see arquebus.

Arcioni, It. the fore and aft peaks of the saddle.

Arcon, the saddle-bow.

Arescuel, the grip of a lance, **R.**

Arest de lance, vamplate, later the lance-rest, **G.**

Arganello, It. the windlass of a crossbow.

Argolets, French mounted arquebussiers, XVI–XVII cent., **R.**

Arma bianca, It. ⎫
Arme blanche, Fr. ⎬ sword.

Armacudium, an indefinite weapon of offence.

Arma d'asta, It. any long-shafted weapon.

Armatoste, Sp. the windlass of a crossbow.

Armes à l'épreuve, pistol-proof armour.

Armet, a close helmet with bevor and movable visor.

Armil, see surcoat.

Armin, an ornamental hand-grip for the pike made of velvet or leather.

Arming-bonett, a padded cap worn under the helmet.

Arming-doublet, worn under the armour.

Arming-hose, long hose worn under leg-armour.

Arming-points, laces for tying on parts of the suit of armour.

Arming-sword, a short sword worn on the right side.

Armkachen, Germ. elbow-cops.

Armoyer, O.F. armourer, maker of sword-hilts, **R.**

Armröhen, Germ. cannon of the vambrace.

Armrust, Germ. crossbow.

Armure cannelée, Fr. fluted armour.

Armzeug, Germ. brassard.

Arnesi, It. harness as used for "armour."

Arquebus, a musket of XVI cent.

Arret, Fr. small decorated tabs used on straps for armour and horse-furniture, **G.**

Arrêt de lance, Fr. lance-rest.

Arrière-bras, Fr. see rerebrace.

Arrière-hilt, the counter-guard or knuckle-bow of the sword.

Asbergo, a breastplate or cuirass, a vamplate, **F.**

Asper, aspar, the "grip" of the lance.

Asperges, O.F. a mace, **R.**; see holy-water sprinkle.

Astile, It. the shaft of a lance.

Astonne, a lance, **R.**

Astregal, a moulding on a cannon.

Atilt, the position in which the lance was held in charging.

Attry, O.E. artillery.

Auber, see alborium.

Ausfatz, Germ. the "sight" of a firearm.

Avance, Fr. the front peak of the burgonet.

Avant-bras, see vambrace.

Avant plat, see vamplate.

Aventail, breathing aperture in helmet, the earliest form of visor.

Azza, It. a long-shafted axe.

Azzimino, It. fine inlay work on Oriental weapons, **F.**

B

Bacchetta, It. a ramrod.

Back-sword, sword with single-edged blade.

Bacul, O.F. crupper of horse-trappings, **R.**

Bacyn, see bascinet.

Badelaire, Fr. a short cutlass.

Bagonet, ⎫ a dagger fitted to the musket, *circ.*
Bayonet, ⎬ 1672.

Bagordare, O.It. to hold a burlesque tournament.

Baguette, ramrod, also brayette, q.v.

Bainbergs, shin-defences of metal or cuir-bouilly.

Baldrick, ⎫ an ornamented belt to carry the sword,
Bawdric, ⎬ XIV cent.

Balestra, It. see arbalest.

Balloch knife, a knife or dagger with balls instead of quillons, XV–XVI cent.

Balayn, ⎫ whalebone used for crests or the swords
Balon, ⎬ for tourneys.

Balottera, a stone bow, **F.**

Banded mail, mail formed of rings through which a leathern thong was passed horizontally on the hauberk.

Bandes, Fr. see lames.

Bandes de bout d'affust, trail-plate of a cannon, **H.**

Bandes de dessus, axle-tree bands, cape squares, **H.**

Bandolier, musketeer's belt to carry gun-charges in separate cases of wood or metal.

Bannerets, those knighted on the field of battle and entitled to carry banners.

Banquelets, Fr. strips of decorated metal on a sword-belt to keep the belt rigid, **G.**

Barbazzale, It. the "grummet" of a bridle.

Barbera, Sp. see mentonière.

Barbière, Fr. ⎫
Barbote, Sp. ⎬ see bevor.
Barbotto, It. ⎭

Barbuta, a piece of head-armour, a bevor, **F.**

Barbute, ⎫ a form of bascinet of unknown type, also
Barbet, ⎬ a light horseman.

Bardes, ⎫ horse-armour.
Barding, ⎬

Barde de crinière, Fr. see crinet.

Bardiche, a variety of pole-axe.

Barducium, see morning star.

Barthaube, Germ. chin-guard of plate.

Barriers, the division of wood which separated combatants in foot-jousts, also the jousts themselves.

Bascinet, a light helmet of ovoid form tapering to a point at the summit, worn with or without a visor, XIII–XV cent.

Bascuette, O.E. see bascinet.

Base, O.F. a short sword or cutlass, **R.**

Bases, skirts of fabric or, in armour, of plate, XVI cent.

Basilard, a curved civilian sword, XIV cent.

Bask sword, a stout, single-edged blade.

Bassinet, Fr. priming-pan of a firelock.

Bastard sword, a long sword for cut and thrust with grip sufficiently long for two hands, or a blunted sword for practice.

Baston, a mace or club with polygonally cut head.

Baston, gros, O.F. large ordnance, **R.**

Battecul, see garde-rein.

Batticuli, taces or loin-guards of plate, **F.**

Bauchreifen, Germ. see taces.

Baudik, see baldrick.

Baudrier, Fr. cross-belt.

Bavier, Fr. ⎫
Baviera, It. ⎬ see bevor.

Bergaman, O.F. a cutlass or dagger from Bergamo, **R.**

Bear-paw, ⎫ a form of solleret with obtuse point.
Bec du cane, ⎬

Becco di corvo, It. see martel de fer.

Bec de faucon, Fr. a war-hammer.

Beckenhaube, Germ. see bascinet.

Beinröhren, Germ. see jambe.

Beintaschen, Germ. see tassets.

Beinzeug, Germ. see cuissard.

Beringt, Germ. ringed mail.

Beruier, Fr. a light head-piece with ear-flaps and chin-strap, XV cent., **G.**

Besagues, O.E. small plates to protect the armpits, any small plates of metal.

Bessa, a pickaxe used by pioneers, XV cent.

Beavor, ⎫ the chin-piece of an armet or a sallad.
Bevor, ⎬

Bicoquet, Fr. a species of bascinet with neck and chin piece, XV cent., **G.**

Bicorn, ⎫ small anvil.
Bickiron, ⎬

Bigateno, O.F. a javelin or dart, **R.**

Bilbo, a small rapier.

Bill, a weapon with scythe-like blade and six-foot shaft.

Billette, F., see toggle.

Biro, O.F., a dart, javelin, or arrow, **R.**

Bisacuta, ⎫ the military pick or two-edged axe,
Bisague, O.F., ⎬ XIII–XIV cent.

Bishop's mantle, a cape of mail.

Blacon, O.F., a buckler or shield, **R.**

Blanc haubert, Fr., coat of mail.

Blanchon, O.F., a kind of pike, **R.**

Blank wafte, Germ., see arme blanche.

Boetes, boxes, **H.**

Bohordicum, a burlesque joust in which sham lances (bohours) were used.

Bombarde, an early form of ordnance resembling a mortar.

Bonbicinium, see bascinet.

Bordon, ⎫
Bordonasse, ⎬ a lance used for jousting.
Borto, ⎭

Boson, an arrow with a blunt point.

Bossoirs, the bosses on the peytral of a horse.

Botafogo, Sp. see linstock.

Botta a, It. ⎫ armour proof against sword, axe, or
Botte à, Fr. ⎬ lance blow.

Botte cassée, Fr., armour proof against all weapons, "high proof."

Botton, a button or buckle for fastening the gorget to the breast-piece.

Bouche, the hole cut in the corner of the shield through which to point the lance; also the circular hole in the vamplate.

Boucles, Fr. see genouillière.

Boudrier, Fr. see bandolier.

Bougeran,
Bougran, } buckram used for tournament armour.

Bougon,
Boujon, } blunt-headed arrow for shooting game.

Bougeon,
Boujon, } a crossbow quarrel, **R.**
Boulon,

Bourdonasse, Fr. see bordon.

Bourlet, Fr. a coif.

Bourlet, Fr. the swell of the muzzle of a cannon.

Bourlette, Fr. a mace.

Bourrelet, à, Fr. a method of attaching two plates together sliding in burrs or slots.

Boutefeu, Fr. linstock.

Bouterolle, Fr. the chape of a sword.

Boutreaux, Fr. the pendent strips of leather or fabric which decorated the horse-trappings of the XV–XVI cent., **G.**

Bracciale, It. brassard.

Bracciaiuola, It. a small shield with arm-guard and "sword-breaker" in one piece.

Bracciali, It. see brassard.

Bracconnière, Fr. see taces.

Bracelet, Fr. the ring of metal which joined the vambrace to the rerebrace, the elbow-cop, **G.**

Bracer, a leathern wrist-guard used by archers of the long-bow.

Bracheta, O.It. }
Braghetta, It. } see brayette.

Brandistocco, It. a three-pronged spear, a swine-feather.

Braquemart, a short, broad-bladed cutting sword.

Brasalot, O.F. see elbow-cop.

Brassard, the whole arm-defence, including vambrace, elbow-cop, and rerebrace.

Brasselet, see bracer.

Bratspiess, Germ. see ranseur.

Brayette, O.F. for codpiece.

Brazale, Sp. brassard.

Brechenmesser, Germ. see falcione.

Brechränder, Germ. neck-guards on the pauldrons.

Bretelles, Fr. straps for joining breast and back pieces.

Briccola, O.It. a tiller or crossbow to shoot stones or arrows, **F.**

Brichette, armour for loins and hips.

Brichette,
Brikette, } breast-armour, XV cent.

Brigandine, a body-defence of small plates riveted to a cover and lining of fabric.

Briquet, Fr. a sword of cutlass form, early XIX cent.

Brise-cuirass, Fr. a short, strong dagger.

Brise-épée, Fr. see sword-breaker.

Brochiero, It. a small buckler used for sword and buckler fights.

Broigne, a shirt of mail.

Broke, O.F. a kind of dagger, **R.**

Broquel, Sp. see rondache.

Brújula, Sp. see visor.

Brunt, O.E. the front or peytral of a horse-trapper.

Brustpanzer, Germ. see peytral.

Brustschild mit schönbart, Germ. tilting-breastplate with mentonière.

Bruststück, Germ. breastplate.

Brygandyrons, see brigandine.

Budrière, It. cross-belt for a sword.

Bufe, a movable bevor used with an open casqe.

Bufeta, Sp. neck-guards on a pauldron.

Buffa, the buffe or face-plate of a burgonet.

Bufle, a coat of buff leather.

Buffletin, Fr. see colletto.

Burdo, see borto.

Bukel, Germ. see rondache.

Burghera, a gorget, **F.**

Burgonet, a light, open helmet, generally found with ear-flaps and sometimes a face-guard, XVI–XVII cent.

Burr, the iron ring on the lance below the "grip" to prevent the hand slipping back.

Buttafuoco, It. see linstock.

Buttèire, Fr. a type of arquebus.

Buzo, It. see quarrel.

C

Cabasset, a helmet with narrow brim all round, XVI cent.

Cairelli, O.It. see quarrel.

Caissia, It. a case or quiver for arrows.

Calce, the vamplate of a lance, also the butt end, also stockings, **F.**

Caliver, a short firelock.

Calote, a skull-cap worn under the hat by cavalry, XVII cent.

Caltrop, a ball with four spikes placed on the ground to receive cavalry.

Calva, Sp. skull or bowl of a helmet.

Camaglio, It. see camail.

Camail, a hood or tippet of chain mail, XIV–XV cent.

Camba, O.It. see jambs.

Camberia, see jambières.

Camisado, It. the wearing of white shorts over armour for night attacks.

Campane,
Campanelle, } O.F. the part of the horse-trappings on the haunches, decorated with large bells, XV–XVI cent.

Cambrasia, O.It. a dart or arrow, **F.**

Cannon, the tubular vambrace.

Cantle, the rear peak of the saddle.

Capel de nerfs, a whalebone or leather helmet, XIV cent.

Capelina, It. a skull-cap of steel.

Capellum, the sword sheath or scabbard.

Caperuza, Sp. see chapel-de-fer.

Carcasse, Fr. a bomb.

Carcasse, It. a quiver.

Cardelli, It. see quarrel.

Cargan, a collar or gorget of mail.

Carnet, the visor.

Carosella,
Carousel, } a mimic fight with clay balls and shields.

Carquois, Fr. a quiver.

Carreau, Fr. see quarrel.

Cartouche, Fr., a charge of powder and shot wrapped up in paper; a cartridge.

Casque, open helmet, often of classical design, late XVI cent.

Casquetel, an open head-piece with brim and back peak reaching far down the neck, XVII cent.

Cassa, It. the stock of a firearm.

Castle, O.E. a variety of helmet.

Cataffratto,
Cataphractus eques, } a mail-clad horse.

Cataye, O.F. a javelin or a catapult, **R.**

Catchpole, a long-handled spring fork used to catch the opposing knight round the neck and unhorse him.

Catocio, the charge of powder for musket or cannon, **F.**

Caxeo,
Caxa, } Sp. see casque.

Cazoleta, Sp. the "pan" of the arquebus.

Celada de engole, Sp. a helm worn for foot-jousts with axe, sword, or spear.

Celata, It. see sallad.

Celata da incastro, It. see armet.

Celata Veneziana, It. a Venetian form of sallad with a nose-piece, XV cent.

Cerbatane, some kind of ordnance, **G.**

Cerveliera, It. a metal skull-cap, a secrete.

Cervicale, Fr. see crinet, **G.**

Cesello, It. repoussé-work used in the decoration of armour.

Chamfron,
Chanfrein, } defence of plate for the horse's head.
Chanfron,

Champ-clos, O.F. see lists.

Chape, the metal tip at the lower end of a sword or dagger sheath.

Chapel d'acier, Fr. a steel war-hat.

Chapel-de-fer, Fr. a broad-brimmed helmet used from XII to XVI cent.

Chapel de Montauban, Fr. a steel war-hat made at Montauban, XIV cent.

Chapewe, see chapel-de-fer.

Chapras, the brass badge worn by a messenger.

Chard, the string of a sling.

Charnel, O.E. the bolt that fixed the tilting-helm to the breastplate.

Chausses, covering for the lower leg and foot of chain mail.

Chaussons, trews or breeches of chain mail.

Cheeks, the strips of iron that fix the pike-head to the shaft.

Chéminée, Fr. the nipple of a gun.

Cherval, a gorget.

Chastones, rivets.

Chianetta, a helmet, **F.**

Chiave da mota, It. key for a wheel-lock.

Chien, Fr., cock of a firelock.

Chiodo da voltare, It. a turning-rivet.

Choque, some kind of firearm, variety unknown.

Cimier, the crest on the helm.

Cinquedea, It. a short, broad-bladed dagger for ceremonial use, made in Venice and Verona, five fingers (*cinque ditta*) wide at the base.

Ciseau, a blunt-headed quarrel for the crossbow, **G.**

Clavel, O.F., a lace for fastening the coif of mail or the hauberk, **G.**

Clavones, rivets.

Claid heamh, a sword, Gaelic.

Claid mor, a broadsword, Gaelic.

Claid crom, a sabre, Gaelic.

Claid caol, a small sword, Gaelic.

Claymore, a Scottish two-hand sword (see above). The modern use of the word is erroneous.

Clef, trigger.

Clevengi, studs to fasten the fendace or gorget.

Clibanion, a jack of scale armour, **G**.

Clipeus, It. a circular shield.

Clous perdus, Fr., false and useless rivet-heads found in XVII-cent. armour.

Cnémide, Fr. see jambs.

Coche, the notch of an arrow, the nut of a cross-bow, **C**.

Coda di gambero, It. see lobster-tail.

Codole, Sp. elbow-cop.

Codpiece, a piece of plate to protect the fore-body.

Coif de mailes, hood of chain mail, see camail.

Colichemarde, swords invented by Königsmark about 1661–86.

Colet,
Coletin, } Fr. a gorget, also a jerkin.
Collettin,

Colletto, It. a buff coat.

Collo, It. see crinet.

Colodrillo, Sp. the plate of the helmet that covered the nape of the neck.

Coltellaccio, It. see cutlass.

Cophia, a coif of mail.

Coppo, It. the skull of a helm or helmet.

Corale, see cuisses.

Coracina, Sp. cuirass.

Corium, armour composed of leather.

Cornel, } O.E. the rosette or button fixed on the
Coronall, } tip of the lance in some forms of tilting.

Corpel, O.F. the hilt of a sword, **R**.

Corregge, It. see bretelles.

Corseque, Fr. a species of partizan, **G**.

Corsesca, It. see ranseur.

Cosciale,
Coscioni, } see cuissard.
Costale,

Coschewes, O.E. see cuisses.

Costa, It. the wings on the head of the war-mace.

Coat-armour, see surcoat.

Coterel, O.F. a large knife, **R**.

Cotta di maglia, It. a coat of mail.

Cottyngyre, cold-chisel.

Coude,
Coudière, } elbow-pieces of plate.
Coute,

Coup de poing, Fr. a small pistol.

Coursel, Fr. windlass for a crossbow, **G**.

Coussart, a demi-glaive, XV cent.

Coustile, Fr. a knife and possibly a staff-weapon with cutting point, **G**.

Coustil à croc, } short, single-handed sword with
Coutel, } two-edged blade.

Couvrenuque, Fr. the neck-plate of the back of the armet or sallad.

Cracowes, } sometimes used for poleynes and also
Crakoes, } for pointed shoes, XIV cent.

Crampon, a bolt for attaching the helm to the cuirass.

Cranequin, the wheel and ratchet machine for bending the crossbow.

Cravates, French mounted militia.

Cresta, It.
Cresteria, Sp. } crest of a helmet.
Crête, Fr.

Crête-échelle, a support fixed from helm to back-plate to take the shock when tilting.

Crêtu, O.F. a sword-breaker, **R**.

Crinet, armour for the horse's neck.

Crochets de retraits, trail-hooks of a cannon, **H**.

Crinière, see crinet.

Croissante, see moton.

Crosse, the butt of a gun or a crossbow.

Croupière, armour for the hinder part of a horse.

Cubitiera, It. elbow-cop.

Cubrenuca, Sp. see couvrenuque

Cuirass, body-armour, originally of leather, afterwards of plate.

Cuir-bouilly, } defences for horse and man made of
Cure-buly, } boiled and moulded leather.

Cuissards, leg-armour, comprising cuisses and knee-cops and jambs.

Cuishe,
Cuisse, } thigh-pieces of plate.
Cuyshe,

Cuissots, see cuisse.

Culasse, the breech of a gun.

Culet, kilt or skirt.

Cullotes, Fr. breeches.

Culverin, a hand-gun or light piece of ordnance, XV, XVII cent.

Curatt, see cuirass.

Curtale, O.It., a variety of cannon, **F**.

Curtana, the blunted "sword of Mercy" used at the Coronation.

Curtelaxe, O.E. for cutlass.

Ciclaton, } a tight-fitting surcoat shorter in front
Cyclas, } than behind, XIV cent.

Cyseau, O.F. an arrow or dart, **R**.

D

Daburge, a ceremonial mace.

Dag, Tag, a short pistol, XVI–XVII cent.

Dague à couillettes, Fr. see balloch knife.

Dague à oreilles, a dagger with the pommel fashioned like two circular wings.

Dague à rognons, Fr. a dagger with kidney-shaped projections above the quillons.

Dague à ruelle, Fr. a dagger with thumb-ring.

Dard, Sp. javelin.

Degen, Germ. sword, dagger.

Demi-poulaine, pointed sollerets of medium length.

Demy-teste, O.E. a steel skull-cap, **C.**

Destrier, a war-horse.

Détente, Fr. the trigger.

Diechlinge } Germ. see cuisse.
Dieling

Dilge, Germ. leg-guard for jousts.

Dobbles, O.E. probably moulds or patterns on which armour was made.

Dolch, Germ. poniard.

Dolequin, a dagger, **R.**

Doloire, a short-handled axe, **G.**

Dolon, O.E. a club, **R.**

Dorso, It. the back of a gauntlet.

Dos, Sp. back-plate of a cuirass.

Dossière, Fr. the back-piece of the cuirass.

Dussack, Hungarian and German sword of cutlass form.

E

Écrevisse, Fr. see lobster-tail.

Écu, Fr. shield.

Écouvillon, sponge of a cannon.

Eisenkappe, Germ. a skull-cap of steel.

Eisenschuhe, Germ. see sollerets.

Elbow-cops, elbow-pieces of plate armour.

Elbow gauntlet, a metal or leather glove with cuff reaching to the elbow, XVI, XVII cent.

Elingue, O.F. a sling, **R.**

Ellenbogenkachel, Germ. see coude.

Elmo di giostra, It. a tilting-helm.

Elsa,
Elso, } the hilt of a sword or dagger, **F.**
Elza,

Enarmes, the loops for holding a shield.

Encoche, see coche.

Enlace, see anelace.

Épaulière, } shoulder-defence, of plate.
Éspalière,

Épaule-de-Monton, Fr. see poldermitton.

Epieu, a spear; a spear with crossbar or toggle, **G.**

Esca, It. tinder.

Escarcelas, Sp. tassets.

Escarpes, Sp. sollerets.

Esclaivine, O.F. a dart, **R.**

Escopette, a pistol or carbine with a firelock, **C.**

Espada, Sp. a long sword.

Espadin, Sp. a short sword.

Espaldar, Sp. pauldron.

Espare, O.F. a dart, **R.**

Espieu, see epieu.

Espingardier, an arquebussier, **C.**

Esponton, Fr. see spontoon.

Espringale, a siege crossbow on wheels, a piece of siege ordnance, **G.**

Espuello, Sp. spur.

Estival, leg-armour for a horse; exceedingly rare in MSS.; only one example of this armour exists, in Brussels.

Estoc, a thrusting sword.

Estradiots, Greek horsemen, temp. Charles VIII.

Estramaçon, the edge of a sword, a sword-cut.

Etoupin, a quick-match.

Etrière, a military flail, **G.**

Étrier, Fr. stirrup.

Exsil, O.F. the scabbard of a sword, **R.**

F

Falcione, It. see falk.

Falda, It. see taces.

Falarique, an arrow headed with tow, for incendiary purposes, **G.**

Faldaje, Sp. taces.

Falk, a primitive weapon formed of a scythe-blade fixed on a pole; a glaive.

Falsaguarda, Sp. the wings on the blade of the two-hand sword.

Fan-plate, the " wing " on the outside of the knee-cop.

Fauchard, see glaive.

Faucre, Fr. a lance-rest.

Fautre, Fr. thigh-armour.

Faux, see falk.

Feather-staff, a staff in which are concealed spikes released by a spring.

Federzapfen, Germ. spring-pins to which the pauldrons are hung, XVI cent.

Fendace, a species of gorget, XV cent.

Feure, O.F. a scabbard, **R.**

Fiancali, It. see tasset, also flanchard.

Fioreti, It. a thrusting foil.

Flail, the military flail was like the agricultural implement, but as a weapon of war the thresher was of iron instead of wood.

Flambard,
Flamberge, } a two-hand sword with wavy blade.

Flamberg, Germ. rapier with wavy blade.

Flanchard, O.E.
Flancois, Fr.
Flankenpanzer, Germ. } armour for the flanks of a horse.
Flanqueras, Sp.

Flaon, Fr. a wedge fastened to the breast-piece which took the shock of the shield; see poire.

Fleau, Fr. military flail.

Flechière, see flanchard.

Fletcher, a maker of arrows.

Fleuret, thrusting foil.

Flight, an arrow for distance shooting.

Flo, O.E. arrow.

Forcina, It. a gun-fork.

Forconi, It. a military fork for escalades.

Fornimento, It. the hilt of a sword.

Fouchard, see glaive.

Fouloir, the rammer of a cannon.

Framée, O.F. a mallet or mace, **R.**

Francesca, It. a battle-axe or pole-axe.

Francisque, a long-handled axe, **R.**

Freccia, It. an arrow.

Freiturnier, Germ. a joust run without a barrier, XVI cent.

Frête, O.F. a variety of arrows, **R.**

Frog, the hanger of a sword-belt.

Fronde, Fr. a sling.

Frontale, It. see chamfron.

Fronteau, F. see chamfron.

Fueille, the blade of a sword, **C.**

Fusetto, It. see misericorde.

Fusil, short musket with a firelock.

Fussturnier, Germ. joust on foot, XVI cent.

Fust, the stock of a firearm.

G

Gadlings, knuckle or finger spikes fixed to the gauntlet.

Gagnepain,
Gaynpayne, } Gay derives this from canepin, sheep or goat leather, hence a glove of leather, mail, or plate. Meyrick explains it as a sword.

Galapentin, O.F. a sword or sabre, **R.**

Galea, It. a helm.

Gambeson, a quilted tunic, XI cent.

Gambiera, It. see jambs.

Gardaignes, O.F. arms, clothing, etc., **R.**

Garde-de-bras, reinforcing piece for the left arm, used in tilting.

Garde-faude, Fr. see codpiece.

Garde-ferre, O.F. the rest of the lock of the arquebus (pan cover?), **C.**

Garde-collet, Fr. neck-guards on the pauldron.

Garde-rein, E.Fr. loin-guard of armour.

Garde-queue, Fr. the tail-guard of a horse.

Garrock,
Garrot, } used for the quarrel of the crossbow and also for the lever.

Gaudichet, O.F. a mail shirt.

Gaveloc,
Gaveloche, } a species of javelin.
Gavelot,

Gavette, It. the string of the crossbow.

Genestare, O.F. a javelin, **R.**

Gedritts, a German form of joust in which the challenger fought two opponents in succession.

Gefingerte handschuh, Germ. gauntlet with separate articulated fingers.

Geldière, O.F. a kind of lance, **R.**

Genetaire, a javelin, XV. cent.

Genouillières, jointed knee-pieces of plate.

Gentilhomme, a wooden cannon bristling with spikes, XVI cent., **G.**

Gesäfreifen, Germ. rein or loin guard.

Gestech, various forms of the joust as practised in Germany, run without barriers.

Ghiazarino, It. see jazerant.

Gibet, a military mace.

Gibicière, Fr. a cartridge box, also pouch.

Ginocchietti, see genouillière.

Gisarme, a staff weapon of the glaive order.

Giostra, It. joust.

Glaive, a species of bill with a large blade.

Glazing-wheel, polishing-wheel for armour plates.

Gliedschirm, Germ. see codpiece.

Goat's-foot, a lever for bending the crossbow.

Godbert, see hauberk.

Godendar,
Goedendag, } a species of short club at the top of which is a spike, XIII–XIV cent.
Goudendar,

Goie,
Goy, } a hedging-bill, **C.**

Goiz, O.F. a sword, **R.**

Gola, Sp. }
Goletta, It. } gorget.

Gonpillon, Fr. see holy-water sprinkle.

Gonfanon, Fr. a flag or standard.

Gorget,
Gorgiera, It.
Gorjal, Sp. } a wide plate collar to protect the throat, XVIII cent.; purely ornamental.
Gougerit, Fr.

Gossets, see gussets.

Graffe, Fr. a small dagger.

Grand-guard, reinforcing piece for tilting, worn on the left shoulder.

Grano d'orzo, It. chain mail closed with a rivet.

Grappes, Fr.
Grappers, } a toothed ring on the "grip" of the lance which held the weapon firmly against the wood or lead block behind the lance rest.
Grates,

Greave,
Greve, Fr. } shin-defence, of plate.
Greba, Sp.

Gronda, It. see couvrenuque.

Groppa, It.
Grupera, Sp. } see crupper.

Guanciali, It. ear-flaps of a burgonet.

Guardabrazos, Sp. see pauldron.

Guardacorda, It. see garde-queue.

Guardacuore, It. see mentonière.

Guardagoletta, It. the neck-guards on the pauldrons.

Guarda-o-rodillera, Sp. knee-cop.

Guardastanca, It. see grand-guard.

Guige, the strap round the neck to carry the shield, XII cent.

Guiterre, O.F. a small buckler of leather, **R.**

Gusset, pieces of chain mail, tied with points to the "haustement" to cover those portions of the body not protected with plate armour; they were usually eight in number, viz. for armpits, inner side of elbows, knees and insteps.

Guyders, straps to fasten the various pieces that went to make up the suit of plate armour, also gussets.

Gynours, the servers of catapults and the like siege engines.

H

Hackbuss, see arquebus.

Hake, demi-hake, O.E. the former an arquebus, the latter a short firearm, XVI cent.

Hagbuttes, arquebus.

Haketon, see gambeson.

Halacret, see alacret.

Halagues, crossbowmen, **R.**

Halebarde,
Halbert, } a long-shafted weapon with crescent-shaped blade on one side and a hook or spur on the other, surmounted by a spear-head; sometimes found with double blade, XV and XVI cent.
Harlbart,

Halsberge, Germ. see gorget.

Hampe, the staff of a halbert or pike.

Hand and half sword, see bastard sword.

Hansart, O.F. a missile weapon of the javelin order, **R.**

Harnischekappe, Germ. the padded cap worn under the tilting-helm.

Hars, O.F. a bow, **R.**

Harthstake, a rake or poker for the forge.

Haubergeon, short } shirt of chain mail, XI to XII
Hauberk, long } cent.

Haulse-col,
Hausse-col, } Fr. see gorget.

Hauscol de mailes, Fr. see standard of mail.

Haustement, Fr. a close-fitting undergarment to which the hose and the chausses were fastened with points.

Haute barde, Fr. a high-peaked saddle.

Haute cloueure, Fr. high-proof armour, especially mail.

Hauste, O.F. the staff of a pike, **R.**

Heaume, a heavy helm without movable visor and only an eye-slit or occularium, mostly used for tilting.

Hendeure, Fr. the "grip" of the sword.

Hentzen, Germ. mitten gauntlets.

Hinterarm, Germ. see rerebrace.

Hinterfluge, Germ. the back-plate of the pauldron.

Hinterschurz, Germ. see garde-rein.

Hobilers, common light-horse troopers.

Hoguines, see cuisse.

Holy-water sprinkle, a shaft of wood fitted with an iron spike-studded ball, XVI cent.

Horse-gay, a demi-lance, XV cent.

Hosting harness, armour for war as distinct from that of the joust.

Hufken, a light head-piece worn by archers, XVI cent.

Huque, a long surcoat worn over the armour, XV cent.

Huvette, Fr. a head-piece of leather or cloth stiffened with wicker or metal, XIV cent.

Hwitel, Anglo-Saxon, knife.

I

Imbracciatura, It. see enarmes.

Imbricated mail, see jazerant.

J

Jack, a loose-fitting tunic of leather, either quilted or reinforced with plates of metal or horn.

Jambers,
Jambeux, } see jambs.

Jamboys, skirts of plate, XVI cent., see bases.

Jambs, armour for the lower leg.

Janetaire, see javelin.

Jarnac, Brassard à la, a jointless arm-piece of plate reaching from shoulder to wrist.

Jarnac, Coup de, a cut on the back of the leg or a " hamstringing cut."

Jazerant, body-armour made of small plates, of the brigandine type.

Jeddartstaff, a long-shafted axe.

Jupon, a short surcoat, XIV–XV cent.

Justes of peace, jousts at barriers.

K

Kamm, Germ. the crest or ridge of the helmet as distinct from the heraldic crest.

Kamfhandschuhe, Germ. gauntlet.

Kehlstück, Germ. the neck-plate in the front of an armet.

Kettyl-hat, a wide-brimmed steel war-hat, XIV cent.

Kinnreff, Germ. bevor.

Knee-cops,
Kniebuckel, Germ.
Kniestück, Germ. } knee-defences, of plate, first worn over chain-mail chaussons, and afterwards with complete plate armour.

Knuckle-bow, the part of the sword-guard that protects the knuckle.

Kragen, Germ. gorget.

Krebs, Germ. see tasset.

L

Lama, It. sword-blade.

Lama a biscia, It. see flamberge.

Lamboys, see jamboys.

Lambrequin, a species of hood of cloth attached to the helmet with " points," and falling down at the back to protect the wearer from heat and rain.

Lames, narrow strips of steel riveted together horizontally as in the taces.

Lance a boëte, a lance with blunted point.

Lance de carrière, a lance for tilting at the ring, **C.**

Lance a rouèt, or *courtoise*, blunted lances for tournaments, **R.**

Lance-rest, an adjustable hook or rest fixed on the right side of the breastplate.

Lancegay,
Launcegay, } O.F. a short spear, hence light horseman, **R.**

Lanciotto, It. javelin.

Lansquenette,
Landsknecht,
Lanzichenecco, It. } a broad-bladed double-edged sword, and also German mercenary infantry, XVI cent.

Leva, It. see goat's-foot lever.

Lendenplatte, Germ. a large cuisse for tilting.

Lingua di bue, It. see cinquedea.

Linstock, a combination of pike and match-holder, used by gunners for firing cannon.

Lobster-tail, back peak of a helmet, or cuisses, made of overlapping lames like a lobster-shell, XVII cent.

Lochaber axe, a long-shafted axe. Scottish, XVII, XVIII cent.

Locket, the metal socket at the top of the sword sheath with button for hanging to the belt.

Locking gauntlet, a gauntlet of plate in which the finger-plates lap over and fasten to a pin on the wrist, used for fighting at barriers, XVI cent.

Loque, O.F. a quarter-staff, **R.**

Luchet, O.F. an iron pike, **R.**

Luneta, Sp. rondel.

Lunette, Fr. open sword-guard, late XVII cent.

M

Maglia gazzarrina, It. see jazerant.

Maglia piatta, It. see ringed mail.

Mähenpanzer, Germ. see crinet.

Maillet, Fr. a martel de fer, XIV cent.

Mainfaire,
Manifer, } a right-hand gauntlet.

Main gauche, dagger used with the left hand when the right hand held the sword.

Maleus, a falchion, **F.**

Mamillières, circular plates worn over the breast to hold chains to which the sword and dagger were attached, XIV cent.

Mancina, It. see main gauche.

Manetta, It. the trigger of a gun, also a spanner.

Manezza di ferro, an arming-gauntlet, **F.**

Manicle, gauntlet.

Manico, It. the grip of a sword.

Manoglia, It. the handle of a small buckler.

Manopla, Sp.
Manople, It. } gauntlet.

Manteau d'armes, a rigid cape-like shield fixed to the left breast and shoulder for tilting.

Mantling, see lambrequin.

Martel de fer, Fr. } a war-hammer used by horse
Martello d'arme, It. } and foot.

Martinetto, } It. see cranequin.
Martinello, }

Mascled, mail, } { lozenge-shaped plates of metal, sometimes overlapping, sewn upon a tunic of leather or quilted linen, XI, XII cent. (Meyrick).
Macled, mail, }

Massüe, Fr. a mace or club.

Matchlock, a firearm with touch-hole and fired with a match, early XV cent.

Mattucashlass, a Scottish dagger carried under the armpit.

Maule, a mace or club.

Maximilian armour, a style of plate armour distinguished by shallow vertical flutings, said to have been devised by the Emperor Maximilian I, XVI cent.

Mazza d'arme, It. war-mace.

Mazzafrustro, It. see flail, also morning star.

Mêche soufrée, a slow-match.

Mell, see maule.

Mentonière, a piece used with the sallad to protect chin and breast.

Merlette, O.F. a sergeant's staff, **R.**

Meris, O.F. a javelin, **R.**

Meusel, Germ. see elbow-cop.

Mezail, Fr. visor.

Miccia, It. a gun-match.

Migerat, O.F. a dart or arrow, **R.**

Minion, a four-pounder, XVI cent.

Misericorde, short dagger used for the *coup de grâce*.

Missodor, O.F. a war horse, **R.**

Mitten-gauntlet, } gauntlet in which the fingers are
Mittene, It. } not separate.

Moresca, It. see taces.

Morion, light helmet with crest and inverted crescent brim, latter end of XV cent.

Morning star, a spike-studded ball hung by a chain from a short staff, XIV–XV cent.

Morso, It. the horse's bit.

Moschetto, It. see matchlock.

Mostardo, a musket, **F.**

Moton, plates to protect the armpits, especially the right, XIV cent.

Moulinet, the windlass used for drawing the crossbow.

Moyenne, see minion.

Murice, a caltrop, **F.**

Musacchino, see pauldrons.

Muschettæ, It. projectiles used with the crossbow.

Muserag, a missile weapon of some kind, **F.**

Musoliera, It. a horse-muzzle.

N

Nackenschirm, Germ. neck-plate at the back of an armet.

Naide, anvil.

Naitoules, some appliance for closing rivets.

Nasal, a bar of steel fixed or movable on the front of the helmet to protect the nose, in more general use during XI cent., revived afterwards in XVII cent.

Neighletts, the metal tags of the arming-points.

Nowchys, embossed buckles and ornaments for armour, XV cent.

Noyeau, the core of a gun.

O

Oberarmzeng, Germ. rerebrace.

Occularium, the eye-slit in the helm.

Oreillettes, ear-pieces, found in the later forms of the casque and burgonet.

Orle, the wreath or twisted scarf worn on the helmet immediately beneath the crest.

Oriflamme, the ancient banner of the Abbey of S. Denis used by the kings of France.

Ospergum, see hauberk.

Ottone, It. brass or latten, used for edging armour, etc., **F.**

P

Paefustum, a battle-axe, XV cent.

Palet, a small skull-cap of cuir-bouilly or steel.

Palettes, circular plates to protect the armpits.

Panart, O.F., a large knife, **R.**

Panache, Fr. the plume of feathers on the helmet.

Pansier, Fr. the lower portion of the cuirass when it is formed of two pieces.

Panzer, body-armour, XI–XIV cent.

Panziera, It. see codpiece.

Parement, a surcoat or ceremonial dress of rich fabric.

Parma, It. a small shield or buckler.

Partigiana, It. } { a long-shafted weapon with broad-pointed blade, in form allied to the pike and the halbert.
Partizan, }

Partlet, O.E. gorget, **F.**

Pas d'âne, Fr. loops of bar steel immediately over the cross-hilt of the sword.

Pasguard, a reinforcing piece for the left elbow, used in tilting.

Passe-garde, Fr. the French, following Meyrick, use this word *wrongly* for neck-guards.

Passadoux, a Gascon arrow, **C.**

Passe, the rack for stringing the crossbow, **C.**

Passot, O.F. a dagger, **R.**

Patelet, a padded vest worn under armour, XVI cent.

Patrel, see poitrel.

Patron, a case for pistol cartridges.

Patula, a short sword or dagger.

Pauldrons, shoulder-pieces of plate.

Pavade, a long dagger.

Pavache, Fr.
Pavesche, } a large shield used by
Pavise, } bowmen.
Pavois d'assout, O.F. }

Pavon, a large triangular flag.

Peascod, a form of breastplate made with a central ridge, and pointed slightly downward at the lower extremity, XVII cent.

Pectoral, a breast defence of mail. See also peytral.

Pell, } a sharpened stake used by the Norman
Pill, } peasants.

Pellegrina di maglia, It. mail cape or collar.

Pennacchiera, It. } see porte-panache.
Penacho, Sp. }

Pennon, a pointed banner used by knights bachelor and esquires.

Pentina, O.I. a short pike, **F.**

Pertuisan, Fr. partizan.

Peto, Sp. breastplate.

Petail matres, a large-headed dart or arrow, **R.**

Petronel, a short firearm fired with a flint or pyrites (the common explanation that it was discharged held at the chest is erroneous).

Pettiera, It. see peytral.

Petto, It. breastplate.

Peytral, the breastplate of a horse.

Pezonaras, Sp. see bossoirs.

Pfeifenharnisch, Germ. embossed armour to imitate puffed silk or velvet, XVI cent.

Pheon, a barbed javelin used by the sergeant-at-arms.

Picca, It. see pike.

Picière, Fr. see peytral.

Pieces of advantage, reinforcing pieces for the joust.

Pied de biche, Fr. see goat's-foot lever.

Pied de chèvre, a crowbar.

Pike, a long-shafted weapon used by footmen only. It had a lance-like head, and was shod at the butt-end with iron for fixing in the ground to receive cavalry, XIV–XVIII cent.

Pike-guard, a ridge of metal set upright on the pauldrons, on the left side, erroneously called pasguard.

Pile, the head of the arrow.

Pistolese, a large dagger or knife, **F.**

Pizane, Fr. breastplate.

Placard, } a reinforcing breastplate, XVI–XVII
Placcate, } cent.

Plater, the maker of armour plates as distinct from the armourer who made up the plates into armour.

Platner, Germ. armourer.

Plastron, the upper portion of the cuirass when it is formed of two pieces.

Plastron-de-fer, a defence of plate, usually circular worn on the breast under or over the hauberk.

Plates, Pair of, back and breast plates, XIV–XV cent.

Platine, Fr. the lock of a firelock.

Plommée, Fr. a leaden mace; also holy-water sprinkler.

Poignard, a dagger.

Poinçon, the stamp or trade-mark of the armourer.

Points, laces for securing the gussets of mail to the undergarment, and also the lambrequin to the helm.

Poire, Fr. a pear-shaped button through which the laces passed that held the shield to the left breast, XVI cent.

Poitrel, breast-armour for a horse.

Poldermitton, a defence for the inner bend of the right arm, used in the joust.

Pole-axe, a long-shafted axe with beak and spear point.

Poleynes, see knee-cops, XIII–XIV cent.

Polion, some part of the crossbow.

Pommel, the finishing knob of the sword-grip; also the fore peak of the saddle.

Pompes, see poleynes.

Pontale, the chape of a sword or dagger; also the tag on an arming-point or lance, **F.**

Porte-panache, Fr. the plume-holder on the helmet.

Posolino, It. see croupière.

Pot, a broad-brimmed helmet worn by pikemen, XVII cent.

Poulaine, À la, sollerets with extremely pointed toes, XIV cent.

Pourpoint, a padded and quilted garment of leather or linen.

Pourpointerie, quilted material with metal studs at the intersection of the quilting seams.

Pryke-spur, a spur with a single point and no rowel.

Pugio,
Pugnale, } It. a small dagger.

Pully-pieces,
Putty-pieces, } see poleynes.

Pusane,
Puzane, } see pizane.

Q

Quadrelle, It. a small mace with leaf-like projections, also quarrel.

Quarrel, the bolt or projectile used with the crossbow.

Quetyll, O.E. a knife.

Queue, a projecting hook on the back-piece of the cuirass to take the butt-end of the lance when held in rest.

Quijotes, Sp. see cuisse.

Quillions, the cross-hilt of the sword.

R

Raillon, O.F. a kind of arrow, **R.**

Rainoise, an unknown type of arquebus.

Ranfort, the reinforce ring of a cannon.

Ranseur, a large trident with sharpened blades set on a long shaft; a species of partizan.

Rennen, German jousting courses with sharp spearhead.

Rennhutschraube, Germ. see crête-échelle.

Rerebrace, armour for the upper arm.

Rest of advantage, some detail of armour forbidden in jousts of the XVI cent.; possibly some kind of lance-rest.

Resta
Restra de muelle, Sp. } lance-rest.

Ricasso, the squaring of the base of the sword-blade next above the quillons.

Ringed mail, formed of flat rings sewn side by side on a tunic of leather or quilted linen, XI cent.

Rivet, a suit of armour; afterwards the small nails that hold it together.

Rochet, the blunt lance-point for jousting.

Rodete, O.F. a spur, **R.**

Roelle, O.F. a buckler or small shield.

Roncone, It. see gisarme.

Rondache, a circular shield, XV–XVI cent.

Rondel,
Rondelle, Fr. } circular plate protecting the armpit; also at the back of early armets.

Rondel of the guard, possibly a vamplate.

Ross-stirn, Germ. see chamfron.

Rodela,
Rotela, It. } a circular shield.

Rotellina da bracciale, It. rondel.

Rüchenstück, Germ. back-plate of the cuirass.

Rüsthaken, Germ. lance-rest.

Rustred mail, see banded mail (Meyrick).

Rustung, Germ. armour.

S

Sabataynes,
Sabatons, } O.E. see sollerets.

Sacheboute, O.F. a horseman's lance, **R.**

Sagetta, a casque or helmet, **F.**

Salade,
Salett,
Sallad, } helmet with wide brim at the back, worn with or without visor and mentonière, XVI cent.

Sautoir, O.F. stirrup.

Sbalzo, It. see cesello.

Scarpa a becco d'anatra, It. see bear-paw.

Scarpa a punta articolata, It. see poulaine.

Scarpa a piè d'orso, It. see bear-paw.

Scarsellone, It. see tasset.

Schale,
Schalern, } Germ. sallad.

Schamkapsel, Germ. see bravette.

Scheitelstuck, Germ. skull of the helmet.

Schembart, Germ. the lower part of the visor, the ventail.

Schenkelschiene, Germ. see cuishe.

Schiavona, It. a basket-hilted cut-and-thrust sword.

Schiena, It. the back-plate of the cuirass.

Schiessprügel, Germ. see holy-water sprinkle.

Schiniere, It. see jambs.

Schioppo, O.I. a dag or pistol, **F.**

Schlaeger, Germ. student's fencing-sword.

Schulterschild, Germ. see grand-guard.

Schulterschild mit Rand, Germ. a pauldron with neck-guard attached.

Schwanzel,
Schwanzriempanzer, } Germ. the tail-guard of a horse.

Schwebescheibe, Germ. see vamplate.

Sciabola, It. sabre.

Scudo, It. a triangular shield.

Scure d'arme, It. battle-axe.

Seax, a dagger.

Secreta, } a thin steel cap worn under the hat,
Secrete, } XVI–XVII cent.

Sella d'arme, It. war-saddle.

Semitarge, O.F. a scimitar, **R.**

Serpentina, It. the cock of a matchlock.

Setzschild, Germ. see pavise.

Shaffron, see chamfron.

Sharfrennen, Germ. variety of joust with sharp-pointed lances, XVI cent.

Sharfrennentarsche, Germ. a shield-like reinforcing piece for the above joust.

Shell-guard, a form of sword-guard.

Sfondagiaco, It. see misericorde.

Sisarmes, see gisarme.

Slaughsword, a two-hand sword carried by the whiffler, IV cent.

Sliding rivet, a rivet fixed on the upper plate and moving in a slot on the lower plate.

Snaphaunce, an early form of flint-lock in which the pan has to be uncovered before firing.

Sockets, a thigh-defence similar to the German diechling.

Soffione, It. a musket or caliver.

Sollerets, shoes of laminated plate, usually pointed.

Spada, It. sword.

Spadone, It. a long sword.

Spadroon, flat-bladed sword for cut-and-thrust.

Spallacci, It. pauldrons.

Spallière, Fr. see pauldrons.

Spasmo, O.It. a dart or javelin, **F.**

Spetum, } see ranseur.
Spiede, It. }

Spight, a short or flight arrow.

Spigo, O.It. the plume-holder of a helmet, **F.**

Splint armour, narrow overlapping plates as opposed to armour made of large plates.

Spright, a wooden arrow discharged from a gun.

Springal, see espringale.

Spontoon, a half-pike carried by officers, XVIII cent.

Squarcina, O.It. a short sword or cutlass, **F.**

Staffa, It. stirrup.

Standard of mail, a collar of chain mail, XV cent.

Stecca, It. the locket of a dagger.

Steccata, It. the place of combat for duels.

Stechhelm, Germ. heavy tilting-helm.

Stechen, Germ. jousting course with coronal-tipped lances.

Stechtarsche, Germ. a ribbed tilting-shield used in the " gestech " courses.

Stinchieri, O.It. armour for the shin, **F.**

Stirnstulp, Germ. the upper part of the visor of an armet.

Stithe, O.E. anvil.

Striscia, It. rapier.

Sturmhaube, Germ. see burgonet.

Sturmwand, Germ. see pavise.

Supeters, O.E. see sollerets.

Surcoat, a garment worn over the armour to protect it from sun and rain, and usually blazoned heraldically.

Sword-breaker, a short heavy sword with back edge toothed for breaking opponent's sword, XVI cent.

Swyn-feather, see feather-staff.

T

Tabard, the armorially emblazoned coat worn by heralds ; see also surcoat.

Taces, laminated plates at the lower edge of the cuirass.

Tache, O.E. strap.

Talevas, Sp. shield.

Tapul, the vertical ridge in the centre of some forms of breast-piece.

Tarcaire, O.F. a quiver, **R.**

Targe, a small circular shield.

Tarques, O.F. some kind of engine of war, **R.**

Tartsche, Germ. a small shield or targe.

Tartschen, Germ. see ailettes.

Tassets, plates, usually lozenge-shaped, attached by strap and buckle to the taces to protect the upper or front surface of the thigh.

Taurea, O.It. a buckler of bull's hide, **F.**

Tegulated armour, overlapping tile-like square plates, end of XII cent. (Meyrick).

Tertiare, to " third " the pike, i.e. to shorten either for shouldering or for receiving cavalry.

Tesa, It. the shade or brim of the burgonet.

Tester, O.E. } see chanfron.
Testiera, It. }

Testière, Fr. a metal skull-cap ; also the chanfron of a horse.

Têtrière, Fr. see tester.

Thyrtel, } O.E. knife or dagger.
Thwyrtel, }

Tilt, the barrier used to separate knights when jousting, XIV cent. and onwards ; first, a stretched cloth ; later, of wood.

Timbre, Fr. the skull of a helmet.

Tiloles, *Arbalest à*, Fr. windlass crossbow.

Toggle, the cross-bar of a boar-spear. In modern use a button for joining two ends of a strap or thong.

Toile, see tilt.

Tolys, O.E. tools.

Touch-box, probably a box for flint and steel carried by the musket.

Tourney,
Tournois, Fr. a contest of many knights in the lists as opposed to the joust or single combat at barriers.

Tournicle d'eschaille, Fr. a small tunic or a large gorget composed of overlapping scale armour.

Toyle, a contrivance fixed over the right cuisse to hold the lance when carried upright; a lance bucket.

Trubrico, Sp. blunderbuss.

Traguardo, It. see visor.

Trapper, horse-trappings of fabric or mail.

Trellised armour, quilted linen or leather with leather bands sewn trellis-wise and having studs of metal in the trellis openings (Meyrick).

Tresses, plaited laces or arming-points.

Trilobed scales, triple scales in one piece sewn upon the brigandine.

Trombone, It. a heavy pistol, blunderbuss.

Trousse, Fr. a quiver.

Trumelière, Fr. see jamb.

Tuck, see estoc.

Tuile, Fr. see tassets.

Tuilette, Fr. small tassets as on tomb of Rich. Beauchamp, Earl of Warwick.

Turcasso, It. quiver.

Turves, probably a turban or orle worn on the helmet.

U

Umbo, the boss upon a shield.

Umbril, the shade or brim of head-pieces of XVII cent.

Uncin, war pickaxe.

Uncino, O.It. a broad-pointed arrow, a hook, **F.**

Unterarmzeug, Germ. vambrace.

Usbergo, O.It. breastplate, vamplate, **F.**

V

Vambrace, the plate defence for the fore-arm.

Vamplate, a circular shield through which the tilting and war lances were fixed above the grip.

Vedoil, a weapon used by foot-soldiers, possibly a voulge.

Velette, O.It. a horse-soldier's coat, **F.**

Venetian sallad, a sallad of the XV–XVI cent.; formed like the ancient Greek helmet with fixed visor, but evolved from the bascinet.

Ventaglio, It.
Ventail, Fr. the lower part of the visor when it is made in two parts.
Ventalle, Sp.

Vervelles, the staples on the bascinet to which the carvail was laced.

Vireton, an arrow for the crossbow with curving wings, to produce a spinning motion.

Visera, It.
Visor, that part of the helmet, movable or fixed, which protects the eyes.
Vista, Sp.

Volant-piece, reinforcing piece for the tilt to protect the breast and lower half of the face; possibly a spring breastplate.

Volet, the round disc at the back of the armet.

Volet, Fr. an arrow or dart.

Vor-arm, Germ. see vambrace.

Vorderfluge, Germ. the front plate of the pauldron.

Vorhelm, Germ. see placcate.

Voulge, a weapon somewhat similar to the Lochaber axe; used mostly by the peasants.

Voyders, see gussets.

Voyding knife, a knife for disembowelling deer.

Vuiders,
Vuyders, see gussets.

W

Wafter, English dummy blade for fencing, XVI cent.

Wambais, see gambeson.

Wappen rock, Germ. a cloak decorated heraldically.

Welsches gestech, German name for the Italian course of jousting over the tilt or barrier with blunted lance.

Whiffler, a two-hand swordsman who cleared the way in processions.

Wifle, a practice-sword, possibly a two-hander.

Winbrede,
Wynbred, see gagnepain.

Wire hat, see coif.

Z

Zucchetto, It. a species of burgonet, XVII cent.

Zweyhander, Germ. two-handed sword.

APPENDIX A

DOCUMENT FROM THE RECORDS OF THE ARMOURERS' COMPANY, LONDON, 1322

THIS is a regulation that no armourer should attempt to sell *Bascuettes* (Bascinets) covered with fabric, but should show them uncovered, so that the workmanship might be seen and approved.

ARMOURERS' COMPANY OF LONDON
Lib. C, fol. 33, 15 Edw. II, 1322

Edward ye Second

Be it remembered that in ye hustinge of comon plaes holden ye Mondaie in ye feaste of ye conversion of Saint Paule, ye yere of ye reigne of our Lord ye king Edward, ye son of king Edward, xv th., in ye presence of Sir Hamen de Chigewelle then Maior, Nicholas de farringdon and by assent of Hugh de Auggeye, &c. Armorers.   It is was ordeyned for ye comon proffyt and assented that from henceforth all Armor made in ye Cytie to sell be good and convenable after ye forme that henceforth   That is to saie that an Akton and Gambezon covered with sendall or of cloth of Silke be stuffed with new clothe of cotten and of cadar and of oldn sendal and not otherwise.   And that ye wyite acketonnes be stuffed of olde lynnen and of cottone and of new clothe wth in and wth out.   Also forasmuch as men have founde old bascuette broken and false now newly covered by men that nothing understand of ye mystery wh be putt in pryvie places and borne out into ye contrye out of ye said Cytie, to sell and in ye same citie of wh men may not gaine knowledge whether they be good or ill, of ye wh thinge greate yill might fall to ye king and his people, and a greate slaunder to ye Armorers aforesaid and to all ye Cytie.   It is ordeyned and assented that no Farrar ne other man that maketh ye Irons of bascuette hereafter so to be covered no bascuett by himself to sell be free but that he shall sell out of his hande will open and ungarnished as men have used before this tyme.   And ye which shall abide ungarnished until they be sene by the myor that shall be sworn or by ny of Cz'ens whether they be convenable to garnishe or no.   And there be found in any Court of Armorers or else where in wch Court is Armor for to sell, whatsoever it be, that is not proffytable or otherwise than is ordeyned and none be it taken and brought before ye Maior and Aldermen and hys Czens to be demed good or ill after their discretion.   And for the wch thing well and lawfully to be kept and surveyed Roger Savage Willm. De Langgull, Richard Johonnez (John Conny) being sworne. And if they myor may not attend that ij of them Do that longeth thereto.

Fol. 135.   ffirst it is a general Article ordeyned for all ye crafte of London and centred in ye Chamber of ye Guildhall of ye said City in ye booke wth ye letter

169

C in ye xxxv leaffe in ye tyme of Adam Bury Maior, in ye yere of ye reigne of king Ed. ye thirde after ye conquest.

Lib. v. xd.   It is ordeyned that all ye crafte of ye citie of London be truely ruled and governed every person in his nature in due maner so that no falsehood ne false workemanshipp nor Deceipt be founde in no maner wise in any of ye foresaid crafte for ye worshipp of ye good folke of all ye same crafte and for the comon proffytt of ye people.

APPENDIX B

REGULATIONS OF THE HEAUMERS, 21 EDWARD III, 1347
City of London Letter Book F, fol. cxlii

The Points of the Articles touching the trade of Helmetry accepted by Geffrey de Wychingham, Mayor, and the Aldermen at the suit and request of the folks of the said trade :—

In the first place that no one of the said trade shall follow or keep seld of the trade aforesaid within the franchise of the City of London until he shall have properly bought his freedom, according to the usages of the said City, on pain of losing his wares.

Also forasmuch as heretofore some persons coming in who are strangers have intermeddled and still do intermeddle in the making of helmetry, whereas they do not know the trade, by reason whereof many great men and others of the realm have been slain through their default, to the great scandal of the said trade : It is ordained that no person shall from henceforth intermeddle with or work at helmetry if he be not proved to be a good, proper, and sufficient workman by the Wardens of the said trade on pain of forfeiture to the use of the Chamber.

Also that three or four if need be of the best workmen of the said trade shall be chosen and sworn to rule the trade well and properly as is befitting for security and safety of the great men and others of the realm, and for the honour and profit of the said City and of the workers of the said trade.

Also that no apprentice shall be received by any master of the said trade for less than seven years ; and that without collusion or fraud on paying to the said Chamber 100 shillings.

Also that no one of the said trade or other person of the Franchise shall set any stranger to work who is of the said trade if he be not a proper and lawful person, and one for whom the master will answer as to his good behaviour, on pain of paying to the said Chamber 20 shillings.

Also that no apprentice of the said trade who shall be indebted to his master in any sum of money at the end of his term shall serve henceforth any other person than his own master, nor shall he depart from such service or be into the service of another person in any way received until he shall have fully given satisfaction for his debt to his master. And he who shall receive in any other manner the servant or apprentice of another person shall pay to the said Chamber 20 shillings.

Also that helmetry and other arms forged by the hammer which are brought from the parts without this land beyond the seas, or from any other place unto the said City for sale, shall not from henceforth be in any way offered for sale privily or openly until they have been properly assayed by the aforesaid Wardens and marked with their mark, on pain of forfeiting such helmetry and arms to the said Chamber as shall be so offered for sale.

Also that each one of the makers aforesaid shall have his own mark and sign, and that no one of them shall counterfeit the sign or mark of another on pain of losing his freedom until he shall have bought the same back again and made satisfaction to him whose sign he shall have so counterfeited, and further he shall pay to the Chamber 40 shillings.

Wardens of the same trade chosen and sworn,

ROBERT DE SHIRWODE,
RICHARD BRIDDE,
THOMAS CANOUN.

APPENDIX C

TREATISE OF WORSHIP IN ARMS, BY JOHAN HILL, ARMOURER TO
HENRY VI, 1434

TRAYTESE OF THE POYNTES OF WORSHIP IN ARMES BY JOHAN HYLL,
ARMORER SERGEANT IN THE KINGE'S ARMORY 1434
Bod. Lib., Ashmole. MS. 856, art. 22, pp. 376–83

[376] Too my leve Lordes here nowe next folowinge is a Traytese compyled by Johan Hyll Armorier Sergeant in the office of Armory wt. Kinges Henry ye 4th and Henry ye 5th of ye poyntes of Worship in Armes and how he shall be diversely Armed & gouverned under supportacion of faveurof alle ye Needes to coverte adde & amenuse where nede is by the high comandement of the Princes that have powair so for to ordeyne & establishe

The first Honneur in Armes is a Gentilman to fight in his Souverain Lords quarell in a bataille of Treason sworne withinne Listes before his souverain Lorde whether he be Appellant or Defendant ye honneur is his that winneth ye feelde.

As for the appellant thus Armed by his owne witte or by his counsaille wch is assigned to him before Conestable & Marchall ye wch Counsaille is ordeyned & bounden to teche hym alle maner of fightynge & soteltees of Armes that longeth for a battaile sworne

First hym nedeth to have a paire of hosen of corde wtoute vampeys And the saide hosen kutte at ye knees and lyned wtin wt Lynnen cloth byesse as the hose is A payre of shoen of red Lether thynne laced & fretted underneth wt whippecorde & persed, And above withinne Lyned wt Lynnen cloth three fyngers in brede double & byesse from the too an yncle above ye wriste. And so behinde at ye hele from the Soole halfe a quarter of a yearde uppe this is to fasten wele to his Sabatons And the same Sabatons fastened under ye soole of ye fote in 2 places hym nedeth also a petycote of an overbody of a doublett, his petycote wt oute sleves, ye syses of him 3 quarters aboute wt outen coler. And that other part noo ferther thanne [377] ye waste wt streyte sleves and coler and cutaine oylettes in ye sleves for ye vaunt bras and ye Rerebrase

Armed in this wise First behoveth Sabatouns grevis & cloos quysseux wt voydours of plate or of mayle & a cloos breche of mayle wt 5 bokles of stele ye tisseux of fyne lether. And all ye armyng poyntes after they ben knytte & fastened on hym armed that ye poyntes of him be kutte of

And thanne a paire of cloos gussetts strong sclave not drawes and thatye gussets be thre fingers withinne his plates at both assises And thanne a paire of plattes at xx li lib weight his breste & his plats enarmed to   wt wyre or wt poyntes.

173

A pair of Rerebraces shitten withinne the plates before wt twi forlockes and behinde wt thre forlocks.   A paire of vaunt bras cloos wt voydours of mayle & fretted.   A pair of gloves of avantage wche may be devised.   A basnet of avauntage for ye listes whiche is not goode for noon other battailles but man for man save that necessitie hath noo lawe, the basnet locked baver & vysour locked or charnelled also to ye brest & behynde wt two forlockes.   And this Gentilman appellent aforesaide whanne he is thus armed & redy to come to ye felde do on hym a cote of armes of sengle tarten ye beter for avauntage in fighting.   And his leg harneys covered alle wt reed taritryn the wche ben called tunictes for he coverynge of his leg harneys is doen because his adversarie shal not lightly espye his blode.   And therefore also hen his hosen reed for in alle other colours blode wol lightly be seyne, for by the oolde tyme in such a bataile there shulde noo thing have be seyn here save his basnett & his gloves.   And thanne tye on hym a payre of besagewes.   Also it fitteth the [378] foresaide counsaille to goo to ye kyng the daye before ye bataille & aske his logging nigh ye listes.   Also ye foresaide Counsaille must ordeyne hym the masses ye first masse of ye Trinitie ye seconde of ye Holy Goste & ye thirde of owre Ladye or elles of what other sainte or saintes that he hath devocion unto

And that he be watched alle that night   hym that he is watched and light in his Chambre alle that night that his counsaille may wite how that he slepeth.   And in ye mornyng whanne he goeth to his Masses that his herneys be leyed at ye North end of ye Auter and covered wt a cloth that ye gospell may be redde over it and at ye laste masse for to be blessed wt ye preist and whanne he hath herde his Masses thanne to goo to his dyner.   And soo to his Armyng in ye forme aforesaide. And whanne he is armed and alle redy thanne to come to ye feelde in forme to fore rehersed, thanne   his counsaille bounden to counsaille hym & to teche hym how he shal gouverne hym of his requests to ye kyng or he come into ye feelde and his entrie into ye felde and his gouvernance in the feelde for ye saide Counsaille hath charge of hym before Constable and Mareschal til that Lesses les aller be cryed.   The whiche requestes ben thus that ye saide Appellant sende oon his counsaille to the kyng for to requeste hym that whanne he cometh to ye barrers to have free entrie wt his counsaille Confessour & Armorers wt alle maner of Instruments wt breede & wyne hymself bring-ing in in an Instrument that is to saye a cofre or a pair of bouges.   Also their fyre cole & belyes and that his chayre wt [379] certaine of his Servants may be brought into ye feelde and sette up there the houre of his comyng that it may cover hym and his counsaille whanne he is comen into ye feelde this forsaide gentilman Appellant comyng to ye Listes whether he wol on horsebak or on fote wt his counsaille Confessour & other Servaunts aforesaide havyng borne be fore hym by his counsaille a spere a long swerde a short swerde & a dagger fastined upon hymself his swerdes fretted and beasagewed afore ye hiltes havyng noo maner of poyntes for and ther be founden that day on hym noo poyntes of wepons thanne foirre, it shall tourne hym to gret reproof. And this gentilman appellant that come to ye barrers at ye Southeest sone, his visier doune And he shal aske entrie where shal mete hym Constable and Mareschal and aske hym what art thou.   And he shal saye I am suche a man & telle his name to make goode this day by ye grace of God that I have saide of suche a man and tell hys name bifore my Souain Lord and they shal bidde hym putte up his visier and whanne he hath put up his visier they shal open the barrers and lette hym inne and his counsaille before hym & wt hym his Armorers & his servaunts shal goo streight to his chayer wt his breed his wyne & alle his instruments that longe unto hym save his weppons.   And whanne he entreth into the felde that he blesse hym soberly and so twys or he come to before his Souverain Lord And his Counsailles shall do thair obeisaunce before thair souverain Lord twys or they come to the degrees of his scaffolde and he to obeye him wt his heed at both tymes. Then whanne they to fore thair souverain Lord they shal knele a downe and he also they shal aryse or he aryse he shal obeye hym at his heed to his souverain Lord and then aryse and whanne he is up on his feete he shal blesse hym and turne hym to his chayre and at the entryng of his chayr [380] soberly tourne hym his visage to his souverain Lord wards and blesse hym and thanne tourne hym againe and soo go into his chayre and there he maye sitte hym downe and take of his gloves and his basnet and so refresh hym till the houre of hys Adversarie approche wt breed and wyne or wt any other thing that he hath brought in wt hym.   And whanne the Defendaunt his Adversarie cometh in to the feelde that he be redy armed againe or that he come into the feelde standing withoute his chayre taking hede of his Adversaries comyng in and of his countenance that he may take comfort of.   And whanne the defendant his Adversarie is come int ye felde and is in his chayre thanne shal the kyng send for his wepons and se him and the Conestable and the Marschal also and if they be leefull they shal be kept in the feelde & kutte the same day by ye comaundement of the kyng and the Conestable and Mareschal in ye kynge's behalve. And thanne fitteth to the foresaide counsaille to arme hym and to make hym redy against that he be called to his first ooth and whanne he is called to his first oothe thanne fitteth it to alle his counsaille to goo wt hym to his first ooth for to here what the Conestable and Mareschal seyen unto hym and what contenaunce he maketh in his sweryng And whanne he hath sworne they shl ryse up by ye comaundement of the Conestable and Mareschal. And whanne he is on his feete he shal obey hym to his Souverain Lord and blesse hym and thanne turne hym to his chayre his visage to his souveraine Lord wards and in his goinge blesse hym twys by ye weye or he come to his chayre. And at ye [381] entryng to his chayre soberly tourne hym his visage to his Souverain Lord wards and blesse hym and soo go into his chayre. Thanne fitteth it to his fore saide Counsaille to awayte where the defendaunt shal come to his first ooth and that they be ther as sone as he for to here how he swereth for he must nedes swere that al that ever th appellant hath sworne is false substance and alle.   And if he wol not swere that every worde & every sillable of every worde substance and alle is false the Counsaille of ye saide appellant may right wisly aske jugement by lawe of Civile and raison of Armes forafter ye juge is sette there shulde noo plee be made afore hym that daye.

And if so be that the Defendant swere duly thanne ye Counsaille of the foresaide Appellant shal goo to his chayre agayne and abide ther til they be sent for.   And thanne shal they bringe hym to hys second Ooth and here how he swereth and whanne he hath sworne they shal goo wt hym to hys chayre againe in the forme aforesaide.   And whanne he is in his chayre the saide Counsaille shal awayte whanne ye Defendaunt cometh to his seconde ooth and here how he swereth and if he swere under any subtil teerme cantel or cavellacion the foresaide Counsaille of th appellant may require the jugement.   And if he swere duely thanne shal ye Counsaille of ye foresaide Appellant goo to his chayre againe and abide there til they be sent for. And thanne shal they brynge hym to his thirde ooth and assuraunce.   And whanne they be sworne and assured the saide appellant wt his Counsaile shal goo againe to his chayre in the fourme afore saide and there make [382] hym redy and fastene upon hym his wepons and so refresche hym til ye Conestable and Mareschal bid hym come to ye feeld.   Thanne shal his Armorers and his Servaunts voyde the Listes wt his chayre and alle his Instruments at ye Comandement of ye Conestable and Mareschal.   Thanne fitteth it to the Counsaille of the saide Appellant to ask a place of ye kyng afore hym withinne the barres upon his right hande that ye saide Counsaille of th appellant may come and stande there whanne they be discharged of ye saide Appellant.

The cause is this that suche pyte may be given to ye kyng if God that noon of hem shal dye that daye for he may by his prowaie royal in such a cas take it into his hande the foresaide Counsaille of the Appellant to abyde in the saide place til the kyng have geven his jugement upon him—And thanne ye Conestable and Mareschal shal deliwer the foresaide Appellant by ye Comandement of the kyng to his foresaide Counsaille to govern hym of his going out of ye feelde as wele as they did of his comyng in his worship to be saved in al that lyeth en hem.   And soo to bryng hym to his Logging agayne to unarme hym comforte hym and counsaille hym   And some of his Counsaille may goo to the kyng and comon wt hym and wite of the kyng how he shal be demeaned.   This enarmyng here aforesaide is best for a battaille of arreste wt a sworde a dagger an Ax and a pavys til he come to th asseblee his sabatons & his tunycle evoyded   And thanne the Auctor Johan Hyll dyed at London in Novembre the xiii th yere of kyng Henry the Sixt so that he accomplished noo mor of ye compylyng of this [383] trayties on whose soulle.God have mercy for his endles passion   Amen.

APPENDIX D

TRAITÉ DU COSTUME MILITAIRE, 1446
Bib. Nat., Paris (fonds Français, 1997)

Given in full in *Du Costume Militaire des Français en 1446*, René de Belleval, 1866

Mais quant à la façzon de leur harnoys de jouste, suis content de le vous déclairer plus largement, affin que pour lavenir ceulx qui voudront jouster y preignent exemple, soit de y adjouster ou de y oster, comme mieulx verront et congnoisteront y estre nécessaire.

Et tout premièrement vueil commancer au harnoys de teste, cest assavoir au heaume, lequel est fait en ceste façzon, comme cy après me orrez déclairer ; et premièrement lesdiz heaumes sont, sur le sommet de la teste jusques à la veue, fors et espes et ung pou sur le rondelet, par façzon que la teste ne touche point encontre, ainçois y peut avoir espace de troiz doiz entre deux.

Item, de dessobz de la veue du heaume, qui arme par davant tout le visaige depuis les deux aureilles jusques à la poitrine et endroit les yeulx qui s'appelle la veue, avance et boute avant troiz bons doiz ou plus que n'est le bort de dessus ; entre lequel bort de dessus et celuy de dessobz ny a bonnement despace que ung bon doy et demy pour y povoir veoir, et n'est ladicte veue, tant dun cousté que dautre, fendue que environ dun espan de long, mais voulentiers vers le cousté séneftre est ladicte veue plus clouse et le bort plus en bouty dehors que n'est de lautre cofté droict.

Item, et ledit dessobz ladicte veue marche voluntiers sur la pièce de dessus la teste deux bons doiz, tant dun cousté que dautre de la veue, et cloué de fors clox qui ont les uns la teste enbotie, et les autres ont la teste du clou limée affin que le rochet ny prengne.

Item, la pièce dessusditte qui arme le visaige est voluntiers large et destendant presque dune venue jusques à la gorge, ou plus bas, affin quelle ne soit pas si près des visaiges quant les cops de lance y prennent. Ainçois qui le veult faire à point fault quil y ait quatre doiz despace du moins entre deux. Et à ceste dicte pièce, du cofté droict de la lance, endroit la joue, deux ou trois petites veues qui viennent du long depuis le hault de la joue jusques au collet du pourpoint, affin que l'en nait schault dedens le heaulme, et aussi affin que on puisse mieulx ouir ou veoir celuy qui le sert de la lance.

Item, l'autre pièce dudit heaume arme depuis les aureilles par darrière le long du coul jusques trois doiz sur les espaulles par bas, et par hault, aussi jusques à trois doiz sur la nuque du coul. Et vient façzonnée une areste aval qui vient en estroississant sur le collet du pourpoint, et se relargist sur les espaulles en deux ; laquelle pièce dessusdicte nest jamais faicte forte ne espesse, ainçois la plus legière que on la peult faire eſt la meilleure ; et pour concluſion faire ces trois pièces deſſuſdiĉtes font le heaulme entier.

. . . .

Item, quant à larmeure du corps, il y en a de deux faczons ; ceſt aſſavoir : la premiere comme curaſſe à armer ſaufve que le voulant eſt clox et arreſté à la pièce, par faczon que le voulant ne peut aller ne jouer hault ne bas.

Item, lautre faczon eſt de brigandines ou aultrement dit curraſſines, couvertez et clouées par pièces petittes depuis la poitrine en a bas, ne ny a aultre différance de celle cy aux brigandines que on porte en la guerre, ſinon que tout ce que contient la poitrine juſques aux faulx eſt dune ſeulle pièce et ſe lace du coſté de la main droite ou par darrière du long de leſchine. Item, larreſt eſt eſpès, grox et matériel au plaiſir de celui qui le fait faire.

Item, oudit harnoys de corps y a principallement deux boucles doubles, ou une boucle double et ung aneau limé, ou meilleu de la poitrine, plus hault quatre doiz que le faulx du corps, et lautre du couſté ſéneſtre longues ; de lautre ung pou plus haulte : leſquelles deux boucles ou aneau ſont pour atacher ledit heaume à la curaſſe ou brigandine ; ceſt aſſavoir : la première ſert pour metre une treſſe ou corroye oudit heaulme à une autre pareille boucle comme celle là, qui eſt oudit heaume clouée ſur la pate dudit heaume davant le plus à lendroit du meillieu du travers que len peult, et ont voulentiers leſdiĉtes treſſes et couvertures de cueur trois doubles lun ſur lautre ; lautre ſeconde boucle ou aneau à main ſéneſtre reſpont pareillement à une aultre boucle ou aneau qui eſt oudit heaume à la ſéneſtre partie ſur la pate dudit heaume ; et ces deux boucles ou aneaux ſéneſtres ſervent eſpéciallement pour la buffe, ceſt aſſavoir que quand le rochet atache (*a touché*) ſur le hault de leſcuczon ou heaume, ceſte treſſe ou courroye deſſuſdiĉte garde que le heaulme ne ſe joigne à la joe ſéneſtre par la faczon que ledit jouſteur en puiſſe eſtre depis.

Item, en ladiĉte brigandine ou curaſſe y a en la ſeneſtre partie en la poitrine, près du bort du braz ſeneſtre, à ung doy près endroit le tour du braz hault, troiz doiz plus bas que la boucle de quoy on laſſe ladiĉte brigandine ſur leſpaulle, ung crampon de fer du gros dun doy en ront, dont les deux chefz ſont rivez par dedens et ladiĉte pièce au mieulx quil ſe puet faire, et dedens dudit crampon ſe paſſe deux ou trois tours une groſſe treſſe bonne et forte qui depuis paſſe parmy la poire, laquelle poire eſt aſſiſe et cache ledit crampon ; de laquelle poire la haulteur eſt vouluntiers dun bon doy, ſur laquelle leſcu repoſe, et eſt ataché par leſdits pertuys dudit eſcu de la treſſe qui eſt atachée audit crampon, laquelle ſort par le meilleu de ladiĉte poire.

Item, en ladiĉte curaſſe y a darrière, ou meilleu du creux de leſpaulles, une boucle ou aneau qui ſert pour atacher une treſſe ou courroie à une autre boucle du heaulme darrière, ſi que le heaulme ne chée davant, et affin auſſi que la veue ſoit de la haulteur et demeure ferme que le jouſteur la vieult.

Item, oultre plus en ladiĉte curaſſe y a ung petit aneau plus bas que nul des aultres, aſſis plus vers le faillement des couſtez à la main ſéneſtre, auquel len atache dune aultre legière treſſe la main de fer, laquelle main de fer eſt tout dune pièce et arme la main et le braz juſques troiz ou quatre doiz oultre le code.

Item, depuis le code juſques au hault, cache (*cachant*) tout le tour de leſpaulle y a ung petit garde braz dune pièce, et ſe deſcent juſques ſur le code quatre doiz.

Item, à la main droite y a ung petit gantellet lequel ſe appelle gaignepain ; et depuis le gantellet juſques oultre le code, en lieu de avant braz, y a une armeure qui ſe appelle eſpaulle de mouton, laquelle eſt façonnée large endroit le code, et ſe eſpanouiſt aval, et endroit la ploieure du braz ſe revient ploier par façon que, quant len a mis la lance en larreſt, laditte ploieure de laditte eſpaulle de mouton couvre depuiſ la ploieure du braz ung bon doy en hault.

Item, pour armeure de leſpaulle droite y a ung petit garde braz fait à lames, ſur lequel y a une rondelle joignant une place, laquelle rondelle ſe haulſe et ſe beſſe quant on vieult metre la lance en larreſt, et ſe revient recheoir ſur la lance quant elle eſt oudit arreſt, par telle façon quelle couvre ce que eſt défarmé en hault dentre la lance et ledit garde braz.

Item, auſſi oudit royaulme de France ſe arment de harnoys de jambes quant ilz jouſtent.

Item, quant à la façon des eſtacheures dudit harnoys par bas, ſi que il ne ſourmonte point encontremont par force des copz, je men paſſe à le déclairer pour le préſent, car il y en a pluſeurs façons. Ne auſſi daultre part ne me ſemble pas ſi quil ſe doye divulguer ſi publicquement.

Item, quant eſt des lances, les plus convenables raiſons de longueur entre grappe et rochet, et auſſy celles de quoy on uſe plus communuement eſt de treze piez ou de treze piez et demy de long.

Item, et leſdiz rochez ſont vouluntiers de ouverture entre chaſcune des trois pointes de deux doiz et demy ou trois au plus.

Item, leſdictes grappes ſont voulentiers plaines de petittes pointes agues (aiguës) comme petiz dyamens, de groſſeur comme petites nouzilles, leſquelles pointes ſe viennent arreſter dedens le creux de larreſt, lequel creux de larreſt plain de bois ou de plomb affin que leſdittes pointes ne puiſſent fouir, par quoy vient ladicte lance à tenir le cop : en façon quil fault que elle ſe rompe en pièces, que len aſſigne bien ou que le jouſteur ploye leſchine ſi fort que bien le ſente.

Item, les rondes deſſuſdictes lances ne couvrent tout autour au plus aller que ung demy pié, et ſont vouluntiers de trois doiz deſpès de bourre feutrée entre deux cuirs, du couſté devers la main par dedens.

Et oultre plus pour faire fin à la manière que len ſe arme en fait de jouxtes ou pais et contrée que jay cy deſous déclaié, ne diray aultre choſe pour le préſent, ſinon que ung bon ſerviteur dun jouſteur doit regarder principallement trois choſes ſur ſon maiſtre avant quil luy donne ſa lance ; ceſt aſſavoir que ledit jouſteur ne ſoit défarmé de nulles de ſes armeures par le cop précédent ; laultre ſi eſt que ledit jouſteur ne ſoit point eſtourdy ou méhaigné pareillement par ledit cops précédent quil aura eu ; le tiers ſi eſt que ledit ſerviteur doit bien regarder ſil y a autre preſt ſur les rengs qui ait ſa lance ſur faulte, et preſt pour jouſter contre ſondit maiſtre, affin que ſondit maiſtre ne tienne trop longuement ſans faire courſe la lance en larreſt, ou quil ne face ſa courſe en vain et ſans que autre vienne à lencontre de luy.

APPENDIX E

EXTRACTS FROM THE ORDINANCES OF THE ARMOURERS OF ANGERS

STATUTS DES ARMURIERS FOURBISSEURS D'ANGERS, 1448

1. Quiconque vouldra estre armurier ou brigandinier, fourbisseur et garnisseur d'espées et de harnois . . . faire le pourra. . . .

2. It. les quels maistres desd. mestiers seront tenus besoigner et faire ouvrage de bonnes étoffes, c'est assavoir pour tant que touche les armuriers, ils feront harnois blancs pour hommes d'armes de toute épreuve qui est à dire d'arbalestes à tilloles et à coursel a tout le moins demie espreuve, qui est a entendre d'arbaleste a crocq et traict e'archiers, et pour tant que touche les brigandiniers ils seront tenus pareillement faire brigandines, c'est assavoir les plus pesantes de 26 à 27 livres poix de marc tout au plus, tenant espreuve d'arbaleste a tillolles et marquées de 2 marques, et les moindres de 18 a 20 livres, tel poix que dessusu et d'espreuve d'arbaleste a crocq et traict d'archier, marquees d'une marque. Et seront icelles brigandines d'assier, trampees partout et aussi toutes garnies de cuir entre les lames et la toile, c'est assavoir en chacune rencontre de lames, et ne pourront faire lesd. brigandines de moindre poix de lame. . . .

3. It. et fauldra qe lesd. lames soient limees tout a l'entour a ce que tes ettoffes durent plus largement. . . .

10. Que las marchans et ouvriers desd. mestiers, tant faiseurs d'espees, haches, guysarmes, voulges, dagues et autres habillemens de guerre, seront tenus de faire tout ouvrage bon, loyal, et marchant.

11. It. que tous fourbisseurs et garnisseurs d'espees, tant vielles que neuves, seront tenus de faire fourraux de cuirs de vache et de veau, et les jointures de cuir de vache, la poignee d'icelles nouee de fouer [fouet ?] et se aucunes poignees sont faictes de cuir, icelles poignees seront garnies de fisselles par dessouez, led. cuir.

12. Et pareillement les atelles des fourreaux seront neufvs et de bois de fouteau sec. . . .

18. It. que nuls marchans ne maistres forains ne pourront tenir ouvrouers ne boutiques de harnois, brigandines, javelines, lances, picques ne espees, ne choses deppendantes desd. mestiers en ceste ville s'ils ne sont maistres en cette ville.

Ordonn. des rois, T. XX, p. 156, etc.

AGREEMENT TO SUPPLY ARMOUR BY FOREIGN ARMOURERS IN BORDEAUX

1375. Conegude cause sie que Guitard de Junquyères, armurer de Bordeu, Lambert Braque, d'Alemaine, armurer de cotes de fer, reconegon e autreyan e en vertat confessan aver pres e recebut de la man de Moss. de Foxis 100 florins d'aur d'Aragon, per los quans lo prometan e s'obligan aver portat a Morlaas 60 bacinetz ab capmalh e 60 cotes de fer o plus si plus poden, boos e sufficientz.

Arch. des B. Pyrénées, E, 302, fol. 129.

PERMISSION GRANTED BY LOUIS XI TO FOREIGN ARMOURERS TO PRACTISE IN BORDEAUX FOR TWENTY YEARS

1490. Sachent tous . . . que cum le temps passe de 6 ans ou environ Estienne Daussone, Ambroye de Caron, Karoles et Glaudin Bellon natifs du pays de Mylan en Lombardie et Pierre de Sonnay natif de la duché de Savoye, les quels ce fussent associés, acompaignés et adjustez entre eulx l'un avecques l'autre, de faire leur résidence pesonnelle et continuelle a ouvrer et trafiquer du mestier de armurerie et pour l'espace de 20 ans ou environ. . . .

Min. dec. not. Frapier, Arch. de la Gironde, Rev. d'Aquitaine, XII, 26.

APPENDIX F

EXPENSES OF THE ROYAL ARMOURIES, *TEMP*. HENRY VIII
Brit. Mus., Cotton., Appendix XXVIII, f. 76

1544

The charges of the king's own armoury accounting the Master of the Armourie's fee, the Clerk & Yeoman's wages and 5 armourers for his Highness' own person with 1 Gilder 2 Lockyers, 1 Millman and a prentice, in the year.

	c. li.	s.	d.
In primis the Master of the Armouries fee by the year and is paid by the Customer of Cichister's hands .	xxxi	xi	
Item the Clerk and Yeoman both, for their wages 22/- the month apiece and is paid by the Treasurer of the Chamber by the year	xxviii	xii	
Item Erasmus the chief Armourer hath for his wages by the month 26/8 and is paid by the said Treasurer	xvii	vi	viii
Item Old Martyn hath 38/10 the month which is by the year	xxv	v	x
Item Mathew Dethyke hath 24/- the month which is by the year	xv	xii	
Item Hans Clinkedag hath 24/- the month which is by the year	xv	xii	
Item Jasper Kemp hath 24/- the month which is by the year	xv	xii	
Item the Gilders wages by the year		xl	
Item the 2 Lockyers have 20/- a month apiece which is by the year	xxvi		
Item 1 Millman 24/- a month which is by the year .	xv	xii	
Item for the prentice 6d. for the day	ix	x	
Item for 8 bundles of steel to the said armoury for the whole year 38/- the bundle	xv	iiii	
Item for the costs of the house at £7 0 0 the month which is by the year	xxiiii	xi	
Sm.	iii viii	viii	iiii

182

	£	s	d
In primis the wages of 12 armourers, 2 locksmiths and 4 prentices to be divided into two shops, every of the Armourers their wages at 24/- the month and the Locksmiths at 20/- a month and every prentice 6d. the day amounteth by the year to . . .	clv	xii	
Item the wages of 2 millmen at 24/- the month . .	xxxi	iiii	
Item to every of the said shops 4 loads of charcoal a month at 9/- the load	xlvi	xix	
Item for 16 bundles of steel to serve both shops a whole year at 38/- the bundle	xxx	viii	
Item 1 hide of buff leather every month for both shops at 10/- the hide	vi	x	
Item for both shops 1 cowhide a month at 6/8 the hide	iiii	vi	viii
Item one 100 of iron every month for both shops at 6/8 the 100	iiii	vi	viii
Item in wispe steel for both shops every month 15 4⅛ at 4d. the lb.		lxv	
Item in wire monthly to both shops 12 lb. at 4d. lb. .		lii	
Item in nails & buckles for both shops monthly 5/- .		lxv	
Item to every of the said Armourers Locksmiths & Millmen for their liveries 4 yards broad cloth at 5/- the yard and 3 yards of carsey at 2/- the yard which amounteth in the year for 12 armourers 2 Locksmiths and 2 Millmen at 26/- for a man . .	xx	xvi	
So that these 12 armourers 2 Locksmiths 2 Millmen and 4 prentices will make yearly with the said 16 bundles of steel and the other stuff aforesaid 32 harnesses complete, every harness to be rated to the kings Highness at £12 0 0 which amounteth in the year towards his Grace's charge	c xx iii iiii iiii		
Item of the said Armourers to be divided into 2 shops as is aforesaid 4 of them shall be taken out of Erasmus' shop wherein his Grace shall save yearly in their wages and living the sum of . . .	lxviii		

APPENDIX G

PETITION OF THE ARMOURERS OF LONDON TO QUEEN ELIZABETH
July 13th, 1590 (Lansdowne MS. 63, 5)

To the Right Honourable the Lords & others of the Queens Most honourable Privie Counseil.

In most humble wise shew & beseche your honours your poor suppliants the Armourers of London that whereas we having been at great charges these six or seven years as well in making & providing tools & instruments as in entertaining and keeping of foreign men from beyond the seas to learn & practice the making of armour of all sorts which by the goodness of God we have obtained in such sort that at this time we make not onlie great quantitie But also have farre better armors than that wch cometh from beyond the Seas as is sufficiently proved, and fearing that for lack of sale and utterance of the same we shall not be able to keep & maintain the number of our apprentices & servants which are vy well practised in making of all sorts of armors. Our humble suite therfore to yr honors is that it shall please you to be a means to Her Mtie that we may be appointed to bring into her Mties Store at reasonable prices monthly or quarterly the Armor that we shall make till Her Mties Store shall be furnished with all sorts of Armor in such numbers as Her Mtie shall think good & appoint. And we and our posterity shall not only pry for your Honors but also being strengthened by your Honors we do not doubt to serve this land of Englishe Armor in future years as well as it is of Englishe Calyvers and muskets wch within this thirtie years or thereabouts was servd altogether with Outlandish peces with no money in respect of those wch are now made in this land, And we are the more bould, to make this our sute to your Honors because it is not a particular Comoditie to us but a benefit to the whole land as may be proved by these reasons viz :

1. Armour made in this land being not good, the makers may be punished by the laws provided for the same.

2. It is a means to set a great number of Her Majesty's subjects on work in this land, which now setteth a great number of foreigners on work in other lands.

3. It will furnish the land with skillfull men to make and fit armour to men's bodies in far better order than it hath been heretofore.

4. We shall be provided within this land of good armour, what restrayntments or quarrels so ever be in other lands, whereas hertofore we have been beholding to other countries for very bad armour.

5. We shall be free from all those dangers that may ensue by the number of bad and insufficient armour which are brought into this land by unskilfull men that

184

know not what they buy and sell it again to them that know not where to have better for their money although they know it to be very bad.

Her Majesties armories at this parte are very weakly furnished and that wch remaynes is neither good in substance nor yet in fashion. So as if it might stande in wth yor. LL. good liking it is very needfull the same should be supplied wth better choise.

The armor that is here made is accompted far better than that wch cometh from beyond the Seas and would well servi for he Mties store So as it might be delivered in good tyme wch the Armorers will undertake to prove but the armor wch they make is wholly blacke, so that unless they will undertake to serve white wth al it will not be so serviceable The proportion that shall be delivered I refer to yor ll. consideracion theire offer is to deliver to the number of eight thousand wthin fyve yeres and so after a further proporcion it so shall seem good to yor LL. Theire severll prices are hereunder written wch is as lowe as can bring it unto.

Launce armor compleat   iii li   vi s   viii d.
Corslets compleate   xxx s.
Curate of proofe wth poldrons   xl s.
Ordinary curate wth poldrons   xxvi s   viii d.
Target of proofe   xxx s.
Murrions   iii s.   iiii d.
Burgonetts   iiii s.

Endorsed the humble petition of the Armorers of London.

It is signed by RICHARD HARFORD.

JOHN SEWELL.

RICHARD WOODE RW.

WM. PICKERING.   13 July 1590.

Lee to inform.

APPENDIX H

UNDERTAKING OF THE ARMOURERS' COMPANY OF LONDON TO MAKE CERTAIN ARMOURS EVERY SIX MONTHS AND THE PRICES OF THE SAME

From records of the Company dated 17th March, 1618

The Privy Council on the 15th of March, 1618, made inquiry :—

" Who be the ingrossers of Plate to make Armor in London, and secondly what is the reason of the scarcity of Armor, and how it may be remedied ? "

The Company agreed to the following answer being sent :—

" That concerning the first we know no ingrossers of such Plate and we have called to our Hall all the workmen of Armor in London and we find them very few, for that in regard of the long peace which, God be thanked, we have had, they have settled themselves to other trades, not having imployment for making of Armor, nor the means to utter the same if they should make it, for the remedy of which scarcity, if it please the Privy Council to take order that the Armorers' work to be by them made in London, may be taken and paid for at every six months end. They will undertake, if continually employed, to use their best means for provision of stuff to make armor in every six months to furnish One hundred Lance Armor, Two hundred Light Horsemen's Armor, and Two hundred Footmen's Armor at such rates and prices as followeth."

The Lance Armor, containing Breast, Back, Gorget, Close Head piece, Poulderons and vambraces, Gushes, and one Gauntlett, to colored Russet, at the price of £4 0 0

The Light Horseman's Armor being Breast, Back, Gorgett a barred Head piece, Pouldrons, and an Elbowe Gauntlett, to be Russet, at the price of £2 10 0

The Footman's Armor, containing Breast, Back, Gorgett, head piece, and laces, with iron joints, to be colored russet, at the price of . £1 10 0

APPENDIX I

PROCLAMATION AGAINST EXCESSIVE USE OF GOLD AND SILVER FOLIATE, WHICH IS TO BE CONFINED TO ARMOUR AND ENSIGNS OF HONOUR

S.P.D. Jac. I, cv, February 4th, 1618.   Procl. Collec. 65

. . . . and furthermore the better to keepe the gold and silver of this kingedome not onely within the Realme from being exported, but that it may also bee continued in moneys and coyne, for the use and commerce of his Majestie and his loving subjects and not turned into any dead masse of Plate nor exhausted and consumed in vanities of Building and pompous use of Gold and Silver Foliate which have beene in the Reignes of divers kings of this Realme . . . and the better to prevent the unnecessary and excessive waste of Gold and Silver Foliate within this realeme ; His Majestie doth likewise hereby prohibit and forbid That no Gold or Silver Foliate shall be from henceforth wrought, used or imployed in any Building, Seeling, Waniscot, Bedsteds, Chayres, Stooles, Coaches or any other ornaments whatsoever, Except it be Armour or Weapons or in Armes and Ensignes of Honour at Funerals.

Feb. 4. 1618.

APPENDIX J

ERECTION OF PLATING-MILLS AT ERITH BY CAPT. JOHN MARTIN
1624
State Papers Domestic, Jac. I, Vol. CLXXX, 71

King Henry the eight being resolved to have his armorye alwayes stronge and richly furnished wt thirtie or fowertie thousand armes to be in Rediness to serve all the necessities of th times (how suddaine so evr) caused a batterie mill to be built at Detford nere Grenew^ch for the batteringe of plaetes for all sorts of armes but dyed before the bsiness was perfected.

In the time of Queen Elizabeth Captain John Martin and myself resolvinge on endeavors to the furtheringe so good a worke resolved y^t I should go to Inspurge wch is uppon the Germaine Alpes and into Lukland likewise to bring over into England seven or eight plaeters, the beste that might be found (wch was donne to ow^r very great chardges) and im̄ediately ther uppō fallinge to worke in a batterie mill wch we likewise erected nere unto Erith in Kent and in y^t place wrought as many plates of all sorts as served very nere for twentie thousand armors and targets never having the misterie of plaeting mills in England before. All wch plaeters formerly brought over are now dead save one, and he of so cunninge and obstinate a disposition that he would nev^r yet be brought to teach any Englishman the true misterie of plaeting unto this day.

The beste plaetes that have been formerly knowen to be in Christendome have been made of Inspurg stuff wch place hath continually served Milan Naples and other nations, and latelie England also, wch place beinge so remote and in the Emperor his owne countrie, it is not possible that wth any conveniencey any stronge plaetes can be now bought from thence as formerly we have had. But if his Matie will be plesed to have his armorie continually furnished wth thirtie or fortie thousand armes or more to what number he shall be beste plesid as hath been the course and resolution of his Roiall pdecessors, y^t may now be done wth Englishe Irone, by a misterie yet unknown, either to smolten plaetes or armour and to be of such strength and lightnes, for the ease and pservation of the life of the souldier as none can be better found in any nation in Christendome from the pistole to the musket.

It hath been observed in all antient histories and in the rule of our later moderne wars, that the goodness strength and lightness of armes hath been so great an incoradgement unto the souldier as hath made him stand faste in the time of great and strong chardges of the enemye, and to give valiant and couradgeous chardges, and assaults when they have been assured of the strength and goodness of theyre armes.

The raetes for Plaetes and armors exactly examined for the prices the strength and lightness considered are thus reduced.

	£	s	d
The chardge of a tun of Armor plaetes	18	0	0
Two chaldron of coles wt. carriage will be	1	12	0
The workmen for battering this tun of plaetes will have uppon every hundred 4/-	4	0	0
Reparation weekly for the mill		12	0
A clarke's wages weekly		12	0
Extraordinary chardges toe & froe for carridges		10	0
These particular chardges come to	£25	6	0

The true chardge of all such sorts of armor as they will stand you in wt. their severall p̄portions and such apporveable goodness as we never heretofore have had.

	£	s	d
Sixe hundred of iron will make five hundred of plaetes wch. will be a skore of ordinary curatts of pistoll proofe wch. cometh toe wth pouldrons	5	10	0
The Armourers may make them wt due shape black nayle and lether them for	7	10	0
These twentie armours will yeild	26	0	0
So in these twentie armours is clerely gained the sum of	13	0	0
Fower hundred of plates will make 20 paier of curatts wt out pouldrons	3	12	0
The Armorers may p̄portion them, black lether & naile them for	6	0	0
These 20 paire of curatts will yeld	20	0	0
In these 20 paire of curatts is clerely gained	10	8	0
The chardge of 20 lance armours. Sixteen hundred of plaetes will make twentie lance armours wch come to	14	8	0
The Armourers may finishe them upp for fourtie shillings the armour wch comes to	40	0	0
These 20 launce armours will yeld fower pounds a piece wch amounteth unto	80	0	0
So yt in these 20 launce armours is clerely gained	25	12	0
Five hundred of plaetes will make twentie proof targetts wch will come to	4	10	0
The armourers may finishe them lether them and blacke them with all other chardges for	12	0	0
Thes targets will yeld (24s.[1]) the piece	26	0	0
In these targetts may be cleared	9	10	0

[1] An error in the original—this should be 26s.

Twelve hundred of plaetes will make 20 paire of stronge
curatts with stronge capps wch will stand in   .   £10 16   0
The Armourers may finishe them for (30s.) the paire
wch amounteth unto   30   0   0
These 20 paier of stronge curatts wt their capps will
yeld 4 li. the paier wch cometh toe   .   .   80   0   0
So that by these 20 paier of stronge curatts will be
clerely gayned   .   .   .   .   .   39 10[1] 0

With fower plaeters may be wrought up in one weeke
3700 weight of plates.   The pfitt of wch weekly,
as by the particulars may appear will be   .   .   98 14   0
And if these fower plaeters be emploied the whole year
(abating one month in the year for idle dayes) it
amounteth unto per ann   .   .   .   4737li.12   0

[1] Should be 4s.

APPENDIX K

HALL-MARK OF THE ARMOURERS' COMPANY
Carolus I, ann. 7, 1631.   Rymer, Vol. XIX, 309

"John Franklin, William Crouch, John Ashton, Thomas Stephens, Rowland Foster, Nicholas Marshall, William Coxe, Edward Aynesley, Armourers & freemen of the company of Armourers ar ordered to deliver 1500 armours each month with arms, pikes &c. and to train prentices and to mend, dress & stamp armours." The document goes on to state " you ar to approve of all such armour of the said common armes & trayned bands as shall be found fit for service, and shall trye all sorts of gunnes, pikes, bandaliers of the said common armes and trayned bands before they be used or excersied and to approve of such as are serviceable for warres at the owners charges and being proved shall allow as fit for service and allowing shall stamp the same with A. and a Crown being the hall mark for the company of workmen armourers of London which marke or stamp our pleasure is shall with consent of the lord lieutenant or his deputy lieutenant remayne in their custodye who shall have the charge to be intrusted with the execution of this service. . . . And because diverse cutlers, smythes, tynkers & othe botchers of armes by their unskilfulness have utterly spoiled many armes, armours gunnes and pykes, and bandoliers . . . we doe hereby prohibit that noe person or persons whatever, not having served seven years or been brought up as an apprentice or apprentices in the trade and mysterie of an armourer, gunmaker, pyke-maker and bandolier-maker and thereto served their full tyme of seven years as aforesaid . . . do make, alter, change, dress or repayr, prove or stamp any armes, armours, gunnes, pykes or bandoliers . . . we do absolutely forbid that no iron-monger, cutler or chandler or other person whatsoever doe vent or sell any armours, gunnes, pikes or bandoliers or any part of them except such as shall be proved and stamped with the said hall marke of the company of workmen armourers aforesaid being the proofe marke . . . that hereafter there shall be but one uniform Fashion of Armour of the said Trayned Bands throughout our said Kingdome of England & Dominion of Wales . . . whereof the Patterns are and shall remayne from tyme to tyme in our said Office (of Ordinance)."

APPENDIX L

PETITION OF THE WORKMEN ARMOURERS OF LONDON TO THE COUNCIL

S.P.D. Car. I, cclxxxix, 93, May, 1635

Petitioners being few in number & most of them aged about 7 years past sued to Her Mtie for some employment for preservation of the manufacture of armour making within the kingdom. Her Mtie on advice & report of the Council of War granted petitioners a patent which 2 years passed the great seal & was then called for by the Council for further consideration. Pray them to take the same into consideration and the distress of petitioners & either to pass the patent or if there be any omission in it to give orders for drawing up another.

APPENDIX M

EXTRACT FROM SURVEY OF THE TOWER ARMOURY, 1660

Harl. MS. 7457

Greenwich. Wee doe find aswell upon our owne view as upon the information of diverse officers of the Armoury stoorekeeper and others That dureing the time of the late distraccions The severall Armes amunition and Habiliments of Warre formerly remaineing in the greene Gallery at Greenwich were all taken and carryed away by sundry Souldiers who left the doore open ; That sundry of the said Armes were afterwards brought into the Tower of London by Mr. Anneslye where they are still remaineing ; That the Wainescot in the said Gallery is now all pull'd downe and carryed away ; and (as We are informed) was imployed in wainescotting the house in the Tower where the said Mr. Anneslye lived ; That a great part of the severall Tooles and other utensils for makeing of Armour formerly remaineing in the Master Armourers workehouse there and at the Armourers Mill, were alsoe within the tyme of the said distraccions taken and carryed away (saving two old Trunkes bound about with Iron, which are still remaineing in the said workehouse, One old Glazeing wheele, still at the Mill, and one other glazeing wheele sold to a Cutler in Shoo lane) : That sundry of the said Tooles and other utensills have since byn converted and sold to private uses, by those who within the tyme of the late distraccions had the Command and care of the said armes and Tooles, both at Greenwich and at the Tower : That diverse of the said Tooles are still in other private mens hands, who pretend they bought them : That the great Anville (called the great Beare) is now in the custodye of Mr. Michaell Basten, locksmith at Whitehall, and the Anville knowne by the name of the little Beare, is in the custodie of Thomas Cope, one of His Majesties Armourers ; And one Combe stake in the Custody of Henry Keeme one other of his Majesties Armourers And that the said Mill formerly employed in grinding and glazeing and makeing cleane of Armes, is destroyed and converted to other uses by one Mr. Woodward who claims it by virtue of a Graunt from King James (of blessed memorye) but the officers of the Armorye (for his Majesties use) have it now in their possession.

Memorandum. That the severall distinguishments of the Armors and Furnitures before mencioned, vizt The first serviceable, The second defective, and to be repaired, The third unserviceable, in their owne kinds, yet may be employed for necessary uses, are soe reported by Richard Kinge and Thomas Cox, two of his Majesties Armorers at Greenwich, who were nominated and appointed in his Majesties Commission, under his signe Manual before recited, to be assistant in this Service : And we doe thinke the same to be by them faithfully and honestly soe distinguished.

WILL. LEGGE, Master of his Majesties Armories.   J. ROBINSON, Lt: Ten: Toure.

Jo. WOOD, Barth Beale.

INDEX